Swami Vivekananda
the Monarch of Monks

Dushyanta Pandya

Readworthy
New Delhi

Disclaimer from the author: All religions/beliefs and schools of philosophy are equally respected and statement of any kind does not endorse or prefer one over the other. The beliefs, thoughts, convictions, suitability, benefits, etc. expressed are all personal to me. Any narration, belief, indication, conclusion, method or similar statement should not be construed as recommendations. Those may and would not suit to all or even anybody in some cases. These are not to be taken as a panacea. Nothing is promised. The reader may or may not follow what is stated; he or she may do so only by using his or her own personal discretion and at his or her own responsibility.

First published 2009

Readworthy Publications (P) Ltd.

Regd. Off.: A-18, Mohan Garden
Near Nawada Metro Station
New Delhi – 110 059 (India)
Phone: 011-2537 1324
Fax: +91-11-2537 1323

Branch: 4662/21, Ansari Road
Daryaganj
New Delhi – 110 002
Phone: 011-4354 9197
Fax: +91-11-2324 3060

Email: info@readworthypub.com Web: www.readworthypub.com

Cataloging in Publication Data–DK

Courtesy: D.K. Agencies (P) Ltd. <docinfo@dkagencies.com>

Paṇḍayā, Dushyanta, 1916-

Swami Vivekananda, the monarch of monks / Dushyanta Pandya

p. cm.

Swami Vivekananda, 1863-1902, Indian philosopher and religious leader.

Includes index.

ISBN 13: 978-81-89973-84-1 ISBN 10: 81-89973-84-3

1. Vivekananda, Swami, 1863-1902. 2. Hindus--India--Biography. 3. Ramakrishna Mission--Biography. I. Title.

DDC 294.555 092 22

Printed at D.K. Fine Art Press, Delhi - 52

Swami Vivekananda
the Monarch of Monks

About the Author

Dr. Dushyanta Pandya has a long association of over six decades with the Ramakrishna Math and Mission. Presently, he is the president of the Ramakrishna-Vivekananda Centre, Jamnagar. Earlier, he was the convener of the centre. He is also closely associated with Ramakrishna Jyot, a Gujarati monthly published by the Ramakrishna Ashram, Rajkot.

Dr. Pandya has written a good number of books, including one on Montessori Method of teaching. Also, he has translated several books of Swami Ranganathananda, Swami Jitatmananda and Swami Chetanananda into Gujarati, as well as fifty Gujarati poems of Umashankar Joshi into English. He is a recipient of Best Teacher's Award and Gujarat Sahitya Academy Award.

Contents

The Great Deliverer

A man in a hapless condition, says an Indian saying, leaves the world and becomes a *sadhu* - a monk. When Narendranath Dutta, a "brilliant graduate of Calcutta University took the vows of *sannyasa*, the condition of his family could not have been worse. His father, who was a leading advocate of Kolkata, the capital of the British Empire then, and who was living like a lord, died all of a sudden in 1884. And the pomp and show all vanished as if engulfed by a severe earthquake. A family of younger brothers, sisters and mother had to be supported. But Narendra, then only twenty three years of age, chose the path of a *sannyasin* instead of that of a householder.

Haridas Desai, then Diwan of Junagadh state in Gujarat, with whom Swami Vivekananda had come to be closely attached, happened to visit Swamiji's house in Kolkata and after seeing the dire straits Bhuvaneshvari Devi, the Swami's mother, and other relatives were living in, wrote a letter to Swamiji in America disapproving the latter's choice of life of a *sannyasin*. The Diwanji was like a father to Swamiji, and the Diwanji's remonstrance, howsoever mild it might have been, touched Swamiji to the quick and he appears to have been very much moved by it. His letter from Chicago, dated 29th January, 1894, to 'Dear Diwanji Saheb' (C.W. Vol. VIII p. 297 Mayawati Mem. ed., 1989) makes it clear to the whole world:"... "Without my giving up the world, the great mission which Ramakrishna Paramhansa, my great Master, came to preach would not see the light..."

These words of Swamiji in the letter to one whom he respected like his father, mark out very clearly Vivekananda's choice of the path of life, his goal in life. And that choice he had made when he was just twenty three years old. He had come in contact with his guru during 1881-1882 and after his first meeting with Shri Ramakrishna at Dakshineshwar, he had left the place with a very odd impression about the person who was to mould him, guide him and declare him to be his first apostle. Once the guru had simply shocked Naren-the future Vivekananda-and others present in his room by suddenly declaring that Naren was eighteen times more intelligent, more capable, and spiritually greater than Keshub Sen. And Keshub Sen, was the leader of his Brahmo Samaj, a sincere seeker, a brilliant orator and a powerful writer. This sudden burst of Shri Ramakrishna had shocked everyone present there, Naren the most.

And this prophecy of the guru came true on September ll, 1893, at the World Parliament of Religions at Chicago, about a decade after it was made. And one has also to remember that Vivekananda had gone to the Parliament absolutely unprepared, simply because, he had not been sent as a delegate to the Conference by any religion, any sect or, any subsect. The portals of the Conference were opened to him at the very last moment at the instance of Professor Wright of the Harward University.

And Swamiji's introductory speech was a spiritual atom bomb, the speech in which he pithily put forth his Master's living message of toleration and acceptance of all religions. He had not mentioned the name of Shri Ramakrishna, but he had quoted from history and ancient scriptures. The speeches he later gave at the Parliament of Religions made a deep impact. Even Romain Rolland, who did not know English, was moved by the 'tongue of flame' of Swamiji. The powerful force of Swamiji's words completely upset the apple cart of Dr. Barrows and others of his kind who had cloaked their intention of spreading the message of Christianity, 'the only religion,' in their myopic view. It is this obstinate belief in 'my religion is the only true religion,' that Shri Ramakrishna never accepted and Vivekananda, one might say, was upholding his great guru's preaching, the preaching he had actually lived.

All of a sudden from down in the valley, Swami Vivekananda had taken a Hanuman-like leap to the Everest of fame. From an unknown, wandering, undeputed pennyless monk, he had been suddenly transformed as a spiritual leader of the world. But the true *sannyasin* that Shri Vivekananda was, cared neither for fame nor for money. His great master had taught him to shun lust and lucre. His life mission was to spread the message of toleration and acceptance given him by his master.

Swamiji's departure from Mumbai in the summer of 1893 had gone quite unnoticed. So unnoticed was his arrival at Vancouver in July of the same year. But his landing at Colombo on January 15, 1897 was of a totally different kind. No conqueror of the world had ever received such tumultuous and enthusiastic welcome as Swamiji had. One of his *gurubhais* had reached Colombo from Kolkata. Vivekananda's boat was standing still in the Indian Ocean. The Lankan shore heaved by the ocean of men shouting welcome and waving flags and holding garlands in their hands. Thus his arrival sounded the awakening of India. Even if Swamiji was not a political leader, he had awakened the masses of India from their slumber of centuries.

Although India felt his influence the most, Swamiji was not merely a leader of India. His contribution to the spiritual wealth of the world was unparalleled.

Like the great Buddha, Jesus Christ and his own master Shri Ramakrishna, Vivekananda's words were *spoken* words. They came out on the spur of the moment. May be, that's why they have such tremendous power, as testified by Romain Rolland. His ministration was a short one: it did not last a decade even. And yet, after a century, their penetrating appeal has not diminished a bit. On the contrary, the message of toleration and acceptance has become the need of the day. Religion and politics have got mixed up and the measure of intolerance seems to have squared up. No 'grammar of politics' would be able to solve this crisis which seems to be getting murkier and murkier.

This small book is a humble attempt to draw the attention to the 'still, small voice' of Vivekananda preaching toleration and acceptance. I must hasten to thank all the great writers who have written about Swami Vivekananda.

I only hope this attempt would be tolerated and accepted. I thank all who have written on Swamiji. I have borrowed from many sources available to me. I am indebted to the various biographer and writers.

Dushyanta Pandya

1

An Incarnation of Nara

It was a November afternoon of 1881. The vast Kali temple complex, situated about four miles north to the city of Kolkata, standing on the bank of the great river Ganga wore a quiet look. The thuds of a horse's hoofs audible from a long distance were piercing the quiet. It was an indication that some visitors were arriving in a carriage. The sound of the horses' hoofs became more clearly audible and then it slowed down and came to a stop near the temple courtyard.

About four people got down from the hackney carriage. One of them was a middle aged man of more than thirty five years and he was accompanied by three young men in their late teens. Entering the courtyard of the Kali temple, they veered to their right and walked towards the last room, standing on the bank of the Ganga, a few feet away from the last of the twelve Shiva temples. These visitors, except a youth of nineteen, entered the room from the door nearest to them. This young man walked a few steps further on and entered the room from the western door, close by to the Ganga.

Why did this young man choose an entrance different from the choice of others? There might not be any specific reason behind the choice. But he was noticeably different from his companions. He was tall and stout as he was a gymnast. His face was so chiselled as to attract the attention of others. His big and brilliant forehead indicated the sharpness of his intelligence. His eyes seemed to be looking for something beyond, and he appeared neither particular about his dress, nor about his hair, nor about his general appearance. To a keen observer, he appeared to be in search of something outside the normal range of vision.

On entering the room, the visitors bowed down to a man sitting on a small wooden platform with due reverence. He was forty-five years of age, with dishevelled hair and a small unkempt beard. His clothes were quite ordinary and were worn quite carelessly. He wore a constant smile on his face, which bewitched many an onlooker and revealed his shining white teeth. He welcomed all his visitors with warmth and beckoned the young ninteen year old, different looking, young man to sit on the mat on the floor, in front of the low wooden platform he himself was sitting on. He controlled himself with great difficulty at the sight of this youth. He had heard the young man sing once at the house of Surendra, who was leading the party that particular afternoon. Surendra appeared to treat this forty-five year old man, Ramakrishna Paramahansa, respectfully as his guru.

Shri Ramakrishna asked the young man, whom he had invited to sit in front of him, to sing a *bhajan*. Ramakrishna had heard the youth sing soulfully at the house of Surendra, some two or three weeks ago. Ramakrishna's penetrating eye had measured the youth there and then, when he had first seen the young man at Surendra's house. The young man's total involvement with the *bhajan* he had sung had cemented the impression Ramakrishna had formed about the youth. Then he had checked the antecedents of the boy with Surendra and his friend, Ramachandra Datta, who was a close relative of the youth. Like Surendra, Ramachandra also looked at Shri Ramakrishna with great respect. Then Ramakrishna had called the boy to him and got himself assured of the boy's worthiness. Only then he had asked the youth to come to Dakshineshvar to meet him. And today he had come along with Surendra and other friends. The young friends accompanying the youth Ramakrishna had asked to sing were deeply attached to the world. The young carefree boy was entirely different. This was what Ramakrishna's X-ray like eyes had discovered at his very first glance on the youth.

We have the most authentic report of this first meeting of Shri Ramakrishna and his would be apostle from the two persons themselves. Swami Sharadananda has obliged the world by quoting the actual words of both. The comments by both tell us that they are not mere words. Let us recreate the event as the two persons themselves narrated it.

When Shri Ramakrishna asked the young boy to sing, he learnt that the boy knew only two or three Bengali songs. Shri Ramakrishna had said about it, 'When I asked him to sing, he sang the Brahmo Samaj song;

'O mind, let us go back to our own home,
Why do you wander aimlessly
In an alien land, in a non-native garb?'

'He started singing pouring his entire soul into it, as if he was completely engrossed in it. On hearing it, I could not control myself. I got into an ecstatic state.' This is Ramakrishna's version.

The young man, Narendra, carried the story further. 'I sang the song. Immediately thereafter, he got up and holding me with his hand, he took me to the verandah on the north of the room. It being winter, the pillars of the verandah were holding matting curtains to prevent the cool northerly winds. As soon as we entered the verandah, he shut the door of the room and so I thought that he wanted to preach me alone. But what he said and did was most astonishing, and was beyond imagination. He held my hand tight, started shedding tears profusely and speaking to me as if I were a close acquaintance of him since a long time. He spoke to me with great affection: "Do you have to come after so many days? Do you not think even once of the eagerness with which I have been longing to see you? My ears have been parched by listening to the useless prattle of sensuous persons. And since I am not able to tell any one what I feel within my heart, my stomach has swollen like a big drum.' He spoke many things in the same strain and continued weeping. And the very next second, he stood facing me with folded hands and showing respect to me as if I was a god. He said, "I know my Lord, you are that same ancient sage, Narayana in the form of Nara, born again to relieve souls from going to hell etc."'

'I was simply struck dumb at his strange behaviour. I couldn't even move: I started thinking, "Whom have I come to meet here? This man is totally mad: or else, why should he say such things to me, son of Vishvanath Datta of Kolkata? Whatever it might be, I kept mum and that strange maniac went on speaking whatever came to his mind. Then, next minute, asking me to be where I was, he went back to the room and brought with him butter, sugar and a few pieces of *sandesh* (a Bengali sweet) and forced me to eat those things. I told him to give those things to me to share with my friends. But he said, "They'll have it later on. All these are for you to eat," and made me eat all the stuff. Then holding me with his hand he spoke, "Promise me that you'll come here once more, and *alone*." I was forced to give an assurance and then only, he opened the door. Both of us walked back into the room and I sat there along with my friends.'

It was not merely a change of scene but the change in the behaviour of Ramakrishna was noticable too. All the abnormality young Narendra had noticed a couple of minutes ago in the verandah appeared to have been left there only. And how gratifying was his talk! The young visitor Narendra, asked a question, tormenting him: 'Sir, have you seen God?'

And forthwith gushed forth the reply: 'Yes, I have seen him, as I am seeing you now, but more intensely. 'Then he added, 'One can see God. But who wants to see Him? One sheds a potful of tears for wife and children and for money. Does any one so weep for God?

Motilal (UK) Books of India
367 High Street
London Colney
St. Albans, Hertforshire
AL2 1EA
Tel: (0044)+(0)1727761677
Email: info@motilalbooks.com
Fax: (0044)+(0)1727761357

www.motilalbooks.com

Ray's Books of India Pvt Ltd
14/52, Subhash Nagar,
near Shadley Public School,
Rajouri Garden,
New Delhi, 110027
Tel: 01141548816
Email: raysbooksofindia@gmail.com

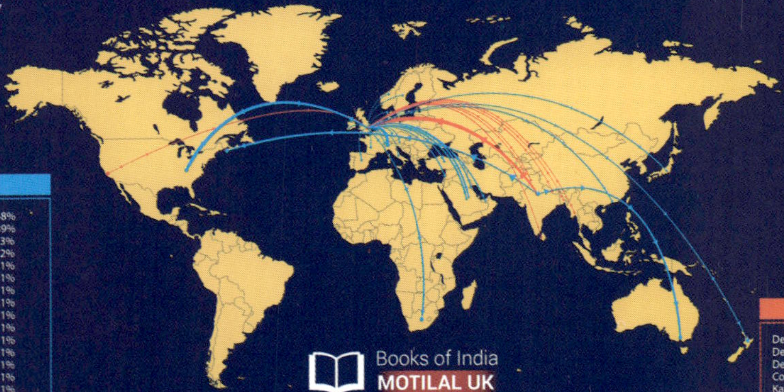

SELL TO

Elsewhere in the UK	48%
USA	39%
To Sth Africa	3%
To Saudi Arabia	2%
To Lebanon	1%
To Germany	1%
To Holland	1%
To Ireland	1%
To UAE	1%
To Hg Kg	1%
To Mid Nth Island	1%
To Switzerland	<1%
To France	<1%
To Italy	<1%
To Belgium	<1%
To Denmark	<1%
To Norway	<1%
To Sweden	<1%
To Australasia	<1%
To Turkey	<1%
To Japan	<1%
To Kuwait	<1%
Spain	<1%

Books of India
MOTILAL UK

THE Indian Book Wholesaler - From India To The World
13,000 books sold per month in 2017
8,978 titles sold in 2017
Over 16,000 titles in stock
The top 200 sellers kept permanently in stock
Also selling books from Pakistan, Nepal, Bangladesh, Sri Lanka & More

IMPORT FROM

Delhi to New York	43%
Delhi to London	43%
Delhi to Melbourne	4%
Columbo to London	4%
Kathmandhu to London	3%
Lahore to London	2%
Dakha to London	<1%
Los Angeles to London	<1%
Kabul to London...	<1%
Rangoon to London	<1%

Unless that intense yearning for God is there, how can one see God? These words of Shri Ramakrishna, uttered, as it were, with the sincerity of a person who had seen God, touched the strings of young Narendra's heart. God for him had been a great puzzle. The various stories of God he had heard in his childhood from his mother seemed to have lost their significance as he grew up. His father was a happy go lucky fellow, enjoying his hookah and his Hafiz and allowing God to have His own way, for God never came between him and his clients and his pleading.

While the young boy was playing with his pets and practising exercises at the gymnasium, God didn't seem to bother him. However, at times doubts arose in his mind and they drove him to the Brahmo Samaj. He liked the atmosphere there. The gathering of men was august, prayers from the *Vedas* were recited with due awe, *bhajans* were sincerely sung and lectures were given from the pulpit. God, however, seemed to have stayed away. These words of Ramakrishna, coming from the innermost depth of his heart, were reassuring. But there was a big 'but.' While going back home young Narendra's mind could not reconcile the two entirely different aspects of the behaviour of Shri Ramakrishna. When they were both alone in the verandah, how ridiculously he had behaved? There was no method in his madness even. What was the old man's meaning in addressing young Naren as an *avatara* of an old sage if not an expression of insanity? And added to it was his act of weeping! No person in his senses would behave in such an absurd manner. How very meaningless was the act of Ramakrishna's folding his hands worshipfully to him, young Narendra? Ramakrishna, thought Narendra, should be sent to a mad house.

And yet, when back inside the room, in the presence of Surendra and other companions, he was wisdom personified. He was completely convincing in every word he spoke, in all his behaviour. Where had his mania disappeared so soon? This sharp contrast in Ramakrishna's behaviour was a great puzzle.

All the logic he had learnt at the college, could not explain this sudden transformation in Ramakrishna's behaviour. 'I must fathom deep and find out,' thought Narendra. There were a few things strikingly positive in the old Dakshineshvar man. His renunciation was exemplary. His simplicity of life was striking. The confidence with which he spoke about 'seeing' God was convincing. The affection the old man had showered on him was simply genuine and unique.

And yet the dichotomy in the old man's behaviour was too obvious to be brushed aside. It was so glaring that all along the way back, Narendra could not think of anything else. He might have laughed inside his mind: could he play a joke with his mother? On reaching home he thought of telling her, "Mom, I am not your son Narendra. I am the incarnation of the great Nara Narayana."

On his way back home, he exchanged no words with any of his friends or with Surendra Mitra, who had taken him to meet Shri Ramakrishna at Dakshineshvar. He was so engrossed in his own self. An enigma was eating up his entire being. He did not believe in miracles or magic. His rational mind would not let him rest unless and until he had solved the problem satisfactorily. In order to find the solution, he would have to go again. He would go again, and again, and resolve the last trace of his doubt.

And Narendra suddenly remembered that it was Ramakrishna himself who had held him, Naren, by hand and forcefully asked him to come again. He also remembered that he was told with slight emphasis to come alone. It would be a good thing to go to Dakshineshvar unaccompanied by anyone. The bearded man with a bewitching smile would then be entirely available to observe and study.

'With my rapier of logic I'll unsheathe every layer of his personality and with my perspicacity lay bare the insanity of his mind, if any.' With these thoughts Naren entered his house. "I am Nara Narayana, not Narendra," he was thinking with a smile on his face.

2

Nara Narayana? Shiva's Demon?

Having seen Narendra only once at the house of his devotee, Surendra, Shri Ramakrishna had asked the teenager to visit him. In the previous chapter, we have seen Shri Ramakrishna exhibiting a very strange behaviour towards the young visitor so much so that the youth thought Shri Ramakrishna to be insane. Naren might not be said to be wrong in his opinion of the Paramahansa of Dakshineshvar for addressing him, Naren who was the son of Vishvanath Datta and Bhuvaneshvari Devi, as 'Nara' the 'Incarnation of Narayana.'

But Ramakrishna had his own logic in so talking to the young boy who was yet to be a sophomore at a Calcutta college. His logic was not based on the normal material or intellectual plane. Ramakrishna's logic was based on the super conscious level, what Shri Aurobindo was to term later on, the supramental level.

Shri Ramakrishna lived more often than not at the super conscious level, what is called the state of *Samadhi*. And in that state he often had visions, which came true later on. In one of his visions, he had described later on to his desciples, he had said, 'One day I felt that my mind was flying higher and higher in *Samadhi* along a luminous path. It soon went beyond the limits of the gross stellar region and entered the subtle region of ideas. On my way on both sides, I saw ideal forms of gods and goddesses. My mind crossed over to the outer limit of that region and saw a barrier of light separating the sphere of relative existence from the sphere of the Absolute. My mind crossed that barrier and entered the transcendental domain, where no embodied being could be visible. Even the gods and goddesses did not have the courage to peep into that sublime realm of luminescence. They were just satisfied to be in the nether region they were in. The very next moment I saw the seven great *rishis* seated in *Samadhi.*

'These venerable sages must have surpassed not only ordinary mortals but also the gods and goddesses in knowledge, divinity, renunciation and love. Dumbfounded with admiration I started contemplating on their greatness. I then saw a small portion of that undifferentiated luminescence take the form of a divine baby. The divine baby went up to one of the meditating sages and putting his tender hands around the neck of the sage spoke to him in a sweet voice and tried to bring down the mind from his *Samadhi*. The divine child gently spoke, "I am going down to the earth. Would you also not go with me?"

'The divine baby waited for a reply. A few seconds later, the great sage came out of the *Samadhi*, opened his eyes just for a moment and gave a sweet little smile. He had agreed to go down to the earth with that divine child. Naren is that great sage.' It was this vision of Shri Ramakrishna that had prompted him to take Naren away to the verandah on the north of his room and suddenly burst into tears and an utterly unexpected utterance which had shocked young Naren greatly. He felt that the old man had gone berserk and what he was saying was utter nonsense. Naren strongly desired to be free from the clutches of the lunatic.

Narendra had no knowledge of what Shri Ramakrishna thought about him, Narendranath Datta. He had first seen Shri Ramakrishna almost casually at the house of Surendra Mitra. Ramakrishna's penetrating eye had, however, pierced the outer sheath of Narendra and had made him invite the young collegian to visit Dakshineshvar. And immediately on Narendra's visit, Ramakrishna had burst forth with his extraordinary utterance. But who was Narendra? For an answer we'll have to delve a little bit into history.

The British had arrived in India in 1611 and had opened a factory at Surat. They had moved from there to Bombay(now known as Mumbai) and had later on made use of Madras(now known as Chennai) and Calcutta(now known as Kolkata) as entrepots and established factories there also. Less with bravery but more with bribery and cunning, Robert Clive had sowed the seed of the British rule in India and it had soon sprouted into an oak tree.

The British had established their own courts and had started administering justice as per the English law. This factor, along with the need to trade with the East India Company, had drawn people of the upper castes to learn English, as they had learnt Persian in the past after the arrival of the Muslims, whose court language and language of administration was Persian. Members of the Kayastha community, along with the Brahmins in Bengal, were in the forefront so far as the state administration was concerned. They occupied important positions in the administrative set-up and also practised law. They naturally studied Persian very well. And now with the establishment of the British rule, they started learning English.

One Datta family was in the forefront and one Ram Mohan Datta had established himself as a leading advocate by the end of the eighteenth century. The Dattas were well educated both in Persian and in English, had acquired wealth by dint of their intellect and hard work and were well respected. Ram Mohan owned a big and comfortable house in the Gour Mohan Mukherjee Lane of the Simla area of Calcutta.

Durgacharan, Ram Mohan's son was to inherit his father's legal practice, wealth and property and name. At a very young age, he was made a partner in the firm of his father. As per the social custom, Durgacharan was married when he was very young. But his bent of mind was quite different and he was interested in the pursuit of the incorporeal. Having been married he begot a son. Everyone in the family was happy that the Datta line would continue. The little child, named Vishvanath became three years old and showed all the signs of a robust growth. Suddenly, the spiritual streak in the personality of Durgacharan became active and, like the great Buddha, he walked out of his house leaving his tender, young wife and, the child, Vishvanath. The tiny boy must have been grieved by the sudden disappearance of his father, but the boy's mother, who was in the prime of life must have suffered the pangs of separation. But there was no trace of Durgacharan. He had renounced the world to become a *sannyasi*, and like all other *sannyasi*s might have been moving from one place to another, from house to house, begging for his food and sleeping, more often than not, under a tree. The poor, young wife must have been wailing and shedding tears. Her fate was like that of a widow, probably worse.

Three long years passed by. The Datta family went on a pilgrimage to Kashi. A pilgrimage in those good old days was not like an organised tour of the modern times, where tourists are pushed from place to place and driven from city to city by tour organisers. Going by a sail boat upstream for nearly five hundred miles must have itself consumed quite some time. The pilgrims must have stayed on the way at a few places and then only they must have reached their destination, Kashi.

Kashi, the abode of Vishvanath, the Lord of the Universe, is a city much older than London, Rome or Athens. When the great Buddha visited it in the sixth century B.C., it was a thriving city and was famous as one of the holiest of places. Pilgrims from all over India and other countries flocked the place. The Datta family of Kolkata approached the place with feelings of great reverence in their hearts. Bathing at the *ghats* on the Ganga and visiting various temples, they spent there quite a few days.

Many temples are situated on the bank of the Ganga and several devotees take a dip in the holy waters before entering the temples. Naturally, the steps leading to the temples are wet and having been there since times immemorial many of them have become slippery. It so happened that going up the steps to the Vishvanath temple once, the young unhappy wife of Durgacharan slipped, lost her balance and tumbled down. Seeing her tumbling down, a *sannyasi* ran down to her, gave her a helping hand and made her sit up properly. After recovering from the accident when the young pilgrim looked up at her benefactor, she received another shock, a mental one. The *sannyasi* was none other than her husband, Durgacharan. The *sannyasi* had also recognised the lady he had helped and the very next moment he turned his face away, started walking quickly and disappeared in the crowd. When the pilgrims returned home, the young, abandoned woman must have returned with a mixture of memories, more bitter than sweet.

A few years later it so happened that as prescribed by the *Shastras*, the *sannyasi*, Durgacharan, came back to Calcutta and was staying there with some old friend. The host in exhuberance informed the family members of Durgacharan who came to where he was staying and took him home. They lodged him in a room and kept strict vigil over him. But the *sannyasi* had his own way of resistance. He refused all food, and kept his mouth completely shut. He did not speak to anyone. This went on for three days. The family members felt that if things went on like that, the *sannyasi* might die and they themselves would be responsible for the mishap. So they relented and keeping open the doors of the room occupied by the *sannyasi*, they moved away. The *sannyasi* quietly slipped away, never to be seen again.

His only son, Vishvanath, though given the name of Lord Shiva, did not have a particularly religious bent of mind. He was an intelligent boy and had acquired mastery over Persian. Hafiz was his favourite poet and he had commited many poems of Hafiz to memory. He quoted them often. He had, probably, been sent to a missionary school for his education and had developed a great love for the *Bible*. He was very fond of reading the holy Gospels. This reading, along with the preachings of Christian missionaries, coupled with the shock of desertion given to him in his infancy by his father, who had left the family by becoming a *sannyasi*, might have affected Vishvanath's attitude to religion. He might not have turned an atheist, despising all idol worship, temple going and priest respecting, yet his attitude towards religion had taken a rational, if not a sceptical turn.

He took to his ancestral profession and became an attorney. His brilliance coupled with his mastery of law and powerful ability of argument put him in the front rank of advocates and he had a roaring practice. His way of life was very lavish and his home, as well as his purse, were open to everyone. People could easily approach him for money for going to a bar even. When his son grew old enough to understand the ways of the world and argued with his father about the latter's odious charity, Vishvanath gave a stunning reply, "What do you know about the miseries of life that drive a man to drown himself in drink and forget his worries even for some time in his life? That temporary happiness is better than no happiness at all. I help some poor people go to a bar to drink to relieve themselves from their worries." This, no doubt, was a strange argument in favour of alcoholism. A few relatives took advantage of the noble nature of Vishvanath and lived with him, enjoying free hospitality. Others approached him with more often false than genuine tears in their eyes and begged for financial help. Vishvanath never questioned anyone and was always ready with money to help. The borrower always promised a quick return but soon forgot his promise, or even made bold to approach Vishvanath for more monetary assistance, which was always forthcoming. Vishvanath never reminded them of their previous borrowings.

He was married to one Bhuvaneshvaridevi, a lady of noble means and nobler nature. She never came in the way of her husband's habit of giving money to people without ascertaining the genuineness of their needs, without any written agreement or without any third party standing guarantor. Vishvanath never questioned her about how she ran the household and placed at her disposal whatever amount of money she needed. By nature, she was also of a generous temperament.

She had no formal schooling but had learnt reading and writing and had a good voice and a good memory. She knew many *pada*s and *bhajan*s by heart. She carried on the tradition of daily worship of the family deities and also paid visits to temples.

After her marriage with Vishvanath, Bhuvaneshvaridevi had given birth to four daughters one after another. Unfortunately two of them had died in infancy. Like almost all Indian men and women, she very keenly desired to parent a son. Possessed as she was with a strong desire for a male heir, she started praying to Lord Shiva, to observe fasts on certain days and to offer special worship to the Lord. Anybody who knew her could understand her craving for a son. She also wrote to some relative of hers at Kashi to make special offerings on her behalf to Vireshvara Shiva, visit the temple on certain auspicious days for prayers, and beg the boon of a son on her behalf. She herself practised self control, and prayed to Lord Shiva intently.

Some time later, she became pregnant and during the period of her child bearing, she started having visions of Lord Shiva. Her mood underwent a change and her noble nature became nobler. Her devotion to Lord Shiva became more intense. It is not known how Vishvanath looked at the single-minded devotion of his wife or shared her belief in her visions. But he was practical enough not to poke fun of his wife's firm faith. If his wife's deep devotion to her deity bore fruit, he would no doubt be happy.

The year 1862 had come to a close. The fanfare of the nativity of Jesus and celebrations of the incoming year 1863 were over. The sun was to commence its northward journey, leaving the house of Capricorn. The night of 11th January was over. The dawn of the early morning of 12th was slowly dispelling all darkness. The Eastern horizon was aglow with crimson and golden hues. Just then Bhuvaneshvaridevi gave birth to a son. And six minutes later, from the Eastern horizon rose the sun to dispel darkness all over the earth. Little did Bhuvaneshvaridevi know that like the sun coming up on the horizon, the tiny boy she had just given birth to was also going to dispel darkness all around and shine in glory.

The new born had to be given a name. People who knew the Datta family saw a striking similarity between the features of the infant with his *sannyasi* grandfather, Durgacharan. They therefore, suggested that the boy be called Durgacharan. But Bhuvaneshavari considered the son to be a gift of Lord Vireshvara and so named him after that God. The name was soon abbreviated to Billay. It was later on changed to Narendranath. The suffix 'nath' was often dropped and 'Narendra' also was abbreviated to 'Naren' as it was easy speak.

There is a saying in Indian language that 'The son lying in the cradle indicates his future.'

In more ways than one, the little boy Naren appeared to prove this. He had a healthy body, keen intellect, sharp memory and a strong tendency for mischief. He would often get quite ungovernable. He would make his mother run after him from room to room, upstairs and downstairs and even in the big compound. He would climb up here and there, jump from heights quite dangerous for his age and trouble his elder sisters and his mother. Bhuvaneshvaridevi would lose her temper and start punishing the boy but in vain. At long last she found out a way to control her naughty son. She would bring a pot of cold water and pour the water on the head of the little boy. The next moment the boy would be as quiet as a lamb.

The exasperated mother would moan, 'I had prayed to Lord Shiva for the boon of a son and he sent me one of his demons instead.'

The transformation from this Shiva's demon of Bhuvaneshvaridevi to 'Narayana' in the form of 'Nara' of Shri Ramakrishna provides an interesting phenomenon.

3

Growing Up

Thomas Babington Macaulay had laid the foundation of the English system of education in India in 1836. He had imposed it. The three universities of Calcutta, Bombay and Madras had came into existence in 1857, the year which witnessed the last unsuccessful effort of the Indian rulers to drive away the British and the formal establishment of the rule of Queen Victoria. Indians, who had cut themselves off from all external contacts and influences, stood on the threshold of a new age. This transformation was to exact its own price.

The imposition of the English language and education was accompanied by the open and subtle attack on the religions and culture of the country by the missionaries. During 1861-62 there were 1153 educational institutions run by the missionaries in India, in which more than 1,00,000 students were studying. The great Raja Ram Mohan Roy had the guts to escape from the clutches of the missionaries. But the Raja's outlook had undergone a lot of transformation. Idol worship, meaningless practices, strict caste rules, untouchability, etc., were attacked by the missionaries and there was hardly anyone capable of challenging the missionaries. The impact of the Western sciences, physical and social, on the minds of those who took higher education was enormous. Some of the people like Michael Madhusudan Datta and Reverend Tilak cast off their ancient religion and converted themselves to Christianity. Others like Raja Ram Mohan Roy gave up traditional religious practises and started their own sects, which were a hotchpotch of the Hindu religion and Christianity. The Brahmo Samaj of Bengal had its echo in the Prarthana Samaj in Bombay and the Western India.

What the Indians did not know, however, was the traffic of influence in the reverse direction. It had started a few centuries ago when some European scholar had translated a few *Upanishads* into Latin from their Persian translation. But the English translation of the great drama Shakuntala of Kalidasa by Sir William Jones began a new era. Sir Jones had also translated the *Isha Upanishad* and some other pieces from the vast ocean of Sanskrit classics. Then some scholar translated the *Gita* into English. The great nature poet Wordsworth's philosophy shows some affinity to the great ancient Indian philosophy. Later on Thoreau, Whitman and Emerson were influenced by the philosophy of India. And Edwin Arnold's great translation of the *Gita*, The Song Celestial, and of the long poem *Buddha Charita*, The Light of Asia, had a widespread influence. In any case, some minds in the West had come to recognise the greatness of the ancient Indian philosophy and culture.

The influence of Indian thought on the West was, however, neither so widespread nor so intense as the influence of the Western education and culture on the Indian mind. Macaulay had run down Indian literature in a devastating manner, even though he had not read any single Indian book. The missionaries were very aggressive in their attacks and no one came forward to parry their well aimed cuts and thrusts. It was left to Dayananda Sarasvati and the Arya Samaj founded by him, who openly opposed the missionaries. As noted earlier, some people turned to Christianity and some others to new sects. Several others who did not have the courage to adopt either of the two paths, showed their lack of interest in the pursuit of religion and in following social customs. They did the things but without their hearts in the matter.

This was the scenario when young Naren was ready to carry a satchel to the temple of the goddess of learning. But the process of learning had started much earlier. As a matter of fact, for all children it starts from the moment of their birth. The assimilation of learning depends upon the grasping and retaining capacity of the infant. Narendra had both the capacities in abundance. He was gifted with a strong physique, good health and was bubbling with energy. He had a good height, big and bright forehead, sharp and big eyes and typical, tartar like jawbones. In his later life he used to say quite often that there was a tartar streak in him. His learning process was strikingly rapid, his grasp was comprehensive, and his retentive memory made repetitions of lessons absolutely unnecessary.

All the prayers and hymns Bhuvaneshvaridevi sang soon became little Narendra's property. He achieved mastery over the three R's effortlessly. His mother taught him the Bengali alphabet as well as several English words. The stories of the Ramayana and the Mahabharata were heard by him with rapt attention. He once heard a story teller say that the monkey god Hanuman lived in an orchard of Banana trees. Hanuman, who could cross over the sea at one jump and land himself from the southern tip of India into Sri Lanka, who could carry both Rama and Lakshmana on his shoulders effortlessly and who could set the whole Lanka on fire, naturally would attract impressive minds. Narendra's mind was one such. As soon as the story teller finished the story for the day, Narendra went to a banana orchard to see Hanuman. But there was neither Hanuman nor any of his soldiers and when it grew quite dark, little Narendra came home, rather dejected. Bhuvaneshvari consoled him, saying, "Well my son, Rama might have sent Hanuman on some other business."

In olden days when there were horse drawn carriages, the coachman was the ideal of the growing up boys. The coachman of his father's coach, perched high in front of the coach in his livery and controlling the powerful horses, naturally, was liked by the little boy. He very much desired to order people, like the coachman asking them to keep away from the path of the coach. Controlling the powerful horses also was a great thing in itself to young Naren. The coachman was unmarried and he liked the unmarried Hanuman and condemned marriage. Little Naren had installed clay idols of Rama and Sita in his room and had started worshipping the idols. But on hearing the coachman condemn married life, Narendra lost all his respect for Rama as he had married Sita and threw out the idols on the street.

Right from early childhood his uncommonness could be seen. Without anybody telling him, he had started sitting in meditation. Once, when he didn't respond to repeated calls by his elders, they started searching for him. They found him sitting in a room upstairs absorbed in meditation. Fortunately for him, they did not disturb him after locating him. He made his friends also play the game of meditation. Once when a few of his friends had joined him in the meditation game in a room of his house, in a few minutes the friends got up and fled away from the room. The young friends just could not concentrate their minds and in a couple of minutes they opened their eyes. When they did so, to their great horror, they saw a big snake crawling nearby to where they were seated. They were frightened and they soon took to flight. Not so did Narendra. He was totally unaware of the snake, nor was he at all aware of the noisy running away of his frightened friends. He was sitting absorbed, completely unaware of the outside world, as if meditation was natural to him. In later life he told his guru that every night while going to bed, he used to see some bright light in front of his eyes. This light hovered around for some time and then he fell asleep. He believed that it was a common occurence and everyone else must be seeing the effulgent light while going to bed.

The growing-up boy used to have two distinct ideals set before him in his visions. In one of them he saw himself as a very wealthy and successful man, rolling in luxuries, commanding men and controlling them. In another vision he saw himself as a mendicant *sannyasi*, who had renounced everything and yet, who commanded the world.

Right from early childhood, he exhibited another characteristic of his nature. Whenever a *sadhu* or a mendicant stood near the entrance of his house and begged for something, little Narendra would be the first person in the house to offer something to the begging person. He had given away a brand new dhoti of his to a *sadhu*. He would pick up anything handy and simply rush to the entrance to give it over to the *sadhu* at the door. The elders started locking him up in his room. But he would shower something on the begging *sadhu* at the door from the window of his room on the first floor. His elders who locked him up had no idea of how much he was to give later on and to how many people.

His father, who mainly remained engrossed in his clients, their law suits and his friends, had his own approach to the various problems of life. Little Naren once used some improper words while talking to his mother. Vishvanath was a witness to the scene witness scene and heard what his son had spoken and how. He did not punish his son for the impropriety, but with a piece of chalk wrote on the door of the room of Narendra, 'While talking to his mother today, Narendra had used these words.' Every friend of Narendra entering the room would read that. This taught young Narendra a lesson. On one occasion he asked Vishvanath, 'What have you done for me?' The great advocate's plea was, 'Look yourself into a mirror and find it out yourself.'

Under the preponderance of caste system, the drawing room of Vishvanath had many hookahs, different ones for people of different castes and one of them to be used by his Muslim friends and clients. Young Narendra could not understand the 'subtle' differences of the caste system and one day when there was no one in the drawing room, Narendra sneaked in and picking up the hookah pipes one by one, he found that each one gave the same taste. The hookah for the Muslims also was no different. Just when he had the pipe of the hookah reserved for the Muslims in his mouth, his father suddenly walked in and asked his son what he was doing. Narendra truthfully said that he wanted to find out the difference behind the different castes and creeds. 'What a big devil you are,' was the response of his father, accompanied with a smile on his face.

When Narendra was about six years of age his name was enrolled in a school nearby. But before learning anything of the three 'R's, he picked up some foul words from other boys and practised his newly acquired learning loudly at home. His elders wisely discontinued sending Narendra to that school. In another school, he was sent to, he had a different experience. The schools then in India were no different from the schools David Copperfield of Charles Dickens was sent to. A co-student of Narendra was caught playing some small mischief by the teacher and as a result was being punished mercilessly by the teacher. Narendra could not contain himself and spoke out that the punishment was quite out of proportion. The teacher considered it to be a challenge to his authority, left punishing the mischief monger, walked to Narendra and pulled Narendra up by his ear. Narendra's ear almost came out and he started bleeding because of the sudden forceful pull by the teacher. Narendra cried out loudly at the cruelty of the teacher. Just at that very time Ishvarchandra Vidyasagar, the founder of the school, happened to pass by in the lobby. He was horrified at the harshness of the punishment, bordering on cruelty and he intervened. The teacher might have been taught a lesson. But the severe injury caused to Narendra did not make him give up fighting for the right causes.

Narendra had a very receptive mind and retentive memory. One day he was talking with the other boys in the class while the teacher was teaching something. On hearing the noise the teacher asked one or two boys found out talking by him, to repeat what he had spoken. They failed miserably and were asked to stand up on the bench. Then the teacher asked Narendra to do so and the little boy repeated every word spoken by the teacher. The teacher asked him to sit down but Narendra joined his friends on the bench saying, "I was talking too." This shows the sharpness of his memory, his span of attention as well as his sense of truthfulness and loyalty to friends in sharing the guilt.

His strong physique took him to a gymnasium for various exercises. At first he had started a gymnasium in some part of the compound of his house. An uncle of his objected to this so he started visiting a neighbouring gymnasium regularly. Once the boys at the gymnasium were putting up a trapeze. But it was beyond their capacity to raise the two supporting pillars holding the thick and weighty pole linking the two pillars. A British sailor, who happened to pass by, came forward to help the little gymnasts. At long last they seemed to be nearing success when the whole structure they were trying to raise came down. No boy was injured but the falling beam struck the head of the foreign sailor who fell down unconscious. The other boys ran away frightened. Only Narendra had the courage and the presence of mind to apply first aid, pour cold water on the forehead and make arrangements for his stay for a couple of days till he fully recovered. He did not believe in running away out of fear.

He also exhibited qualities of leadership. He took his young friends to various places like the zoo etc. Even when he was turned out by the janitor at an office, he had managed to get into the office by the staircase on the back side and get the naval officer's permission on an application for seeing a man-of-war that had arrived there. This showed his resourcefulness. As he came out of the office with the permission, the janitor, who had prevented him from entering, asked him how he had managed to enter. 'I know magic,' was the ready retort of the young boy.

When Narendra was fourteen years of age, his father had to go to Raipur in the Central Provinces then, in connection with some work and stay there for a long time. He had taken his family with him. As the Bengal-Nagpur Railway had not joined Kolkata with that part of the country, they had to take a detour and go via Allahabad to Jabalpur and Nagpur by train and then reach their destination by bullock carts. It was a slow and long journey involving climbing up and down the Vindhya mountains, going on the edge of hills, going through thick forests, etc. It was a new experience altogether for the city-bred Narendra. The cart journey lasted for about a fortnight and Narendra enjoyed every bit of it. Once while the cart was passing through a narrow opening between two high hills, Narendra's roving eye fell on a beehive hanging high in a big crevice in one of the hills and hundreds of bees going round and round humming. The honeycomb which seemed to have been there since times immemorial, the narrow, widening passage between the hills, the tall trees looking like the fingers of the earth pointed towards the sky, the azure sky itself, all of these things had a strong impact on the mind of young Narendra, who lay down in his cart deeply absorbed, lost completely to everything around him. When he came back to himself, they had covered quite a few miles.

There was no going to school at Raipur. But that did not stop Narendra's education. He was a voracious reader and read anything he could lay his hands on. His father's erudition was a great help in itself. But the greater thing was the approach of Vishvanath, who did not impose anything upon his young son but put him questions, discussed various issues with him and guided him to find his own answers. The spectrum of topics Vishvanath discussed with his son was a very wide one. The advocate did not use his brilliance in the court room to floor down his adversary, but talked to his son in such a manner as would put the boy's imagination on fire, activate his reasoning processes and make him search for answers. Thus, the total environment at Raipur became a classroom for Narendra.

Vishvanath and party had gone to Raipur some time in 1877 and returned to Kolkata in 1879. It was now time for the Entrance Examination—the school final examination—of Narendra. But he had neither attended any school almost for the previous two years, nor had he taken any examination. But the headmaster and the teachers of the school knew Narendra quite well and after some formalities admitted Narendra to the top class in school and allowed him to appear for the Entrance Examination. Narendra was the only boy from the school to secure first class marks at the examination. His father presented him with a beautiful pocket watch.

Narendra joined the Presidency College for higher education. Mr. Hastie, the Principal of the College, while teaching Wordsworth's poem 'Excursion,' made a touching reference to 'the Paramahansa Ramakrishna of Dakshineshvar' while explaining the connotation of the word 'ecstasy' in the poem. But this reference evoked no special response in the mind of young Narendra. He was engrossed in reading literature, history, science, logic, philosophy etc. He seemed to be in search of something. This craving of his led him to become a member of Sadharan Brahmo Samaj. It was an offshoot of the Brahmo Samaj founded by Raja Rama Mohan Roy and after his death it was led by Devendranath Tagore, the father of the great poet Ravindranath. Maharshi Devendranath was highly influenced by the *Upanishads*, but the brilliant young man, Keshub Sen, whom the Maharshi had selected as his follower had come under the strong influence of the *Bible*. The difference in their outlooks, was fundamental and Keshub thought it prudent to leave the Maharshi alone and establish his own brand of the Brahmo Samaj, which came to be known as Sadharan Brahmo Samaj. The Maharshi's Samaj came to be known as the Adi (Original) Brahmo Samaj. Keshub was a learned man, deeply religious, powerful speaker, social reformer and prolific writer. His writings and speeches, coupled with the fame he had earned at home and in England made him an idol for the youths of Bengal. Like many others, Narendra joined the

Brahmo Samaj. Some time before Narendra's enrolment, there was another schism in the Samaj and poor Keshub had to part company with the Brahmo Samaj he had himself established and start the Nava Vidhan Brahmo Samaj. Narendra and his friend Rakhal, however, were members of the Sadharan Samaj, then led by Vijay Goswami and Shivanath Shastri. Both of them had come in contact with Shri Ramakrishna. But their reactions to him were totally different if not opposite. Vijay was slowly attracted towards Shri Ramakrishna and became a close devotee in future. Mr. Shastri stuck to his prejudices and considered the *samadhi*s of Shri Ramakrishna mental delusions.

Narendra's quest had led him to the Brahmo Samaj and had made him eagerly follow the routine of prayers at the Samaj gathering with earnestness, listen to the lectures given from the pulpit with rapt attention, and read the writings of Keshub, Shivanath Shastri and other leaders of the Samaj. Because of his sweet voice and mastery of music, he was one of the leading members of the choir at the Samaj. In spite of practising everything sincerely, his spiritual quest remained unquenched.

This harrowing thirst of him took him to Maharshi Devendra Nath. As Shri Ramakrishna had remarked later on with his inimitable wit, 'Yes, Devendra has best of both the worlds. He has wealth, status, fame and a large number of children. He also meditates on God and pursues the spiritual path.' In his spiritual pursuit, the Maharshi had tried to cut himself from the world and had chosen the seclusion of a boat for undisturbed meditation. The driving quest of Narendra made him break into the castle like boat of the Maharshi, who was astonished at the sudden arrival of the youth. But he was astonished much more when with penetrating eyes the young Narendra asked: 'Sir, have you seen God? The stunned Maharshi, took some time to speak and when he spoke, he did not give any reply to Narendra's query, but he said, 'young man, you have the eyes of a yogi'. Though this was quite flattering, it did not satisfy Narendra at all.

A chance call by his neighbour Surendra to go to the latter's place and sing a *bhajan* or two had placed him in contact with Shri Ramakrishna, who, with his sixth sense, had marked out the young collegian and asked the youth to visit Dakshineshvar. That encounter has been described in the first chapter. As stated there, Naren's mind was turned into an area where two entirely opposite and conflicting ideas about Ramakrishna were fighting a fierce duel. The poor young boy was not able to come to any final decision. But he remembered that he had given a promise to Shri Ramakrishna that he would visit the latter again and do so alone. He must keep the promise. And he kept it.

4

More Shocks

With the conflicting impact of his first encounter at Dakshineshvar, hanging heavily on his mind, Narendra set out to meet Shri Ramakrishna once more. He was very hesitant but he had promised to do so, and the promise had to be kept. He also wanted to understand the truth behind the personality of the Paramahansa, whose behaviour had exhibited two incomprehensible extremes: Was he a lunatic? Was he a saint?

On Narendra's first visit to Dakshineshwar, he had gone in a horse drawn cab, accompanied by Surendra and a couple of other friends. On the way to the Kali Temple, they must have been conversing and joking so he had no idea of the distance. On his second visit, he was alone and was going on foot. The walk was tiresome. But Naren's mind had become the Kurukshetra for the two conflicting ideologies: Was Ramakrishna a lunatic? But he was very saintly and affectionate. This contrast itself was a great puzzle. But there was a greater puzzle too. Narendra had been influenced by the rationalist thinking of Spencer and Mill. Were they insane if Ramakrishna was a wise saint? And what about the lessons he had been learning at the Brahmo Samaj? Narendra could see no meeting ground between his Brahmo learning and the strange behaviour and various utterances of Shri Ramakrishna. But, the utterances welling up from Ramakrishna's heart had a stunning ring of experience, which was simply gripping. All these thoughts were churning in the mind of the young man going to the Kali Temple.The four mile walk was not an easy one. When, after a strenuous walk, he reached his destination and entered the room of Shri Ramakrishna, Narendra found the old man sitting alone on the small, low platform he was sitting on at the time of his previous visit. Narendra noticed that the old man appeared to be a bit lost within himself and muttering something slowly to himself. Ramakrishna invited the young Kolkata boy to sit with him on the same platform. Narendra did that and took his seat a little bit away from Shri Ramakrishna. But Ramakrishna moved closer to Narendra and without uttering a single word touched the young man with his right foot.

That touch of Shri Ramakrishna was a gentle one but it proved to be cataclysmic to young Narendra. This is how he himself has described the encounter:

'He muttered something to himself which was incomprehensible to me. He looked hard at me, then he got up and came close to me. I thought that we were going to have another eccentric scene. But scarcely had the idea passed through my mind, when he touched me with his right foot. That very moment, I had an amazing experience. Both my eyes were wide open and I saw that everything in the room, including the walls and doors, appeared whirling round and round and moving further and further away into eternity. It also appeared to me that my consciousness of self, along with the entire universe was about to fade into a vast, all devouring void. I felt that the destruction of my self-consciousness was tantamount to my death. I experienced death right in front of me. I could not control myself and with a piercing cry, I said, "Oh, what is this that you are doing to me? I have my mother and father, don't you know that?" On hearing my agitated words, Thakur laughed a bit loudly. Then he touched my chest with his hand and said, "It's all right-It's enough for the day. It need not be done all at once. It will happen in its own course, at the proper time." To my utter amazement, the extraordinary vision I had just experienced vanished as speedily as it had come. I then saw that the walls and doors and things inside the room and outside were not moving but were stationary as before.

'The description of that experience has taken so much time, but it had taken place in a few moments only. But my entire thinking process had been changed by it. That experience of mine had begun and ended in obedience to the will of this extraordinary individual. Well, I had read about hypnotism in books. Was this experience of mine such a one? But my heart would not accept that. Because persons with great will-power can create such conditions only when they are working on men with weak minds. But mine was no such weak mind at all. I took pride in my intelligence and powerfull will. This old man could neither bewitch me nor make me a puppet of his. Contrarily speaking, when I had met him here for the first time, I had decided that he was a lunatic. Then, why did I find myself so suddenly in this awkward condition? This was a great riddle to me and it had to be solved. I firmly resolved to be on my guard, lest he overpowered me with his influence in the future.'

When Narendra had become normal once more, the scene changed totally. Shri Ramakrishna was talking with him and joking with him. As on the previous occassion, he gave Narendra things to eat and did it so affectionately as if Narendra was an old acquaintance of him. Narendra, however, was nonplussed at this show of affection, for, this was only his second visit to the strange man. It was nearing sunset and Narendra told his host that he, Narendra, must go back home. The very mention of the idea of Narendra's departure seemed to hurt Ramakrishna. He felt quite disappointed at the idea of separation from Naren. 'Promise me that you will return as soon as you can,' he spoke, holding Narendra's hand in his own. Parting from Narendra for him was all sorrow, without any tinge of sweetness. The young collegian had to promise that he would do so at the earliest.

The second visit to Dakshineshvar was more confusing than the first one for Narendra. It was true that, this time the behaviour of Shri Ramakrishna exhibited no 'lunatic' symptoms. But why was the old man showering so much affection on him who was visiting the Kali Temple for the second time only? A saint exhibiting so much attachment was quite unexpected. This strange behaviour of Ramakrishna was a puzzle. But the other 'terrifying' experience he had when Ramakrishna had just touched him was entirely incomprehensible. Did the old man of Dakshineshwar possess any magical powers? Although Narendra was walking southwards towards the city, his mind was held back by the magnet of Ramakrishna, about whose ecstacies Prof. Hastie had spoken in so glowing terms. What was an ecstasy? Was seeing all things moving round and round as if caught in a whirlpool and moving further and further away as if into nothingness—was that an ecstatic state? If so, of what use was it? Narendra had got frightened at the experience and cried out for a quick return to the normal state. And lo, when in response to his frightful appeal, Shri Ramakrishna had touched him again, the strange vision had disappeared with equal speed, if not greater. The science based on the theories propounded by Newton and Descartes had no explanation to offer. Nor could rationalist thinkers of the stature of Herbert Spencer and John Stuart Mill be of any help. However, fleeting was the experience of the vision that Narendra had at the mere touch of the foot of Shri Ramakrishna, its impact on the personality of the young collegian was very stunning. It seemed to have affected his total personality and to be posing a challenge to his rational, inquisitive mind. His sharp intellect wanted him to accept the challenge. He would unsheathe every cover hiding the riddle. Truth had to be found out.

He reached home, ate and drank and slept and attended his college classes and went out in the evenings. But the unsolved mystery of Shri Ramakrishna and the Dakshineshvar experience kept on needling his mind. He had promised Ramakrishna that he would visit Dakshineshvar once more. Now Narendra seemed to be in a hurry to keep the promise. The reason? The mystery had to be solved. Wasn't it the mystery of touch? At the touch of Ramakrishna's foot, he was transported to, but he did not know where. It was a terrible experience. Totally unbearable. In a few seconds it had made him cry out. And the sharp terror-striken cry made Ramakrishna touch him again. Lo and behold! This touch had made the frightening vision disappear. Was there something in the touch of Shri Ramakrishna? If so, what was it? No other person Narendra knew with different degrees of intimacy possessed any such power. He had shaken hands with many and many elderly people had put their hands on his head or back, uttering blessings. But Narendra had never experienced anything remotely similar to what Ramakrishna's touch had made him experience. Nor did he know anyone else who had undergone such a phenomenal experience. He decided to go at the earliest.

Narendra paid his third visit to Dakshineshwar about a week later. This time he was very conscious and was very much on his guard. He had steeled his will not to fall a prey to Ramakrishna's hypnotism or mesmerism, in case he possessed any such occult power. On the day Narendra visited the Kali temple, there were quite a few persons moving around and offering prayers and talking. Soon after his arrival in Ramakrishna's room, the latter suggested that they would walk together, away from the people, in a nearby garden. Narendra readily agreed. Touching the Kali temple complex of Rani Rasmani, on the city side, was a big garden house of one Yadu Mallik. Yadu had come to know Shri Ramakrishna, was attracted by his spiritual qualities and had always tried to be of help to Shri Ramakrishna. It was in the drawing room of the bungalow of this same Yadu that Shri Ramakrishna had seen the picture of Virgin Mary holding the baby Jesus and was drawn to Christ. Ramakrishna went there with Narendra and after strolling in the garden of the bungalow on the bank of the Ganga for some time, Ramakrishna took his young visitor to the parlour. Yadu had given standing instruction to the housekeeper to open up the parlour whenever Ramakrishna visited the place.

Both of them sat down on a sofa or a bench. Narendra was determinedly on the alert. In a few minutes Narendra saw something quite different. Ramakrishna became silent. His eyes were half open. His mouth wore its usual bewitching smile. But Ramakrishna looked like a log of wood to Narendra, totally lifeless. Ramakrishna had passed into *samadhi*. Narendra sat there observing this state of Ramakrishna. Narendra had never seen anyone in such a state before. The youth was on his alert. All of a sudden, Ramakrishna touched Narendra and the young man's armour of alertness seemed to fall apart totally. In spite of his strong will, Narendra soon lost his consciousness. He had become totally unconscious. He had no idea as to how long he remained in that unconscious state. But when he started regaining consciousness, he experienced the soothing touch of Shri Ramakrishna on his, Narendra's, chest. Not only that, Narendra saw that Ramakrishna was looking at him, wearing a gentle and sweet smile. There was no exchange of words. Ramakrishna exhibited no sign of insanity as he had done when Narendra had met him for the first time and whisked him away into the verandah. Ramakrishna did not utter any precepts either. Young Narendra had absolutely no idea of what had happened in the parlour of Yadu Mallik's house. Both of them must have walked back to the room of Shri Ramakrishna in the temple complex, where Ramakrishna must have made Narendra eat something endearingly and had not felt happy when Narendra must have begged his leave for departure and must have certainly asked him to come again.

Swami Sharadananda tells us in his great biography of his Guru what Ramakrishna told some of his disciples about it. 'Later, on his third visit, when we were sitting in the parlour of Yadu Mallik and Naren had lost his outer consciousness, I put him several questions, such as who he really was, why he had come, how long he would stay in this world etc., etc. I made him dig deep into the innermost recesses of his being and his answers came from there. All his answers precisely confirmed everything I had learnt about him in my visions. It is forbidden to tell all these things to anyone. But I must tell you that, on the very day he comes to know who he really is, he will no longer remain in this world. With his great will power, he will immediately cast aside his body through *Yoga shakti*. Naren is a *Mahatma*. He is perfect in meditation.'

The vision of Shri Ramakrishna about Narendra has been described in the first chapter. At the very first sight of the boy at Surendra's house, Ramakrishna might, rather must, have been reminded of his vision. He just could not control himself when Narendra visited him for the first time at Dakshineshvar and he took the young visitor to the verandah at the back of the room. At the second visit of Narendra, Ramakrishna probably tested him and wanted to guage Narendra's readiness to receive his spiritual inheritance. The third visit of Narendra removed all doubts, if at all there were any, because Ramakrishna had the sixth sense to penetrate in to the innermost depth of an individual at just a glance at the visitor. And yet, Ramakrishna took all these precautions. He did not want to sow the seeds of his unique spiritual wealth on a stone or in sand. In Narendra, he found the most fertile loam of the Ganga plains and the enormous power of the mighty Himalayas to stand firm against the most powerful cyclones.

On his way back, this time, Narendra was a mellowed man. His pride in his will power had now given way to the acceptance of some ability of Shri Ramakrishna, much more superior to his own. It was true that he had so far not succeeded at all to fathom it, yet he decided that he would not blindly accept anything in the traditional manner according to which a disciple submits to his guru. He was entirely opposed to the tradition prevalent in the Hindu religion of blind faith in a guru. 'I would not surrender my freedom of judgement to Shri Ramakrishna or to anyone else. Yes, Shri Ramakrishna is head and shoulders above other human beings. I'll go to him and learn everything he has to teach. But I'll test every word of his teaching. I won't accept anything blindly.' This was the chain of thoughts in Narendra's mind when he was on his way home.

5

Shri Ramakrishna and Naren

One of the reasons which had driven Narendra to Shri Ramakrishna was a social one. His father Vishvanath was a legal luminary and a man of status. His life style apparently indicated his high financial standing. His wife Bhuvaneshvaridevi, apart from being the wife of a leading attorney, was well known for her various qualities, charitable nature and pious disposition. Narendra was their son. Narendra himself had a tall and stout physique, big, bright eyes, affable temperament, a brilliant intellect and he had a wide spectrum of interests. Naturally, he was the cynosure of all eyes. He was now an eligible bachelor. And in those days of the nineteenth century, he had started attracting the attention of several fathers who had daughters of ten years of age and over. The girl may or may not be intelligent or attractive, but the dowry offered by the parents acted as a great magnetic power.

A wealthy father of a young daughter approached Vishvanath and Bhuvaneshvaridevi. Their daughter was good looking and they were willing to offer a good dowry. The parents of Narendra were tempted by the offer, but not Narendra. As mentioned in a previous chapter, in one of his visions he saw himself as a *sannyasi,* abstaining from all wealth and property and not marrying. He had heard the story of his grandfather who had abandoned his young wife and only son and taken orders. Was it not better, he thought, if one wanted to renounce the world, to keep away from marriage itself?

Another proposal, from one point of view more tempting than the first, was received. Its negative side was that the bride-to-be was not fair looking, but its positive side was the offer by the girl's father to send Narendra to England where he might study for the most coveted Indian Civil Service, or may join one of the four inns and return as a barrister at law, join the father's office and have a roaring practice. The worldly wise Vishvanath found it very tempting. He tried to force young Narendra to accept the offer. Though they were both living in the same house and were on friendly terms, Vishvanath had no idea that his teenager son was readying himself for absolutely another kind of life. Narendra had been practising meditation since childhood. He had started abstaining from non-vegetarian food and sleeping on the bare floor. He had no clear vision of the goal of his life, yet unconsciously, he was thus preparing for it. And marriage did not fit into that picture at all. Naturally, he turned down the attractive offer.

This offer, subsequent consultations and discussions and arguing with Narendra by the elders of the house must have taken some time. Ramachandra Datta, a close relative of the family might have come to know of the proposal, so attractive from the worldly point of view, and of its firm refusal by young Narendra. Along with Surendra Mitra and Manmohan, he had been drawn to Shri Ramakrishna and had become a devotee of the Paramahansa. When he learnt about Naren's turning down of the attractive proposal of marriage, he said to Naren, 'If you don't want to marry and lead a worldly life and if you desire to give up the world and become a *sadhu*, you should better go to Dakshineshvar and meet Shri Ramakrishna Paramahansa and seek his guidance'.

Principal Hastie's reverential reference to Shri Ramakrishna, Rakhal's likely references to his visits to Dakshineshwar, or any stray reference to the saint at the Brahmo Samaj Naren so regularly attended, seemed to have failed in making Naren visit

Dakshineshvar. The young boy was groping. His vast and pointed reading of history, literature, science and philosophy had many interesting ideas to offer, but none was able to lead him to his goal. John Mill's 'Essay on Religion' added fuel to the fire. The great motto of the French revolution, 'Liberty, Equality, Fraternity,' was energising in its own way, but it would not bring any peace of mind to the tormented mind of Naren. His friend Brijendranath Seal, who later on earned fame as a well known scholar and rose to be the vice chancellor of Mysore University, tried to counsel him but without any success. The torment in his mind turned into a holy fire, the flames of which were consuming his innards. Like a storm tossed vessel, he was carried hither and thither by the different gusts. Even his regular visits and attentive participation at the Brahmo Samaj had miserably failed to satisfy the earnest cravings of his soul. At this critical juncture in his life, he was called to sing a *bhajan* or two by his neighbour Surendra when Shri Ramakrishna was visiting him. This, though looked like a chance meeting, was a tryst with destiny for the young Naren.

That meeting at Surendra's place, invitation by Shri Ramakrishna and the hint by Ramachandra, all had combined to take Naren to Dakshineshvar. The first meeting between the two, as we have noted in chapter 1, instead of quenching young Naren's spiritual quest, appeared to have made him question the very sanity of the Paramahansa, so praised and respected by Surendra and Ramachandra and so respectfully referred to by such a great person as Keshub Sen in his writings. The queer behaviour of Ramakrishna in the verandah towards him had made Narendra think of the former as a maniac. Ramakrishna's renunciation, his purity, his piety, his affection towards him, Naren, were no doubt impressive. Naren was torn within himself.

His insatiable thirst for truth made him accept the invitation so affectionately given to him to visit Dakshineshwar again. The impact of the slight touch by the person whom he had taken for a mad man previously, had transported him into a world undreamt of by him, from where he just wanted to flee away. Another magic touch by Shri Ramakrishna had brought him back to the room on the bank of the holy Ganga, near Kolkata. For young Naren, this was an equally disorientating experience like the first, if not more. Without any conscious effort on his part, his opinion about Shri Ramakrishna was undergoing change. Did Ramakrishna possess any special power? If yes, what was it? How strong must that superior power of Ramakrishna be, that an intelligent, well-read, strong willed youth like himself crashed down as a sand castle to be blown away with a gust of sea breeze? And he also could not understand the second restoring touch of Shri Ramakrishna, which had completely made him free from that 'harrowing' vision of his. Naren had neither read about, nor heard about anything like that. The riddle of Ramakrishna seemed to get enwrapped into an enigma. But it made Narendra modify his impression of Ramakrishna being insane.

The promise he had given to Shri Ramakrishna and the desire to solve the mystery of the Paramahansa made Naren pay his third visit to Dakshineshvar. The fortress of his strong will, which he thought was invincible, splintered and crumbled down at just a touch of the Paramahansa. The touch, this time, had made him lose all outward consciousness. Every touch of this fragile looking, smiling 'magician' seemed to have a different effect. The chemistry of Ramakrishna's touch posed a big problem for Narendra. He might be able to solve it at any time or not, Naren had to come to a conclusion: Shri Ramakrishna was no ordinary individual and seemed to possess some superior, indefinable power, difficult for Naren to comprehend. Though the tossing of his mind had not stopped, he had come to admit that this poorly clad Paramahansa, so careless about his external appearance, possessed rich spiritual wealth and, may be, he might be able to guide young Naren, in his quest. But he would not submit to Shri Ramakrishna blindly, accepting every word that he spoke. He would apply his critical faculty to every word of Shri Ramakrishna, put it to all sorts of tests possible, weigh it in the light of his own knowledge and throw away what he found as chaff. The apparently opposite ideals of action and contemplation which were pulling in different directions had to be reconciled and a proper path had to be chalked out, Naren didn't know how helpful Shri Ramakrishna would be in that. Would one of the two be jettisonned overboard?

Narendra knew himself to be a voracious reader, gifted with razor sharp intellect and indelible memory. When at Surendra's place, Narendra had first stepped into Shri Ramakrishna's ken and when the Paramahansa had assured himself that the youth facing him was none other than the *rishi* he had seen in his vision, and that he had the *Sheshanaga* like capacity to carry a huge burden, long and strong hands that could reach anywhere and could hold and mould things and persons, energetic and powerful legs that could carry him to wander anywhere in the world and the vision, and decision making faculty of the great Chandragupta Maurya, which made him a born commander of men. The moment Ramakrishna cast his glance on the carefree Narendra, he had resolved to catch the youth in his net and with his spiritual chisel mould the agnostic looking youth into his great successor. As a boy of five or six years of age, Narendra had fallen down from a height and had suffered a serious injury on his forehead. He had taken quite some time to regain consciousness. The injury had left a mark on his forehead. Shri Ramakrishna had said that if that had not happened, Naren would have shaken the whole world.

Ramakrishna also appreciated Narendra's agnostic attitude, which would not take anything for granted. Everything had to be tested on the touchstone of reason. Nothing absolutely should be accepted with blind faith-that was Narendra's attitude. One day when he criticised 'blind faith,' his guru flabbergasted him by the question: 'Well, Naren, Can you show me faith with eyes?' Naren could not think of any reply.

Thus an invisible bond was being formed, a knot much stronger than the one tied by Gordius, a knot that no one could untie, no Alexander could cut. The knot was to revive India, breathe new life into the giant that had been lying dormant for almost a millennium, the giant that seemed to have lost his psyche and all his physical and intellectual and spiritual strength, the giant that had splintered himself into innumerable castes and subcastes, which formed a pyramid, at the bottom of which were placed the poor untouchables, a giant that had fallen a prey to evil customs like child marriage, forced widowhood and evil treatment of widows, a society that had shut itself completely from the outside world and thus had caused stagnation in all areas of knowledge. The new education had, no doubt, opened new vistas, but that was for the fortunate few, who could avail themselves of the facility of schooling. But its great drawback was that the prejudiced influence of the missionaries made most of the educated Indians look down upon everything Indian. Unless one knew wherein lay the real strength of India, educated Indians would turn into brown sahibs. The spirit had to be awakened. The chain of narrow-mindedness had to be broken. The cub, brought up in a herd of sheep and thinking himself to be a lamb, had to be led to a river and made to see his leonine face, his growing mane and then taught to roar like a lion instead of bleating like a lamb. At his very first glance on Narendra, Ramakrishna's discerning eye had found out that the young Datta boy was the person marked out for that job. Yes, Naren was not aware of his guru's vision. Ramakrishna would remove all the wrappings on the youth's awareness. The youth's agnosticism was a positive quality. When the youth places his revelations before the world, he would do so with the authority of personal experience. 'Don't believe in a thing because the *Shastras* say so. Don't believe in it because I say so. Test everything yourself before you believe.' These words of the great Buddha were also the watchwords of Shri Ramakrishna.

This understanding of the mission of Narendra coupled with Ramakrishna's vision, made a spring of affection flow in his heart for young Naren. And the young collegian also reciprocated it. After the first three meetings, Narendra started visiting Dakshineshvar almost every weekend. On occasions, he would arrive on Saturdays and sleep there overnight and would return late on Sunday evenings, and at times, on Monday mornings. Then he started visiting Ramakrishna on weekdays also. In case Naren failed to do so for some reason or another, Shri Ramakrishna felt like a jilted lover.

Baburam, who came to be known later on as Swami Premananda, was taken by Rakhal to Dakshineshvar, some time in 1883. Young Baburam was accompanied by one Ramdayal, who was known to Shri Ramakrishna. When the trio arrived at the Kali Temple and went to the room of Shri Ramakrishna, they found the room empty. Rakhal, future Swami Brahmananda, told, his companions that he would go and bring Shri Ramakrishna back to his room. A few minutes later, he returned holding the old man's hand. The old man, Shri Ramakrishna, walked unsteadily, and was staggering as if drunk, but was under the influence of *Samadhi*. Rakhal had to guide every step of his guru. When, after a lot of conversation and dinner, they retired for the night, Rakhal was offered a bed in the room of Shri Ramakrishna and Baburam and Ramdayal were asked to sleep in the northern verandah. At about 11:00 p.m., Ramakrishna walked into the verandah, asked if the two guests were awake and when Ramdayal answered in the affirmative, Shri Ramakrishna said, 'Please do one thing for me at the earliest tomorrow. You know Naren very well. He has not shown his face for quite some time. His long absence has been causing me much pain. I find it unbearable. My heart feels like a drenched towel being squeezed. Please go to him and tell him to visit here at the earliest.' Baburam was astonished to find that this happened three or four times during the night.

Ramakrishna was found shedding profuse tears and he was also found totally unmindful of his clothes also. At that time Baburam didn't know who Naren was.

Vaikunthnath Sanyal, another devotee of Shri Ramakrishna, had a similar story to tell. He had been to Dakshineshvar some time in I883. He was simply amazed to hear Shri Ramakrishna tell him again and again that he, Ramakrishna, had been simply longing to see Narendra who had not been to Dakshineshvar for quite some time. Ramakrishna's face looked like being chiselled by the deep feeling of separation. He just could not bear Narendra's keeping away for such a long time—about a month or so. Vaikunth was requested again and again to go to the Simla Mohulla and tell Narendra how painful was the effect of his absence from Dakshineshvar on Ramakrishna. It was just unbearable. A few days after this visit of Vaikunth babu, they were celebrating Ramakrishna's birthday. All the young disciples and other devotees were there. Ramakrishna was wearing new clothes, his forehead was bedecked by sandal paste and a nice garland of flowers adorned his neck. Everyone present there was having nice time but not the hero of the occasion. This was so only because his beloved Naren was not there. Ramakrishna was simply missing him and he said so many times. All of a sudden, Narendra walked in and the mood of Ramakrishna underwent total transformation. He was so overjoyed at seeing his beloved disciple that as soon as Naren bowed down to his guru and took his seat on the floor, Shri Ramakrishna rushed towards Naren and got entrenched on his shoulders.

Shri Ramakrishna's affection for Naren was unparalleled and was to express itself much more strongly, later on. But that affection was never allowed to come in the way of the resolution of Narendra's doubts.

6

I See Narayana in him

Shri Ramakrishna never called a press conference to give publicity to the vision he had about Narendra, as described in the first chapter. He spoke about it much later to a few select disciples like Sharadananda. But, as mentioned in the previous chapter, he could not hide his unparalleled affection for Narendra. There was no place for any giving and taking in it. Or rather, there was giving in it only as mentioned in the first chapter, when he had gone out of the way and carried *Prasada* for him in the verandah and almost forced it through the young man's throat.

Apparently, Shri Ramakrishna was completely different from Narendra. Ramakrishna was a rustic, born in a poor Brahmin family in a village. Narendra was born and brought up in the then capital of British India and his father was a well-to-do person. Ramakrishna had very little formal education and he never read any books. Naren was a brilliant student, had graduated from the Calcutta University and was a widely read youth. Physically, Ramakrishna was diminutive in size and had an almost fragile frame. Narendra was tall and stout, he took regular exercises at a gymnasium and his body could withstand any shock. Ramakrishna did not have any intellectual pursuits while Narendra was out and out an intellectual. Ramakrishna was firmly rooted in faith and religion and spirituality. Narendra was groping in the dark, was affected by the so called rationalist thoughts of Spencer and Mill and was on the border of agnosticism, if not out and out atheism. Ramakrishna was an idol worshipper. To Narendra an idol was an anathema. Narendra's first impression of Shri Ramakrishna as a crank had to be added to this. The only thing in Shri Ramakrishna that had appealed to the 'young Bengal' was Ramakrishna's simplicity, truthfulness, renunciation and his convincing assertion that he had seen God.

This vast area of antithesis, however, had not prevented young Narendra from developing close contact with Shri Ramakrishna and the main factor for this kind of development was the limitless love the latter exuded from every pore of his personality for Naren. Other disciples had to adhere to a strict routine, do's and don'ts to follow and rules and regulations to observe. Narendra was allowed full freedom. Shri Ramakrishna was being offered sweets and fruits by all sorts of people. With his unerring instinct, he would immediately know who were the genuine ones and who the pretentious ones. He would not touch any stuff, how very costly it might be, offered by such scum. Nor would he allow any of his disciples to do so. Naren was the only exception. Where others would come down spiritually if they even touched such stuff offered by worldly, selfish, base persons, Naren was allowed to consume it freely, without the slightest fear, because, Naren has the fire of knowledge constantly burning in him. The fire of knowledge in him would purify everything he ate or touched. As mentioned in the fourth chapter of the *Gita* (36-37), the fire of knowledge burns all impure actions and the boat of knowledge takes one across the ocean of life. And Narendra had that fire of knowledge constantly burning in him.

Strangely enough, Narendra was not aware of the presence of this 'great fire of knowledge' in him. No doubt, Narendra was conscious of his high intellectual abilities and it seemed to have given him some intellectual arrogance also. But he did not know, could not understand the full implication of this 'fire of knowledge.' Shri Ramakrishna's knowledge about everything, including this 'fire of Knowledge,' put Naren in an extremely embarrassing situation once.

It had so happened that Keshub, Vijay Goswami and several members of the Brahmo Samaj had been to Dakshineshvar once. They had a very happy time as always in the company of Shri Ramakrishna. Naren, a few other disciples and devotees were also there and enjoying the conversation between the two. As usual, Shri Ramakrishna's room had become a great mart of joy. Some time later, Keshub, Vijay and a couple of other Brahmos bade goodbye to Shri Ramakrishna and left the place. Other Brahmos continued to sit there along with the disciples and devotees of Shri Ramakrishna. Shri Ramakrishna's mood changed and he was lost in thought for some time. That was nothing unusual to the people sitting there. It must have lasted for a few moments, for soon thereafter Shri Ramakrishna burst forth with an astounding statement. He said, 'If Keshub has one shining energy, Naren has eighteen such energies.' Everyone present there was stunned on hearing this statement and sat there with their mouths wide open. Some followers of Keshub might have started casting subtle meaningful glances at Naren also. But the young man with 'eighteen energies' just could not control himself. 'Sir, 'he spoke with a loud and stern voice, 'what odd, meaningless comparisons you are blurting out? Where stands Shri Keshub Sen, a man with international reputation, leader of the Brahmo Samaj, a powerful orator, an eminent writer and where am I, just a school boy, not known fully to everyone in the Simla area also? Please control yourself.'

'Do I say so on my own?' asked Shri Ramakrishna, with a great emphasis on 'I'. He then added, 'It is the Mother who makes me say so!'

No one else in the room, including Naren himself had any idea that these prophetic words of Shri Ramakrishna would come true in about a decade. And when the prophesy came true, Pratapchandra Majumdar, the great lieutenant of Keshub Sen, who looked upon young Naren almost as his protege, would burn with jealosy, turn hostile and pour invectives on Naren.

This incident clearly indicates the solid reason of Shri Ramakrishna, for showering such unique affection on young Naren, who was no kith or kin of his. Whatever angularities were there in the apparently agnostic Naren were smoothened out by Shri Ramakrishna in a manner that would look almost effortless. If Naren became slightly irregular for one reason or another and failed to turn up at Dakshineshvar, Ramakrishna would feel the pangs of separation. Two incidents mentioned earlier, one of Ramdayal and another of Vaikunthnath Sanyal, both of whom had been pestered by Shri Ramakrishna and told again and again to go back and tell Naren to visit Dakshineshvar, bear clear testimony to this.

Another incident of the affectionate longing of Shri Ramakrishna might also be mentioned. He could not bear any separation from his beloved disciple. Unfortunately, Naren was not able to go to Dakshineshvar for quite some time and Ramakrishna didn't know where to locate the young whelp. After some thinking about the matter, Ramakrishna concluded that Naren might be wandering hither and thither all the time on all other days, but being a leading member of the Brahmo Samaj choir, Naren would not miss the Brahmo Samaj meetings held regularly on certain days of the week. So he took some one with him on one particular evening and went to the Brahmo Samaj.

The place was well-known to him, as he used to visit the place when Keshub was the leading light of the Brahmo Samaj. Unfortunately, Keshub had broken one of the Samaj rules, made at his own instance. The Brahmo Samaj, ever since it was founded by Raja Ram Mohan Roy, laid great emphasis on social reform and the rule referred to here laid down that no member of the Brahmo Samaj would arrange the marriage of his daughter until she had completed thirteen years. It had, however, so happened that Keshub who was instrumental for this rule had got his daughter married to the Maharaja of Cooch Bihar before she had attained that age. Naturally, all the members of the Brahmo

Samaj were up in arms and poor Keshub, the founder of the Samaj, separate from the original one led by Maharshi Devendra Nath, had to quit it. Shivanath Shastri and other Brahmos who were occupying the front seats did not like Ramakrishna primarily because he was a man preaching traditional religion and more so because of his influence on Keshub, their ex-leader.

Naturally, therefore, Shri Ramakrishna was an unwelcome visitor. On his own part also, Ramakrishna did not expect any formal welcome. On entering the hall, he started walking towards the altar, where, in former days, he was always respectfully made to sit. Or, he might have designed to go there in order to be able to spot his little lamb. His sudden arrival and his proceeding to the altar caused a commotion. The acharya, the preacher at the altar, was forced by this commotion to interrupt his lecture. This sudden stopping of the ritual made the other devotees quietly sitting and listening, stand up and look up. There was more commotion. Several people rose up from their seats to have a look at the intruder, Ramakrishna. Somebody switched the gas lights off. The resulting darkness confounded the confusion. Naren ran up to where his guru was standing and holding him by his hand, slowly led him out of the hall on the street. In the first instance he felt slighted at the discourtesy shown to his guru by the gathering of people at the Samaj. But the bigger reason for his displeasure was the uninvited visit of Ramakrishna there, which had landed him into such an awkward situation. Naren was no fool to remain unaware of the purpose of Shri Ramakrishna's arrival there.

Ramakrishna told Naren that the latter's long absence at Dakshineshvar was causing him indescribable pain, his longing to see his 'dear Naren' was piercing his heart and the separation had become unbearable for him. Naren almost took him to task for this infatuation, which had landed his revered guru into this insulting condition. 'For your sake Naren,' said Shri

Ramakrishna, 'I am ready to bear any insults and suffer anything. This is so only because I see Narayana in you. The day I'll stop doing so, I'll not even cast a glance at you.'

Narendra who was so conscious of his physical and mental abilities, who was so widely read and had so varied interests could not understand his guru's seeing 'Narayana' in him. One day, at Dakshineshvar, when some such talk was going on, he just could not control himself and said to Shri Ramakrishna: 'It's all nonsense you are talking. It's nothing but a figment of your brain.' He continued to talk in this vein for quite some time and spoke in a manner which would convince ordinary people. But Ramakrishna was not an ordinary individual. As he often used to say, he was merely an instrument in the hands of Ma. Whatever Ma made him do, he did. Whatever Ma made him speak he spoke. So on hearing long winded arguments from Naren when he found himself a bit perplexed, he said, 'Wait a minute. I'll go and ask Ma if I am right or wrong.' So saying he went to the Kali temple with signs of worry chiselled on his face, but only to come back with a broad smile on his face the very next moment. And entering his room, he looked at Naren and endearingly said, 'you wretch, never try to misguide me. Ma tells me you are Narayana, come to earth to perform some great mission of hers.'

The young *Narayana* sat there with a stunning silence.

7

Moulding of Naren

Shri Ramakrishna was one of the greatest teachers. His greatness as a teacher consisted in the fact that he never made all his disciples sit together and gave them a formal lecture on any subject. Shri Ramakrishna's seminary did not have well-defined semesters, it had no listed holidays, it did not have benches and desks, chairs and tables, it did not have a black board and it had no library. His students did not carry notebooks and pencils or pens to write down notes. They were never given assignments. They submitted no papers from time to time. There were no fixed periods, there was no ringing of the bell. And yet he was a unique teacher. And his disciples were also unique. They were so diverse; they were of different ages and different educational achievements and of different mindsets. Yet their common goal was spiritual pursuit.

Rakhal's mother had died when he was yet an infant. Rakhal's father had married again and the stepmother showered all affection on Rakhal. Yet, when he came to Shri Ramakrishna led by his brother-in-law, Manmohan, Ramakrishna could immediately perceive the shepherd boy of Vrindavan he had seen in one of his visions and showered all maternal affection on the seventeen year old lad. He made Rakhal sit on his lap also. He would feed Rakhal with butter and other things freely. But one day, when the same Rakhal took the liberty to consume all the butter lying in the room without his guru's permission, Rakhal was severely reprimanded for that act of indiscipline.

Niranjan was a stout and strong youth with powerful muscles. He was once going by boat to Dakshineshvar. Some of the fellow passengers in the boat started criticising Shri Ramakrishna, called him a fake and a good-for-nothing fellow. Young Niranjan could not bear hearing his guru being so insulted by the people in the boat. He got up instantly and standing with his legs wide apart threatened his co-passengers that he would sink the boat and all the foul mouthed persons would go down with it. So saying, he started giving pressure on his legs alternatively and the boat started moving this way and that and the passengers got frightened, they begged his pardon and begged for mercy. Niranjan relented and got down at the Kali temple ghat, threatening the people in the boat of dire consequences if he ever heard them speaking ill of his guru.

With his face aflush with anger and a sense of victory Niranjan entered Shri Ramakrishna's room and narrated the incident. He thought that he would be congratulated for his act of bravery and for upholding the great name of his guru. But what happened was quite different, entirely opposite. 'You should not lose your temper over such flimsy matters. Anger is very harmful in pursuing the spiritual path. You would have, in your anger, committed a great sin, the sin of drowning the people in the boat. And along with those who were speaking ill of me, there must have been other passengers who were quite innocent. You would have killed such innocent people also. Never let yourself be a prey to anger.' This was the lesson preached to him by Shri Ramakrishna.

Yogin was another disciple of Shri Ramakrishna. Just like his gurubhai Niranjan he took once a boat for going to Dakshineshvar. On hearing about his destination, some fellow passengers started criticising and ridiculing Ramakrishna, someone called him an impostor and another one called him a cheat. This game of abusing went on for quite some time. Yogin heard all this, felt very unhappy at the insults hurled at his Guru, but thought that discretion was better than valour and so kept quiet. 'A word of this is not going to affect the glory of my guru,' he thought to himself and sat quietly all the way. Right till he disembarked at the Dakshineshvar temple ghat, Yogin's fellow passengers kept on poking fun at Ramakrishna and calling him different names. When he climbed up the ghat steps and reached the room of his Guru, his face clearly indicated that he was suffering from some mental agony.

When Shri Ramakrishna came to know that Yogin had remained a silent witness to all the insults hurled at his guru, he took the youth to task. 'Are you not ashamed of your behaviour ? Some people go on insulting your guru all the way and you sit hearing all the foul words as if you are a detached yogi sitting in meditation. You should have fought the critics of your guru. They had formed an opinion of me merely by hearsay. Fie on you.' Poor Yogin hung his head in shame.

These two instances bring out the extraordinary pedagogical approach of Shri Ramakrishna. In both the cases, there was complete similarity of the happening, listening to invectives hurled at one's guru. But Niranjan was scolded for his opposition to the people who were speaking ill of his guru and was advised to control his anger, which might have resulted in the death of many people in the boat, some of whom were absolutely innocent. In the case of Yogin, the guru preached him resistance to evil, not sumbission to it. This is a glaring illustration of the individualistic approach of Shri Ramakrishna's teaching. He very often told the story of a mother who would cook different things for her different children, and so take into consideration their different tastes and different capacities of digestion. He was like that mother.

He was apparently an idol worshipper, who worshipped the image of the Goddess Kali. But he never asked any of his disciples to follow him and fall at the feet of Kali in the temple. Rakhal and Naren were members of the Brahmo Samaj, where all idol worship was condemned. As hinted earlier, Rakhal came to Shri Ramakrishna before Naren. Both the young boys had signed on oath that they would not worship idols and that God was formless. Yet, after meeting Shri Ramakrishna and coming under his influence, Rakhal might have changed his belief or, it might be that he had signed on the dotted line on the Brahmo Samaj form without understanding its full significance. Whatever it might have been, but when Naren, who came in contact with Ramakrishna later on, saw Rakhal going to the Kali temple and making obeissance to the idol of the goddess, Narendra flared up at this and he reprimanded Rakhal for the sacrilege the latter had committed. Naren's indignation was righteous in its own way. Rakhal realised the breach of the oath he had taken at the Brahmo Samaj but he was not bold enough to say that he had signed without understanding, or that his belief had undergone change. He stood silent, with his face bowed down, against the volley of Naren. But Ramakrishna, to whom both the boys were like his own sons, told Naren that Rakhal had done nothing wrong in going into the Kali temple and bowing before the idol standing in the temple. Rakhal might have changed his opinion. 'Don't you believe in freedom of opinion? His signature on the Brahmo Samaj form cannot be taken as a lifelong commitment. Don't be harsh to the young boy.' This was how Ramakrishna took Rakhal's side and made Naren quiet. Quiet Naren did become, and he did not argue further or let Rakhal down. But this did not make him change his firm belief against idol worship.

A couple of years passed by. The Ganga carried her regular seasonal tributes to the mighty ocean. The sudden death of Vishvanath Datta had brought about an unexpected and unhappy change in the life of Naren. Penury stalked every step of Naren who was till then leading the life of a carefree, happy go lucky youth. So bitter were the circumstances that Naren often lied to his mother, saying, 'I have taken my meals at a friend's place.' He chose to remain hungry and thereby save a few grains of rice and some flour. He walked miles and miles, climbed numerous staircases, knocked doors of many offices and begged for a job only to hear, 'sorry, no-vacancy. 'He felt the foundations of his faith shattering. Ramakrishna's sympathy for his dear Naren had become boundless on coming to know of the change in the circumstances of his disciple. Feeling totally enervated and helpless, Naren was driven to request Ramakrishna one day, 'O Thakur, show mercy to me and please oblige me by requesting Ma to make me free from these wretched circumstances.'

'How can I do that Naren, when you deny Ma totally and vehemently?' replied Shri Ramakrishna.

'Please be kind to me. My people have to go without food at times, their clothes are torn and worn out and they have to suffer many hardships. I fall at your feet, Thakur. Please oblige me by asking this boon of Ma for me.'

'Naren, you don't believe at all in Ma. I just cannot plead on your behalf. But there is one way. Why don't you yourself go to the temple, fall at the feet of merciful Ma and with all your heart, beg for your own and your family's welfare? Ma hears a prayer spoken from one's heart, the guru suggested.

This slight pinprick by the guru forced Naren to move towards the temple of the Jagaddhatri, the Sustainer of the Universe. What went on in the mind of Naren when he moved towards the temple never came to light. Had he forgotten the Brahmo Samaj oath? Had he changed his belief? Did devotion suddenly spring up in his heart? But when he returned after some time in the temple, he returned transformed. His face bore signs of bliss. He looked transported to another region.

As soon as he came close to Ramakrishna, the latter asked him if he had begged of Ma for the welfare of his family. These words of Ramakrishna broke the reverie of Naren and he replied, 'Oh no. I asked for renunciation and devotion'.

'What a fool you are! Ma will give you whatever you ask for with earnestness. Go again, quickly, and beg for your family welfare. Ma listens to all earnest prayers and grants them,' Shri Ramakrishna said.

Naren did as instructed. But as he started again going to the temple and climbing up the steps, he underwent a change as on the previous occasion and standing before the idol with folded hands got lost and prayed for renunciation and devotion. When he returned to Ramakrishna's room, the latter noticed the subtle transformation in his disciple and brought him back to this world by asking, 'Well Naren, this time you didn't commit the same mistake. I hope you asked Ma to bless you and shower welfare on your family.'

Again, these words of his guru brought Naren back to reality and he confessed that as soon as he entered the temple, he forgot the sad affairs of his family and prayed to Ma for giving him renunciation and devotion. At this Ramakrishna appeared to scold him. He said, 'How foolish of you to forget what you have come here for? Go once more. Now this is the last chance. Don't forget what you want to beg of Ma.'

Naren entered the temple for the third time. But as he approached and entered the temple this time, he had come to realise the *leela* behind what had happened. His inner voice had now fully awakened and now he had come to realise the purpose of his life. Man does not live by bread alone. There are several things far greater than all the material wealth put together. Naren entered the temple fully conscious, praying not for bread and roof, for the worldly welfare, but for surrender at the lotus feet of Ma, for renunciation, for devotion, for the ultimate good. The idol he was bowing to was not a piece of basalt rock. It was the seat of faith, hallowed by unstinted devotion of thousands of worshippers, the noblest of whom was his guru.

Ramakrishna did not have to ask Naren what the latter had begged for in the temple. On seeing the blessed smile on the face of his young disciple, the guru was happy to learn that the disciple had not fallen a prey to lucre and had passed the test. He, therefore, assured Naren,' Members of your family will not go without bread, and ordinary clothes to wear.' Without ever giving any lecture on idol worship or symbolism, the great guru taught his doubting disciple what idol worship meant. A dozen or so years later, Vivekananda was to pay a glowing tribute to his guru's idol worship. The guru's teaching method was simply unique. It proved to be a hundred per cent effective.

Advaita, the nondual school of philosophy, does not believe in God with a form God with attributes. Like the Christians and Muslims, the *Advaita* school believes in formless God. Moreover, God is nondual, absolute, changeless, indivisible etc. The Brahmo way of thinking accepted this formlessness and Narendra was a faithful Brahmo follower, when he had started visiting Dakshineshvar around the end of 1881 onwards. But the *Advaita* philosophy went very much further. Brahman was all-pervading. It preached that every creature, every single thing was Brahman. Nothing exists but Brahman. This was not at all acceptable to the Brahmos and to Naren.

Shri Ramakrishna had imbibed this philosophy from Totapuri and practised it for six months, forgetting all external world, even his own body. It was with great difficulty that he was able to come out of it and heed to the command of Ma, 'Live at the lower level of devotion and worship,' and he had returned almost from the jaws of death, in order to perform the great work he was destined to do.

And one of the things he was called upon to perform was the training of his disciples. Except for the illiterate Latu—Swami Adbhutananda—they all came from good cultural background. Almost everyone had his own deity, his own religious practises, his own spiritual outlook. Shri Ramakrishna never disturbed anyone but built his own special mansion on the foundation in each one's individuality. If a Brahmin disciple of his was influenced by Christ, it did not matter at all to him. Only when he saw a disciple going on a wrong path he would put his foot down, as in the case of Niranjan, who believed in calling spirits through a medium. He had marked out, however, Naren as his heir apparent and so he desired that Naren should be as perfect as possible. But Naren's opposition to the *Advaita* belief was very vehement. Ramakrishna found a subtle way to breach the castle of Naren's opposition to Advaitism. He, therefore, asked Naren to pick up a book from the shelf and read it aloud for him.

Naren picked up the book and when he saw its title, he felt like jumping back as if he was facing a hooded cobra. The book was *Ashtavakra Samhita,* one of the greatest treatises on the *Advaita* philosophy. He naturally resented reading it.' I don't ask you to believe in what is propounded in the book. You are surely tolerant enough to read it out to me,' said Shri Ramakrishna. Naren could not say no to it. But he found every idea in the book to be unconsumable. 'Every thing is Brahman,' 'this wall is Brahman,' 'this door is Brahman.' Naren just could not gulp it down. This door is a door. How could it be Brahman? And this wall made of stones, sand and lime, how could it be Brahman? The difference between the two was so obvious. How could such dissimilar objects made out of absolutely dissimilar things be the same, i.e., Brahman? He considered the idea to be entirely ridiculous and felt relieved to fold the book after some time and place it back on the shelf. Heaving a sigh of relief, Naren walked out of the room and set his foot in the temple courtyard.

As he stepped out into the open, he found one Pratap Hajra sitting on one of the steps. This Pratap was a very typical person. He wore a rosary of Rudraksha beads round his neck and kept his right hand hidden in an L shaped cloth bag pretending to be constantly counting his beads. All this was to impress upon the visitors to the Kali temple that he was a man of great knowledge, a great practitioner of religion and a devout person. Some people were no doubt fooled by his pretentions, went to him, sat with him for a few minutes and offered him something. In turn he blessed them. But the needs of his family living in some nearby village were great. Naturally he desired more and felt jealous of Shri Ramakrishna, because many people flocked to his room and many of them showered gifts on him. This made Pratap say at times that he was a greater saint than Ramakrishna. Narendra was not at all unaware of these pretentions claimed by Hajra, yet he kept him company because at times Hajra talked quite sensibly and also because Hajra flattered Naren in a very subtle manner. Though Naren would not be affected by a few words of praise, somehow, whenever he visited the Kali temple, he spent a few minutes with Hajra, which pleased the latter quite a lot; so as he came out of Ramakrishna's room, Naren was feeling quite relieved. And seeing Hajra nearby, he felt better.

'Well, Hajra,'Naren said, 'everything is Brahman. The brass lota is Brahman. The tumbler is Brahman. This door is Brahman, you and I are Brahman.' So saying he began to laugh.

'Yes, Naren,' Hajra joined in the laughter and added, 'this step is Brahman, this stone platform is Brahman. The wall is Brahman!' Both of them laughed loudly. Hearing the sound of their laughter, Ramakrishna came out of the room, in a state of *samadhi*, with his dhoti quite out of place and asked what the fun was about. Hajra jokingly spoke about everything being Brahman. Naren was enjoying a puff and was laughing. He said with a certain disdain, 'Everything is Brahman.'

All of a sudden Ramakrishna put his hand on the chest of Naren in that mood of *samadhi* saying, 'yes, everything is Brahman' and went back into his room. But his touch had entirely metamorphosed Naren. All around he saw was Brahman. Everything big and small living or nonliving, still or moving was nothing else but Brahman. On his way home, he found the hackney carriages plying on the road to be Brahman, the horses pulling them to be Brahman and the coachmen driving them to be Brahman. The road was Brahman, the people on the road were Brahman, the shops and houses on the sides were Brahman. He pulled his hair, put his finger in his eyes. He pinched himself. All was Brahman, nothing else but Brahman.

He reached home in this extraordinary state. At home also, the doors, the walls, the clothes, the pots and pans, various pieces of furniture, books, pencils, pins, paper, everything was Brahman, nothing else but Brahman. His mother called him for having his evening meals. He washed his hands. The water was Brahman. He took his seat on the low wooden platform. It was Brahman. The *thali*, the metal plate, was Brahman. The food served by his mother was Brahman. And his mother also was Brahman. Naren found it quite difficult to eat. The piece of the roti he took up for consumption was Brahman. He just could not eat. When Bhuvaneshvaridevi saw her son looking stupefied, and not eating, she asked him why he was not eating. Her words seemed to give him a shock. He started eating again. But after a few morsels, he again stopped eating. This went on for quite some time. Wherever he went all was Brahman. He went to the Cornwalis Square and benged his head against each metal rail surrounding the small lake there. Everything was Brahman. This beautiful feeling lasted for three or four days. Poor Naren could hardly bear it. Then Naren was restored to normalcy.

This was how his guru taught him the *Advaita* philosophy.

8

From the Whirlpool of Miseries to the Summit of Bliss

In the previous chapter a reference has been made to the death of Vishvanath Dutta. It was like a bolt from the blue. The care-free, happy-go-lucky fellow that Naren was, had passed his B.A. examination in 1883 and had joined law studies. It was a vacation to him and young Naren was apparently having a nice time. 'Apparently', because, at home there were pressures on him to get married. All his elders, like normal members of the society, desired to bring a *'bahu'* by getting him married. Naren's grandmother, the wife of Durgacharan who had become a *sannyasin* when she was about twenty, strongly urged Naren to get married. In the would-be grand daughter in law, romping in the house with the tiny bells of her anklets tinkling, the old woman might mentally enjoy the pleasures of life she was forced to miss because of being deserted by her husband, Durgacharan, in the prime of life. Bhuvaneshvari's status would go up in the house the moment she would become a mother in law. And the worldly wise advocate Vishvanath had his own calculations, the dowry the girl would bring with her would add to the coffer. The proposal to send Naren to England would bring in other benefits and the status of the family with an England returned son would notch up much higher on the social ladder, and other relatives might be thinking of free feasts and presents they would get on the occasion of the marriage.

But all these pictures of pleasure were affected by Naren's strong 'denial' to marriage. He just didn't want to marry and enjoy a family life. For practising austerities, he had found out a quiet place. It was the house of his maternal grandmother, in the Ram Tanu Lane, not very far from the mansion of Vishvanath Datta. It was not frequented by clients and relatives and visitors like his own house. A small room on the second floor of the house served Naren as his retreat. It was sparsely furnished and Naren liked that very much. He used this quiet room for his studies as well as for meditation. In the post-examination days, he would go home for meals and would quietly walk away to avoid all discussion about the marriage proposals, and thus avoid unpleasantness at home.

Naren's firm stand against getting married and becoming a householder could not be appreciated by the elders in the house and other members of the family. The worldly life was a quagmire to Naren and he didn't want to fall a prey to the entreaties and temptations and threats even. To be out of the house was an advantage to him in more ways than one. Thereby he was saved from unnecessary arguments and this would also entail peace at home. The elders would no doubt, worry, but it would stop only there. So Naren would take the first opportunity to slip away from home. It was so, when after the B.A. examinations he went out one day, staying at a friend's place in the Varahanagar area that night in early 1884, that he was awakened from his sleep and called home. Vishvanath Datta had suddenly died. The cause of his death was a sudden, massive heart stroke.

The untimely and unexpected passing away of Vishvanath widowed Bhuvaneshvaridevi and cast a dark gloom of sorrow on the entire household. Misery followed and overshadowed the mourning, when, within a couple of days of the death of Vishvanath, creditors came knocking at the door to collect the dues the late Vishvanath, they said, owed to them. None, whom

Vishvanath had generously helped, showed up. The creditors carried account books with them. Vishvanath kept no records of borrowing or lending. The rush of lenders and their demand for settling the accounts, within no time of the death of Vishvanath placed the Datta household in a precarious condition. Even before the mourning period of thirteen days was over, the grim situation at home forced Naren to go out and seek a job, any job that would bring some cash. Before his death, Vishvanath, who desired his son to follow his own footsteps, study law and inherit his own practice, had arranged for Naren to go to a firm of a leading advocate of the time, one Nimaicharan Basu. That had to be abondoned and Naren started hunting for a job.

Times then were not very bad for an educated Indian. But luck was against Naren and his wanderings in search of a job wore out his shoes and tore his iron heart by ever repeated refusals of a job. Naren would walk miles and miles, climb up and down numerous staircases, knock at the doors of many firms and offices for a job, only to hear, 'sorry, no vacancy' from the mouths of various people. Besides tiring him out physically, the constant refrain of 'no vacancy' threw him in great despair because thereby he was not able to alleviate the misery of his family. Hunger was literally stalking the household and the members of the Datta family who had always lived above want and a bit luxuriously, were now feeling the pinch and had to go without many things.

After a full day's unsuccessful wandering in search of a job, when Naren came back home fagged out and hungry, and he would look at the pots containing the measly meals cooked by his mother, he would force a change in the expression on his face and tell his mother that he had had a hearty meal at a friend's. He would thus forego eating, so that the other members of the family might have a few more bites.

His tiring search for a job from morning to evening simply wore him down. Every morning, he would pray to God before setting out on his job-hunt. One day, his mother flared up seeing and hearing him pray. 'What has your god done to us? Who hears your prayers? Either your god is deaf or he is unkind. He has no mercy on us. Why does he keep us starving and so miserable?' This attack on his faith from his mother Bhuvaneshvari seemed to strike a blow at the very root of his faith. His logic and his reading of Spencer and Mill strengthened his disbelief and he started talking against the existence of God and his mercy and justice and benevolence. His recent experiences of fruitless search for a job were like petroleum poured on a burning fire. The flames of disbelief flared up and the extrovert that he was, he started speaking against God, against religion, against faith whenever and wherever an opportunity arose.

The story of this turning of the tide in Naren, like all rumours, spread fast far and wide. Additional hues of Naren having fallen in character were added. Some friends of his came to see him and verify the depth of Naren's 'fall.' Naren's response to them was very typical. These stories were carried to Shri Ramakrishna and attempts were made to paint the picture of Naren's fall with as darker a paint as possible. In the beginning Ramakrishna heard these versions of Naren's fall with stoic silence. Naren's long absence from Dakshineshvar also could not convince him that his dearest disciple had proved to be a humpty dumpty. These tales of Shri Ramakrishna not paying any heed to the stories of his 'fall' surprised Naren. He also came to learn how Ramakrishna was led to break his silence, when Bhavanath, a devotee very close to the guru, was cut down with a sharp reproach while reporting about the 'downfall' of Naren, 'Shut up, you fool. Ma has told me, what sterling gold my Naren is. He would never lose faith in God, whatever happens to him.'

In the meanwhile, two events in the life of Naren in those days deserve mention. One day after fruitless wandering for a job, he was sitting along with a few friends of his under the shade of a tree at the foot of the Ochterlony Monument. Someone in the group sang a song in praise of God. Naren burst up like a bomb, 'Stop that nonsense', he cried out, Where is your God? Where is His mercy? Don't you see the misery I am suffering from? Does He not see it? Does He do anything to alleviate it?' The stupified singer stopped singing. A hush of silence prevailed.

Another incident was entircly different. Naren had wandered for the whole day in search of a job, fruitlessly. The way to home was a long one. He was extremely tired. To add to his trouble, it started raining all of a sudden and Naren got completely drenched. Hungry and fagged out, he fell down on the roadside. He did not know how long he was lying there, but when he came to his senses, he was a changed man altogether. He did no longer hold God responsible for the miseries he and the members of his family were suddenly placed into. His faith which had appeared to be shaking was fully restored. He regained strength. He got up and started moving towards his home firmly, and free from all worries, though drenched to the bones.

Naren reached home, restored in faith and made a decision that like his grandfather, Durgacharan, he himself would renounce the world. The grandfather had done that after marrying and begetting a son. Naren resolved to do so before getting ensnared into the web of *samsara*. The Shukadeva in him started egging him on for renunciation. But before so leaving the world, he desired very strongly to see Ramakrishna. And Ramakrishna on his part also had an equally strong desire, if not stronger, to see his beloved disciple. He was to go to Kolkata on the very day Naren had decided to renounce the world. Naren had started making all preparations secretly and he had also decided on a certain day to bid goodbye to *samsara*. He, some how, came to learn that gurudeva was to visit someone in the city on that very day. Naren thought of making use of that opportunity and decided to meet Shri Ramakrishna there before renunciation.

When both met at the house of someone, before Naren could utter a word, Ramakrishna asked him to go with him to Dakshineshvar and he would not take a 'no' as a reply. All entreaties of Naren to avoid going to the Kali temple fell on a deaf ear. No other word was exchanged, but Ramakrishna's blissful eye kept continuously casting a loving glance on Naren. And every glance of the Guru was acting as a soothing balm to Naren's suffering heart. And when it was time to leave, Ramakrishna made Naren go with him to Dakshineshvar and made the young man ride with him in his carriage. A couple of other people were also there. Naren maintained a stony silence and the guru also allowed Naren to ponder over his own chain of thinking, undisturbed.

After some time they reached Dakshineshvar and alighting from the carriage, they reached the room of Ramakrishna, the room overlooking the placid waters of the Ganga. Ramakrishna took his seat on the floor in the centre of the room and others sat along the wall but Ramakrishna called Naren to him and made the latter sit in front of him. After casting a loving glance at his dearest disciple, Shri Ramakrishna, for a while, got lost into *samadhi.* Then tears trickled down from his eyes. He started singing a song:

I am afraid of talking to you,
I am also afraid of not talking,
A doubt arises in my mind,
Shall I lose you, O Radha...'

Naren's eyes were filled with tears also and they were so profuse that his chest got wet. While singing Ramakrishna had moved closer to Naren and had put his hand on Naren's body. Ramakrishna had understood what Naren wanted to do and Naren also had grasped what Ramakrishna wanted him to do. The song and the touch of Shri Ramakrishna cooled the burning fires in the heart of Naren. He gave a pleasant smile and Ramakrishna also responded with a blissful smile. The guru could see that the dark thundering cloud enveloping Naren had been cleared.

Everybody sitting around and watching the drama noticed the transformation in the two characters but could grasp nothing. Curiosity was writ large on their faces. With a cryptic smile, Shri Ramakrishna remarked: 'oh, that was something that passed between us two.'

Naren had a restful night after a long time. Next morning while Naren was still sleeping, Shri Ramakrishna pointed out Naren to some friendly visitor and showered praises on Naren. This he did again and again. Later on, when they were alone, the guru called his dear disciple to him and said to him, 'I very well know that you are not going to live a worldly life. Ma has marked you out for some great work of Hers. But don't be in a hurry to renounce the world. Be there like the maid servant of the rich householder, until I depart. Renounce every thing then.'

Naren luckily got a job. He was picked up to work as head master in one of Vidyasagar's schools. But he left it and joined some advocate's or solicitor's firm. The idea of becoming an advocate implanted in his mind since childhood led him to this job, even though the salary he was offered was quite low. He started translating books in Bengali to supplement his income. He had also joined a Law College. The family now was able to have two meals a day, though they were not square ones always. The luxury of olden days had become a matter of the past.

Two typical incidents showing the mettle of young Naren happened around this time. As is well known, Naren was tall, square shouldered and had very attractive features. A rich widow proposed to relieve the financial troubles Naren was facing, provided he would keep her company and satisfy her. It was a very tempting offer. But Naren would not sell his soul for a 'bouiled suife.'[1] The room on the second floor of the house of his maternal grandmother, situated in the Ram Tanu Lane, was

---

1 Title of a story by Maupassant. It means, 'a bowl (or ball) of tat'

facing another house, occupied by a young widow. The carefree Naren had never noticed her but the leonine figure of Naren, along with his full throated singing had attracted the widow. And when she approached Naren to offer herself, Naren just turned his face away. In both these cases he did not succumb to temptation. Thus, if one believes in the Freudian approach to man's psychology, Naren proved to be an exception. Lust could not attract him at all. He was not a prey to the sex instinct.

It was some time during these days of misery that Naren had approached Shri Ramakrishna with a request to go to the Kali temple and pray to Ma to relieve the misery of the family, mentioned in the previous chapter. As pointed out there, the incident shows out quite clearly the subtle way of Shri Ramakrishna's teaching. Ever since, Naren had completely changed and his castles of opposition to idol worship were razed to the ground. In one of his lectures on idol worship, delivered in the West, he had made a glowing reference to the idol worship of his guru, Shri Ramakrishna.

Though Naren had got a job, it was not at all a permanent one and the salary he got was not big enough to meet all the needs of the family. Changing the context completely, one might very well say that 'man does not live by bread alone.' Various other needs have to be satisfied and considering the way of life enjoyed by Bhuvaneshvaridevi and the other members of the Datta family, Naren's income was just peanuts. And Bhuvaneshvaridevi was not a person to refrain from comparing the present with the past and this was a constant cause of heart burning. And the greater cause for her worry was the fear of Naren's renunciation and the fear of what terrible effect it would have on the household.

At the Ram Tanu Lane house where Naren went for reading, one of the visitors was Shri Ramakrishna. Naren's grandmother dreaded him most. He was considered instrumental for putting the seed of renunciation in the mind of her grandson. One might say that she was not quite right in saying so, even so it was

Ramakrishna who had been watering the seed of renunciation in the mind of young Naren and showing him the path of spiritual bliss. The old lady was a worldly-wise woman and, probably could not understand what spiritual bliss meant. Every visit of Ramakrishna to her house was resented by her and she would not hide her displeasure at the visit. She would also warn her daughter of the fearful consequences. All this meant a life of constant friction for Naren. He very much longed for the day when he would be a free bird. But he had to pay heed to the word of his guru and continue to be in the world. Unfortunately for him, the stars governing that particular period of his life were not kind and favourable. A year and a half later, the guru was to test him, and agreeing to his Guru's suggestion, he was to come back home, pick up a book on torts or criminal jurisprudence, open it, try to read and concentrate on the contents, but only to throw the book away, run fast and thus swim out of the whirlpool of *samsara*.

9

Under the Refreshing Coolness of the Banyan Tree

In the last chapter we have seen the changes in the life of the happy-go-lucky Narendra and how life had begun to pinch him. There is a belief in India that when a mongoose gets hurt in a fight and is bleeding, he goes to a certain creeper, instinctively, and turns and twists his body on the green leaves of the creeper spread on the ground. His wounds are soon healed and he feels his strength restored. So also was the case with Naren. Whenever he went to the Kali temple complex at Dakshineshvar, sat in the room on the Ganga occupied by Shri Ramakrishna, enjoyed the cool and energising breeze from over the Ganga and the warmth of affection of Ramakrishna, Naren felt transported.

Shri Ramakrishna lived always on a plane spiritually much higher than the one on which all ordinary people live. He never looked 'before and after' and never pined for 'what is not'. And that was why his laughter was unmixed joy. This perpetual joyful ness of his was so contagious that anybody who went near him soon got the contagion of his divine joy and joined in the singing and dancing and mimicry, going on in the great mart of joy, and got spiritually uplifted. As pointed out in an earlier chapter Ramakrishna's teaching methods were unique simply because he himself was unique. He had taken the vows of *sannyasa* yet he had not gone to dwell in a mountain cave or in a wood. He had neither deserted his wife nor had he driven her away. He did not wear the ochre cloth of a *sannyasin* but dressed like an ordinary brahmin of that age. He did not follow a particular sect nor stick to one dogma. He rejected no faith or belief. The comprehensiveness of his belief based on the solid rock of his all inclusive experiences and his practice of the various angles of spirituality made him stand apart from all other religious, preachers and prophets.

This uniqueness of his infinite variety of experiences of the Infinite was naturally reflected in his approach to people, to various religious beliefs and to the great variety of the methods of training his disciples. We have noticed earlier some instances of this. But there are innumerable such instances and each one is so different from the other. A woman devotee complained to him that whenever she sat for meditation as advised by him, the vision of a nephew of hers with whom she was very much attached intervened. 'What of that?' said Ramakrishna; 'concentrate your mind on your nephew.' And soon, the lady was able to achieve her goal. Naren had selected the Panchvati, hallowed by Ramakrishna himself, for sitting in meditation. However, he failed to achieve his goal because he was disturbed by some siren of a factory in the area. When he complained to his guru, the latter told him, 'Don't worry, my boy. Concentrate on the siren.' And within no time, the siren ceased disturbing Naren. Ramakrishna did not preach the dogmas of any particular creed. He did not at all emphasize the principles of one particular school of philosophy. He never desired his disciples to follow the tenets of one particular sect. Like the wind and the sunlight he believed in going to every nook and corner and crevice of human spiritual experience. God can have a form, can be formless and can be beyond both the two and yet, as he had so emphatically told Naren, 'God can be seen and experienced.' However, it cannot be done with our normal human eyes. We have to use a telescope for seeing the moons of Jupiter, rings of Saturn or a nebula. We have to use a microscope to see microbes. Similarly, we have to take the help of 'something' to 'see'

God. We cannot experience God with our normal senses. We can do so with the help of extrasensory experiences. Our normal mind is of no help to grasp the idea of God. We have to rise to the supramental level. Without using any high sounding technical terms, Ramakrishna opened the portals of the infinite to his disciples and some blessed devotees, and they entered the divine region and each one of them had the spiritual experience of what he or she desired.

Debates often took place in the room of Shri Ramakrishna, sometimes at his instance and sometimes sporadically. Ramakrishna often spoke of the incessant burning of the fire of knowledge in Naren. Naren's fire would turn down all his opponents' arguments into ashes within no time. At times, Naren would use his rapier of intellect and maul all his opponents down. Ramakrishna would always be delighted to see his dear Naren overpower all his opponents so sweepingly. At the same time, he did not at all believe in someone arguing for the sake of arguments.

One day the disciples were debating on the subject: 'Does God have a form or is he formless?' Another point, incidental to this, being debated upon was, 'Does God incarnate Himself or is it a mere figment of the brain?' Voices were raised high and seemed to rent the roof, arguments were thrown at one another like javelins and the din had risen sky high. Of course, as always, it was Naren with his burning fire of knowledge who came out victorious with laurels. Ramakrishna came close by and burst into a song. The purport of the song was somewhat as follows:

> *'Oh mind! fumbling like a lunatic in the dark, of what use are your efforts to reach the Supreme Being? You won't find It in the Vedas, nor you'll be able to come across It in the six darshanas; the Tantras also won't be of any help to you; It is fond of love only.'*

The din of the debate died down completely. All the disciples listened to the song with rapt attention. Each one of them, arguing from a different point of view got his own answer. Shri

Ramakrishna knew one language, the language of experience. He had realised Him in his soul. To him reason was not supreme. Spirituality to him did not mean conviction with reason; it was self-experience. He often compared the arguing *pandits* to vultures and kites. Those birds are high fliers but their eyes are always aimed at some dead and decaying stuff on the earth below. The *pandits* would be arguing with great vigour and ability, quoting authorities in support of their arguments but their aim would always be fame, wealth and awards.

As illustrated here, Ramakrishna generally avoided participating in the bouts of his disciples' arguments. However, at times, he would side with the opponents of Naren, who had become crest fallen in their debate with Naren. The guru had intervened once when Narendra had with all the vehemence at his command run down faith, calling it 'blind' and condemned it as misleading. While the other disciples were sitting with their mouths tightly shut for lack of argument, Ramakrishna suddenly hurled his lance of argument and asked: 'well Naren, you run down blind faith. But show me a *'shraddha,'* faith 'with an eye or eyes:' Naren could give no reply.

The Panchavati, the wood like serene place, situated to the north of the temple complex, was a place where Shri Ramakrishna had started his spiritual practices, where he had continued to do so under the guidance of the Bhairavi and Totapuri and achieved oneness with the Absolute, was also the place chosen by Naren-and other disciples-for their *sadhana*. The murmur of the placid Ganga flowing by added to the serenity and the white sails of the boats moving up and down pointed to eternity. Young Naren spent many hours there meditating, even though he had not become conscious of the goal.

A couple of his *gurubhais*, who, like Naren, spent their nights also at Dakshineshvar, meditating and praying, sometimes slipped into unconsciousness for a while, as if in a *samadhi*, or started weeping. Even though Naren used to sit quite long hours in meditation, he did not experience any such state. After observing his friends for a few occasions, he asked Ramakrishna why he, Naren, was not having any such experience. The guru patted him and said,' My boy, don't you know what happens when a huge elephant jumps into a small puddle of water? The water soon gets disturbed and muddier and murkier and a lot of water is thrown out of the puddle. But when the same elephant jumps into the waters of the Ganga, nothing happens. The spiritual experience is like that elephant and these friends of yours so easily affected are like those puddles of water. You are like the mighty Ganga, able to digest your spiritual experiences. Their state is not enviable.' That was how his guru taught him to digest spiritual experiences.

Naren's journey within had not been an easy one. He had set out on the journey in his late adolescence. The bark of his soul was attracted by various forces like the writings of Herbert Spencer. Naren had corresponded with the great thinker and surprised the Englishman by his sharp criticism. Mill, Spinoza, Compte and other philosophers of the West, historians like Green and Gibbon, dare devil conquerors like Alexander the Great, and Nepoleon Bonaparte, the characters and ideas and happenings in the oceans of English and Sanskrit literature he had so avidly read, the great leaders of his days like Devendranath Tagore and Keshub Sen, whose reputation had spread beyond the frontiers of India: all this had influenced Naren. The course of his bark, naturally, was not steady and even. It was tossed in one direction once and in another direction next. This tossing, this lack of direction, this lack of a definite goal had turned his inner self into a maelstrom and the turmoil he was suffering from was indescribable.

Principal W. W. Hastie who happened to be a friend of India and who was one of the few foreigners who had seen Shri Ramakrishna and understood him properly, might have given a soothing touch to the agonising Naren. But that reference to

Ramakrishna had not prompted Naren to go to the Paramahansa at Dakshineshvar. The advice of the erudite friend Brijendranath Seal did not help soothe his agonising heart. Naren joined the Brahmo Samaj. Though he was attracted to it because of Keshub's name and fame, Keshub had to leave the Brahmo Samaj he himself had established, after leaving the Brahmo Samaj established by Raja Ram Mohan Roy and Dwarkanath Tagore and being tended by Devendranath Tagore after the death of both the founders. Keshub was a seeker no doubt but he followed a path different from the one the Brahmo Samaj was following under the leadership of Devendranath. Keshub was highly influenced by the *Bible* and the missionaries. He was a brilliant orator and writer and edited various journals and periodicals, in Bengali and English. He had been to England and had met there many important people. He was an idol for the youth of Bengal of the age. The Brahmos were placing equal if not more emphasis on social reforms like breaking the barriers of the caste system, education of girls, remarriage of widows etc., and this had created a rift in the contemporary Bengali society. Rabindranath has painted a vivid picture of the cleavage in one of his great novels. Naren was attracted to the Brahmo Samaj, became quite active though young, was a leading member of the choir and listened to the preachings from the pulpit with rapt attention. They satisfied his intellect, that too partially, but his spiritual well remained as dry as ever.

And when he came in contact with Shri Ramakrishna, apparently almost accidentally but really speaking by the force of destiny, he dreamt of the effect the impact would have on him in future. As a matter of fact, after the first casual meeting at Surendra's house, when Naren went to meet Shri Ramakrishna at the latter's insistence, Naren was shocked at Ramakrishna's odd behaviour in the verandah behind the room and the impression of the old man on his mind was that Ramakrishna being an insane person, though this impression of him had undergone change. When later on they were back in the room, Shri Ramakrishna had talked sensibly and with authority about seeing God. Neither that first meeting at Dakshineshvar, nor the next had quelled the fires burning in Naren's heart. But Ramakrishna's touch had awakened a spiritual spring in Naren's heart, the old man's affectionate care and consideration for Naren as if he was an old acquaintance, the old man's conversation carried on in his slightly stammering, rustic Bengali, the perpetual and magnetic smile adorning his face and his deep, penetrating eyes showering divine love had gripped young Naren. And with every visit of his to Dakshineshvar, the grip was getting tightened more and more.

Naren was not a man easy to surrender. Reason was his God and he would weigh every word and action of the guru in the scales of his reason. His doubts would raise their heads at every step and the guru would remove them with the skill of a master surgeon. Shri Ramakrishna never scolded Naren, nor spoke to him harshly nor ever ran him down for raising doubts, because Ramakrishna had himself prayed to Mother Kali, 'O Ma! Please give me someone who raises doubts about my visions and my spiritual experiences!' Naren was thus, Ma's gift to Ramakrishna. As noticed earlier, Ramakrishna silenced Naren by asking the latter to show him 'faith with eyes;' the guru stopped the din of arguments by singing a song, he could also tell pointed parables. All this made Naren realise slowly that his guru was an intellectual giant also. Naren tested his guru in other ways too. Shri Ramakrishna could not touch any money. Years ago he would stand on the bank of the Ganga with a rupee coin in one hand and a small pod of earth in the other, then would repeat, 'taka, mati', 'mati, taka—'rupee, earth', 'earth, rupee'-and considering the two different things same, would throw both into the flowing waters of the Ganga. Lucre and lust were the deadliest enemies of a spiritual seeker, he firmly maintained. A touch of a coin would give him a sort of a shock.

Naren had heard about this. But he had never come across any proof of it. Belief was one thing but there could be no conviction without an actual proof. So one day, while he was sitting with other disciples and devotees in the room of Ramakrishna, suddenly the latter left the room for a short while. Naren immediately got up and placed a rupee coin on the cot, but underneath the bed, and thus completely out of view. Nobody there knew what Naren had done. A few minutes later Shri Ramakrishna walked in. The people in the room were engaged in conversation of some sort. Ramakrishna went to his bed and as soon as he took his seat on it, he jumped back as if he had received an electric shock. Naren saw this and also heard his Master pronounce, 'Someone has placed some money somewhere on the cot.' Naren's face fell down. The guru noticed it and spoke, 'Naren, that's the right thing to do. Never take anything for granted. Test your guru thoroughly before believing him. Don't accept anything because I have said so. Not by mere argument but after testing everything in the crucible of your intellect only, you should accept it. You should accept it.

Shri Ramakrishna's falcon eye had marked sharp distinction between his other disciples on the one hand and Naren on the other. Whereas others were always eager to listen to the preachings of the guru and accept it without questioning, Naren would weigh every word of Shri Ramakrishna in the scale of his reason, his intellect, compare and constrast it with something he had read or heard—his memory was very sharp—raise doubts if any and when, the guru with his penetrating logic, pointed parables and pleasant smile removed Naren's doubts like a mother dressing her child's wound, Naren would get convinced and then would accept the teaching. Once accepted, it would not be a lip service, or a half-hearted acceptance. The teaching would be absorbed by him fully and it would become a part of every corpuscle of his personality.

Shri Ramakrishna was sitting in his room, surrounded by several of his disciples sometime in 1884. He was talking to them about Vaishnavism as taught by Shri Gaurang, a few centuries ago. He dwelt at some length on the teachings of Shri Gaurang and then, by way of summing up he said: 'This sect preaches doing the following three things: (i) Love for the name of the Lord, (ii) Service to the Vaishnavas, God's devotees, and (iii) Mercy on all creatures. God and His name are one, so go on repeating his name incessantly. Since there is no difference between God and his devotees, love them, love mankind. And understanding quite clearly that the entire world is inhabited by Shri Krishna, show mercy to every creature.'

Immediately on uttering the words, 'show mercy to every creature,' he got carried away into an ecstatic mood and, soon in a semiconscious state, started talking to himself: 'Mercy to every creature! Mercy to every creature! You, an insignificant tiny worm, crawling on earth, who are you to show mercy? No, not at all so. All men are forms of God. We don't show mercy to them. We have to serve them. *Shiva jnane jiva seva*! 'Serve all beings knowing them to be forms of God.'

These words of Shri Ramakrishna reminds us of the words of Kapila (*Bhagavatam*: 3:29:21-28) explicitly stating: 'I abide in all creatures as their souls forgetting this people go in for idol worship. I have constructed my temple in the heart of every creature; donate gifts to them respectfully and lovingly with an eye of oneness and so worship me there.'

So on hearing this great utterance coming out of the mouth of the guru in an inspired state, Naren got electrified. He was beside himself when they were pouring out of the room. All the disciples had heard what Naren had heard. But he was the only one who was illumined by the pregnant speech of the guru. 'The words of Thakur have been greatly illuminating. They were coming from the depth of his soul. With what mastery he has harmonised the truth of the *Vedanta*, always considered harsh and dry, with the path of the poetic *Bhakti*! So natural and grand and sweet! The *Vedanta* is generally believed to be ignoring the society of men and women completely and totally uprooting love, devotion, compassion etc. Naturally, the *vedantin* cuts himself off completely from the normal world, believes the world to be an impediment to the pursuit of the spiritual path. But from the prophetic words that came out of the Gurudev's mouth in an ecstatic mood I have learnt that a *sannyasin* can practise his *Vedanta* living in society as perfectly as he can do by living away from it. The *Vedanta* will be of immense use to us in solving various problems of our life. Whatever vocation an individual might be following, he or she should remember that God pervades every thing and every creature, God pervades the universe and is beyond it. He has taken the form of every creature attracting our love and compassion and yet he is above and beyond these creatures. A man's pride melts away when he realises this. Then he will envy no one and have no pity on anyone. The service rendered through the understanding of a creature as a manifestation of the Divine purifies one's heart and such a person then sees his own self as a part and parcel of the Divine.

'These memorable words of Gurudev, throw a new light on the Path of *Bhakti* or devotion. Genuine devotion is born in a person only when the devotee experiences oneness with God. One must see God, experience Him and serve Him in every being in order to be a true devotee of Him. Since no one can live a moment without performing an action, those who choose the path of action, *Karmayogis*, also will find these words of Thakur as a beacon of light. These words would guide them in directing all their activities in the form of service to humanity. God willing, I'll proclaim this great truth before the whole world and help all men irrespective of their caste or creed, their sex, their social status, their learning, realise this.'

And we shall see later on, how, with the grace of his guru, Naren successfully achieved this goal within a decade or so.

The story of Naren's transformation from a doubting youth to a devoted disciple can never be fully put in words. From a 'pious looking lunatic,' Shri Ramakrishna had risen to immeasurable reckoning for Narendranath. This had happened without his knowing, without his effort. Nor was any effort exerted by Shri Ramakrishna. All his colts were free to romp in any direction and as high as they liked. The only control Shri Ramakrishna exerted was the long unseen rope to which each colt had tied himself. There were no do's and don'ts so far as the guru was concerned. Naren could read anything he liked. He could attend the Brahmo meetings and participate in the proceedings. Naren was free to condemn idol worship and shun going to the Kali temple. He might mock at the teachings of the *Advaita* philosophy. This total freedom to disciples was unheard of, except probably in the academy of Socrates. And yet Naren's doubts got dispelled one by one and the beacon light in him, 'eighteen times stronger than that of great leaders like Keshub and Vijay,' started to shine and spread its light, and in almost a decade burst upon the World Parliament of Religions, held at Chicago, with the potentiality of a glaring sun. A bomb destroys; the powerful glow of Naren was life giving, energising.

A typical example of the U-turn Shri Ramakrishna made Naren do was as follows. Under the influence of the Brahmo Samaj, Narendra was led to believe that too much of meditation would harm the mind and too much of *Bhakti*—devotion—leads to a kind of an intoxicating state, leading to loss of self-control. Ramakrishna gave no lectures, made no arguments. He simply asked his young disciple, 'God is an ocean of immortal bliss. Suppose, my son, that there is a big, wide-mouthed pot full of this immortal bliss and you, a fly, are eager to sip it. How will you satisfy your thirst?'

'I'll perch safely on the border of the pot and sip the ambrosial juice. I would not like to jump into the pot for fear of getting drowned,' replied Naren.

'My son, you forget totally that it is an ocean of existence knowledge-bliss, of immortality. Fear of death has no place there. Love for God is exactly like this ocean. Fools only would believe that excessive devotion to God should not be indulged in. Could love of God be ever excessive? That's exactly why I tell you to dive into the ocean that God is. There's no death. It leads to immortality!' These words of the guru penetrated into the heart of Naren and without his knowing, he became transformed.

This transformation in the spiritual make up of Narendranath was slowly bringing up in his mind a hazy notion of the future role he was to play. The childhood dream of total renunciation and of becoming a big monk had given place to this role though not yet well shaped and clear. But it laid down the direction in which the river of his life was to flow.

One day he was talking to his friends. The young collegians were talking about careers and professions. Turning to them Naren said, 'at the most you would become a doctor or an advocate or a judge and go along the charted paths. Friends, I'am going to chart my own path of life.' He exuded self confidence as he uttered these words. The source of this confidence in his own self was, no doubt, inborn, but was greatly buttressed by his contact with Shri Ramakrishna. And this contact was unique and was to prove very fructifying.

This internal change was having its impact on the bodily features of Naren. Right from the birth he had certain typical characteristics. His height was above normal, his physique, supported by spartan way of life and regular exercises at the gymnasium appeared leonine. His shoulders were broad, his chest was manly and powerful, his arms had grown long as would take the whole world in their embrace. His jawbones got sharper, thus emphasising the Tartar in him. His broad forehead and shapely head attracted attention. But the far more attractive feature of his face were his eyes. They were often compared with a lotus. Broad they were but were not protruding. They reflected his tender and loving heart, his sharp intellect as well as the vision of his spirit. They were unfathomable. They were overflowing with love, love for the person or persons he was talking to, for all mankind, for the entire universe. They were the eyes of a conqueror. He was to establish his kingdom in the hearts of men.

It was the Kali temple at Dakshineshvar on the Ganga where Naren's personality was moulded. It was moulded with the care of a jeweller chiselling a diamond. And Naren turned out to be a Kohinoor.

10

The Guru's Illness and Departure

In many parts of India, summer makes its presence felt by mid-March. The summer of 1885 set in a bit early in Bengal, and the heat was quite intense. Many of the regular visitors to Dakshineshvar started carrying ice with them to provide relief to Shri Ramakrishna. Ice-cold water and glasses of cold sherbet became the order of the day. Besides, Ramakrishna, like a little boy, enjoyed placing pieces of ice in his mouth. Like too much of anything causing harm, too much of ice might have caused some pain in his throat, or it brought the pain which was there into focus. The pricking began to lengthen its periods and its intensity. Application of household remedies did not prove useful and a doctor was called in.The physician prescribed some medicines which Shri Ramakrishna took regularly. However, he completely disregarded two other injunctions of the doctor:(1) talking as little as possible and (2) avoiding *samadhi.* Ramakrishna just could not say no to the Sindhu of visitors who flooded in at Dakshineshvar from early morning to late in the evening and continued to answer their questions and talk to them without any rest like the sun traversing the sky. After all, that was the mission of his life. Nor could he control his *samadhis*. As expected, the result was the worsening of the disease.

In May or early June of the year a step taken by Shri Ramakrishna caused a great aggravation of the pain. There is a place called Panihati, a few miles upstream of Dakskineshvar. Every year on a particular day falling in summer, they celebrate the arrival of Nitai there. Nitai had met some *Pandit* there who had served parched rice to Nitai and the celebration is called the parched Rice Festival. Shri Ramakrishna had previously visited the place a number of times and participated in the festival of devotion by singing and dancing. In 1885, an idea struck him: the 'Young Bengal,' the Western educated youth of Bengal, should attend the festival and have a glimpse of the expression of devotion. Almost all he spoke to about this did not support him in view of his diseased throat. The ceaseless singing and dancing on the open streets—mixed with the cloud of dust would aggravate his disease. But Shri Ramakrishna said that he would control himself completely, would not join any singing party, would not dance and would control his *samadhis*. He also emphatically added that they would not spend more than one hour at Panihati and would return soon. He only wanted the 'Young Bengal' to see the festival, he said. The devotees and disciples had to agree.

It was a big party. People started coming to Dakshineshvar early in the morning on the day. Sharadadevi, with the help of a few friends, had cooked for the group and after having their lunch, the party set sail northwards. Girish, Balaram, Mahendranath Gupta and other devotees were there, Naren, Rakhal, Shashi, Sharat and other disciples were there and, a few lady devotees also were accompanying the party, travelling in a different boat.

The boats reached Panihati in the early afternoon. On disembarking, the Dakshineshvar party saw a crowd of people underneath a peepal tree. Several Vaishnava groups were moving to and fro, singing *kirtana*s and dancing. Naren, Balaram, Ramachandra, Girish, Mahendranath Gupta etc., who were close to Shri Ramakrishna requested him individually and jointly to keep away from the *kirtana* groups. In a few minutes they reached the house of Mani Sen, the landlord of the place. Mani Sen welcomed the party whole—heartedly. Resting for a few minutes the party set out for the Radhakant temple.

Right in the compound of the temple a group of Vaishnavas was having a Sanskirtana. In the centre of the group was standing a Vaishanava exhibiting more of sham and less of devotion. The hollowness of the Vaishnava was absolutely clear to everyone. 'What a fake!' remarked somebody. Ramakrishna just could not tolerate any hollowness, any pretention, more particularly in the field of religion. Seized as it were by some inner force, he jumped into the centre of the group encircling the pretender devotee and, naturally, took over the reins. The devotees and disciples accompanying him were taken aback, but they could do just nothing. They saw that their guru had taken over the charge of the *kirtana* group, which had got electrified at Shri Ramakrishna's jumping into their midst and singing and dancing with divine glee. They also followed the master.

It was indeed a rare sight. Shri Ramakrishna was wearing silken clothes of bright orange colours, the colour of the *Pitambara* of Shri Krishna. The dancers were not the *gopis* of Brindavan but Shri Ramakrishna looked every inch like Shri Krishna dancing with great abandon. Sharat, a disciple of Shri Ramakrishna, who had taken the name of Sharadananda, and who was a witness at Panihati, has given a very vivid description of the scene at Panihati. According to him, Shri Ramakrishna looked taller and his face had acquired a luminosity of its own when he was moving in the centre of the circle of the kirtaniyas. Sometimes he would be standing still, next moment he would be whirling with the fastness of a speedy merry-go-round, then he would again be coming to a stop, then advance in one direction, then go backwards in the opposite direction and he would all of a sudden get into a highly emotional state or even step into a *samadhi* and the next moment he would be singing and dancing with abandon. The surcharged Ramakrishna looked superhuman, divine, as noted by Swami Sharadananda in his *Leela Prasanga*.

The whole group of dancers around him got infected by the devotion of Shri Ramakrishna. The performance of the group attracted the attention of others. The circle grew wider, got divided into several circles, mingling with and separating from one another. It was a huge concourse of men, infected by the devotion of Shri Ramakrishna. It took full three hours to cover the distance of about a mile to the house of Raghav Pandit, said to have been hallowed by Nitai and Gaurang. After a few minutes' rest, the party got back into their boats. Shri Ramakrishna landed at Dakshineshvar after 8.00 p.m., and the Kolkata party reached the city two hours later.

Shri Ramakrishna's throat had been strained utmost with continuous singing for over three hours, and gusts of wind mixed with the dust raised by people moving and dancing. The pain in the throat suddenly increased and he started spitting blood. He found it difficult to eat normal food and he had to start consuming liquid foods like porridge or soup. Medicines prescribed by the doctors were found to be ineffective. This was a cause for worry for his wife Sharadadevi, the devotees, the disciples, and for all. He had said earlier that when he would be visiting the city frequently and start eating at various places, when he would offer from his own dish to someone first and then he himself would consume the food and when he would be able to consume liquid diet only, it should be understood that the final curtain was to fall on the drama of his life. And all this had started happening and it had started worrying all, particularly his wife, Sharadadevi. Since Dakshineshvar was far out of the city limits, it was difficult to contact efficient medical practitioners. Naren took the lead and spoke to other devotees that arrangements be made to move the Gurudeva to the city, so that competent doctors could visit him more frequently and also because, that would enable the disciples to stay with Thakur for longer hours and serve him. He was to need personal attention day and night. Everyone willingly agreed to do so, and someone showed his readiness to mortgage his house, while another one was willing to dispose off his uncle's jewellery.

Naren was the first to stay overnight. Others followed: he also arranged duty hours of others. The parents of some of these young men attending colleges did not at all like their sons' singular devotion to their guru, which led to their absence from their homes and colleges. But the young men were adamant. The parents sought solace under the belief that the illness of Ramakrishna would after all be a short lived affair and after that the boys will be back home and back to their studies. Their hopes however, were belied and their sons were never to return and lead life like normal householders. If any of the young men ever faltered, there was Naren, the lion, who would roar and make all weaknesses scamper away.

Dr. Mahendranath Sarkar, a noted homeopath of the age, was summoned. His treatment seemed to produce some improvement in Shri Ramakrishna's health in the beginning. He prohibited Shri Ramakrishna from talking to visitors, who flocked there in large numbers, but was so enamoured by the magnetic power of the patient that he himself would spend there hours listening to the flow of the ethereal talk from his patient's mouth. The doctor was a non believer, he shunned idol worship and considered all talk about *samadhi* baseless. Naren entered into argument with Dr. Sarkar several times and pointed at his Gurudev as the proof of living religion. The doctor and a medical companion of his had an opportunity once of examining Shri Ramakrishna when he was in the state of *samadhi*. The doctors were amazed to find that Ramakrishna's heart had stopped beating, there was no pulse and even Ramakrishna's eyes exhibited no signs of life. And in a few minutes, Shri Ramakrishna regained normal consciousness and every physical function was found to be normal. But Naren put his foot down on some who faked *samadhis*. He would have exposed them if they hadn't come round.

The change for the better noted after Shri Ramakrishna was shifted to the Shyamapukur house, however did not last long. The place was close by to the city and the flow of the river of visitors was incessant. A guard was placed at the foot of the staircase, but some 'brave and bold' persons would brush the guard aside and climb up the stairs to have Shri Ramakrishna's blessings, to take the dust off his feet—the touch of some peculiar persons would give him a shock—and, at the very least, to have his darshan. As a result of all this, and probably because of the nature of the disease itself, Shri Ramakrishna's health started deteriorating. When the guru had started spitting blood and was prevented by the soreness of the throat from consuming anything but liquid foods, Naren had rushed to the library of the medical college and after referring to several books had come to learn with a shock that Shri Ramakrishna was suffering from cancer and that there was no cure for the disease. His discovery had shocked others. So within three months of his stay at Shyamapukur, Shri Ramakrishna had to be moved away from the city to a place in a quieter and healthier area. It was on December 11, 1885 that Shri Ramakrishna was shifted to a house in the Kashipur area.

This house was situated in the midst of a big area with a well kept garden and a couple of ponds. Besides the bungalow in the centre, there were servants' quarters nearby. The Holy Mother Sharadadevi had undergone a lot of inconvenience at the house in the Shyamapukur Lane. Here, she had enough space on the ground floor, a part of which, along with some rooms in the adjacent servants' quarters were occupied by the disciples. Shri Ramakrishna was housed on the first floor. With a terrace opening on one side, he could see the holy Ganga, the witness to his transformation from Gadadhar to Shri Ramakrishna. The open air, the cool, dry season and freedom from the flow of visitors coupled with Dr. Sarkar's drugs seemed to bring about an improvement in the health of Shri Ramakrishna. The attending disciples and devotees became happy at this. On the New Year day of 1886, unexpectedly, a great event took place.

The day being a public holiday, many devotees from the city had thronged at the Kashipur house since early afternoon. The idea of the visitors was to be as near Shri Ramakrishna as possible. They would consider themselves lucky if they were able to have his *darshan* and luckier if they would be able to offer him *pranams*. Some were strolling in the garden, some resting under the shade of one tree or another or sitting under some awning in small groups and talking amongst themselves.

It so happened that Shri Ramakrishna felt a bit better on the day and probably seeing the sun shine in all its glory, he expressed a desire to go down and stroll. As soon as he got ready and stepped down the stairs, Latu and Sharat and a couple of young attendants took up the opportunity to give some sunshine to the bed, sweep the floor of the room and attend to other things in the room. For three weeks Shri Ramakrishna had not left the room since his arrival here. As he started strolling, the first group of persons he came across with was led by Girish. They were all sitting under the shade of a tree and talking amongst themselves. Delighted at seeing Ramakrishna walking, they bowed down to Shri Ramakrishna. Shri Ramakrishna stopped for a moment and, all of a sudden, asked Girish a pointed question: 'Well Girish, what have you seen in me that you are telling everyone about me (being an incarnation)?'

Girish, the man of imagination, suddenly stepped forward and falling on his knees in front of Shri Ramakrishna, he said: 'How can I put anything in words, where the great Valmiki and Vyasa have failed (to describe God)?'. These words of Girish pouring straight from his heart and uttered with great sincerity, coupled with his falling at the feet of Shri Ramakrishna affected the latter very much and he slipped into a higher mood for a while. He put his hand in that state on the head of Girish and blessed him by saying: "Be illumined." Then all of a sudden, he entered the state of *samadhi*. Soon others who were nearby and had seen and heard what had happened rushed there like a sudden flood and forgetting the injunction of not touching the feet of Shri Ramakrishna, each one bent down his head at the feet of the guru, speaking, '*Jai Shri Ramakrishna* (Victory be to Shri Ramakrishna).' The guru placed his hand on the head of each one and blessed each one by the same, or similar, utterance, like, 'Be illumined;' and there was literally an outburst of spirituality. A few of them became ecstatic, a few started seeing visions, a few started smiling, yet a few started weeping. Some went into deep meditation. All present on the occasion felt as if the divinity in Ramakrishna was revealed to them. Naren, who had been by the bedside of the Master during the previous night, was sound asleep. One might also add that the Master had already showered his blessings on him, and the young disciple was already on the way to illumination. So also were Naren's other *gurubhais*. Naren, no doubt, occupied a very special position in the heart of Shri Ramakrishna.

Though his relationship with Shri Ramakrishna was the most intimate, his thinking was quite rational as could be seen from the way of his thinking about the guru's illness which was leaving him weaker and weaker. Girish, who considered Shri Ramakrishna to be an *avatara*, an incarnation of the Divine, was of the opinion that this illness of Shri Ramakrishna was nothing but incidental. He had a few supporters. There was another group of persons who believed in and propagated the idea that Shri Ramakrishna's illness was not of a normal nature, since he had submitted his will completely to Ma Kali. His disease was because of Ma's will, and later on, when She so willed She would take away the disease and then Ramakrishna would be normal once more. But Naren believed differently. He was of the firm opinion that even when Divinity incarnates itself, the laws of nature governing the species of the incarnation apply to the incarnation. Like any other human being, Shri Ramakrishna was subject to everything any other human being was subject to. Naren had read earlier in medical books that the symptoms of Shri Ramakrishna's disease were those of cancer and that, till that time, medical science knew no treatment to cure cancer.

In spite of getting weaker and weaker day-by-day, in spite of the excruciating pain he was suffering from, the guru didn't holler with pain at all, he bore his suffering calmly, and continued to talk even though he was losing his voice.

One Shashadhar Pandit, learned in scriptures, visited Shri Ramakriskna and said,' Why do you suffer so much pain? The cure is easy for you. Concentrate on the diseased part of your body with all your mind and heart and pray to Ma for cure. Your disease will disappear in no time.'

'Well, Shashadhar, you know quite well that I have submitted my mind at the feet of Ma. I just can't bring it back to concentrate on this mortal frame of flesh and bones,' Shri Ramakrishna replied. Shashadhar Pandit had no further argument to offer.

But Naren, who was present at the time of the Pandit's visit, spoke to his guru, after the Pandit had left, on the same topic. When Ramakrishna put forth the same argument, Naren begged of him forcefully to pray to Ma and request her to cure him, Shri Ramakrishna, so that he could take some food and be able to guide the disciples. Naren was so insistent that Ramakrishna at last agreed to do so. When Naren met Shri Ramakrishna after about an hour or so and asked the latter if he had prayed to Ma to enable him to consume some food, Shri Ramakrishna gave him an astounding reply. 'Yes' he said, 'I spoke to Ma about it, prayed to Her to enable me to take some more food. Do you know what Ma said to me? She pointed her hand at all of you and said: "Don't you eat with all these mouths?" I was simply ashamed.' Naren was dumb struck. What oneness Shri Ramakrishna had achieved with his disciples! Did it suggest that he was going to live through his disciples? Naren now began to look at things differently.

Dakshineshvar was near Kashipur and Naren often ran away to Panchavati, the place of his guru's unfolding, to meditate. At times he went to the cremation ground on the Ganga nearby. Sometimes he would be alone, sometimes he would go accompanied by one or two *gurubhais*. One night, Naren and a few other disciples, strolling in the compound of the Kashipur house, found an open space where they sat in a circle. Collecting dry twigs and dry leaves from around the place, they lit a fire to keep warm. Naren started talking. His inspiring talk lifted up his friends from the mundane plane to a higher spiritual level. They felt transformed. Suddenly Naren said, 'this fire is like a *dhuni* of sadhus. Let us sacrifice our worldly desires, desire for love and fame, desire for money and a happy life into this holy fire and let us all get purified. Let us resolve to dedicate our lives to our guru.' Without uttering a single word, all sitting there around the fire, did so and fell silent. Their meditation lasted till the early hours of the dawn.

In spite of steeling themselves like this, they were often overtaken by the idea of the imminent loss of their guru. Their worry was not quite unjustified. They were all silent witnesses to the steady deterioration in the physical condition of Shri Ramakrishna. They felt deeply for just being helpless witnesses to the ebbing away of Shri Ramakrishna's life. They were afraid of the calm of death descending on and enveloping Shri Ramakrishna. Where and to whom would they go for guidance ? Who would lead them later on along the path, described by the *Katha Upanishad*, as razor's sharp edge? They were sitting silent with sullen faces around the bed of the guru once, these expressions on their faces clearly exhibited their fear for the worst as well their sense of helplessness.

Shri Ramakrishna, who could read minds and hearts, slowly started speaking. He did not speak about life or death, about his own terminal illness, about the happy times they all had together at Dakshineshvar or about the thoughts of their future which might be causing them anxiety. Instead, he told them a story. In his low but clear voice, speaking slowly, he said, 'Do you know what happened once? There was a house with people living happily in it. One night a group of baul singers—singers of a typical, mystic bhakti cult—walked into the house unannounced. The minstrels sang and danced with abandon and all the members of the house, big and small, seemed to be transported by the spiritual element in the music of the bauls. And all of a sudden, the baul group left as quickly as it had come, without giving a hint. A calm descended on the house. 'He paused. A calm had prevailed there also. Then he quietly asked: 'Did you understand the purport?' He then fell silent. Though the disciples sitting close by around Shri Ramakrishna like dumb pawns on a chess board might have grasped the meaning of Shri Ramakrishna's parable, their hearts were not at all prepared for the great impact the departure of Shri Ramakrishna would have on their lives. The Master jeweller was chiselling bright diamonds into shape, yet they were young enough to need his guidance and human enough to feel the loss. By stories such as this the Master was trying to steel their hearts.

In one of the rooms occupied by the disciples, they had put up on the wall a beautiful picture of the Great Buddha. Underneath the picture was a Sanskrit verse beginning with the words, 'let my body dry up on this seat.(until I get enlightened).' His life and his great message were discussed quite often, with Naren throwing a lot of light on the subject. All of a sudden Naren set out for Gaya along with two other friends, all wearing ochre clothes like *sannyasins*. The disciples at Kashipur serving Shri Ramakrishna were worried. They knew Naren's attachment to the Buddha and Naren's spirit of adventure also. But Shri Ramakrishna exhibited no such anxiety. He told his disciples not to worry about Naren at all. And he was proved completely right, for Naren and his friends returned a few days later on from their pilgrimage. At Gaya, they had sat under the Bodhi tree for meditation and got inspired by the teachings of the Buddha. On his return, when he went to Shri Ramakrishna, there was an interesting discussion about the teachings of the Buddha between the two. The philosophy of the Buddha, his emphasis on the eightfold path, his stoic silence when asked about the existence of God, his establishment of the Sangha, his opposition to the offering of animals in sacrificial fires and his love and compassion for all creatures were discussed. At the end, pointing to himself with his finger the guru said, 'There is nothing that is not here.' Naren and the other friends had to agree to that.

Naren often felt very miserable, The guru once asked him what he wanted. Naren said that he strongly desired to experience the *advaita samadhi*, that he wanted to remain in that state for a few days at a stretch, only to come out from that state of *samadhi* at intervals for satisfying bodily needs and again get lost into the state of *samadhi*. 'Fie upon you,' said the guru, 'what a selfish creature you are! You must aim to be like a banyan tree enabling hundreds of birds to perch on its various branches and scores to build their nests. No doubt you also can experience the *advaita samadhi* but, Naren, you have several worldly functions to fulfil yet. You have to appear for your law examination and make proper arrangements for the needs of your family. You go to the city, go home, settle all these matters satisfactorily and then come back. Ma will bless you with whatever you want.' Shri Ramakrishna was absolutely right in his own way in drawing Naren's attention to the affairs of his home which he was not able to attend to for quite some time. Naren set out for the city and reached home.

The reception there was absolutely cold. Not only that, Bhuvaneshvaridevi started scolding him for having neglected them. And there was truth in the allegation which Naren could not at all deny. He was keeping himself so occupied with Kashipur affairs and his own meditation that he had not been able to show his face to his own mother. He heard this harangue quietly with his head bent down, then went to his room to collect a few books and turned about to go to the house of his granny in the Ram Tanu Lane to read. There also the welcome was equally frigid, though there were no sparks like the ones he had experienced at the Simla area house. He drank a glass of water, climbed up to his room and banged the books on the table there. The thud of the books failing on the table started a new chain of thoughts in the mind of Naren. The childhood vision of becoming a *sannyasin* flared up in his mind. All the riches of the world were, as the great Maharashtrian saint Tukaram, a contemporary of the Great Shivaji had put it, like the droppings of a pig, to be shunned away. He realised that he was not born to be ensnared by the *maya* of the world. Had not his guru said that he, Naren, was destined to carry out some great mission of Ma Kali? He must not place himself in the strait hole of *samsara*. He must jettison all the temptations of the worldly life and set out in search of God. The sooner, the better.

No sooner did this thought well up in his mind, than he kicked the chair, got out of the room and came out of the house of his grandma in the Ram Tanu Lane with the speed of a cyclone. The next moment he hit the road, running, unmindful of the traffic on the road, unmindful of the people around him. His mind was set on one goal, the Kashipur house, where his great guru was lying on his death bed, the guru whose protege he himself was. He was running like a calf separated from his mother (cow). On the way somewhere there was lying on the road a big heap of hay. It was no impediment for him. He waded through the heap and lost his shoes. He didn't stop to search for his shoes in the heap. At long last he arrived at Kashipur, breathing hard and perspiring.

His arrival was reported to the Master lying in his bed on the first floor. He did not give any verbal reaction but was elated to learn that his dear Naren had not failed him but passed the acid test. With all the thoughts of his home, his legal career also went out of his mind. Naren got settled at Kashipur and got engrossed in the spiritual practices. A couple of days passed and one evening as he was meditating, he felt that he was transported to some other region. He felt his limbs had gone dumb. He cried out: 'O Gopalbhai,' (Gopal was the seniormost of Shri Ramakrishna's disciples, older than Shri Ramakrishna. His monastic name was Advaitananda), 'Gopalbhai, where are my hands and feet?' Gopalbhai struck a couple of blows on, or pinched Naren's hands and feet and said. 'Here they are, Naren.' This state of *samadhi* went on for such a long time as to frighten his friends. One or two of them quickly ran upstairs and reported the matter to Shri Ramakrishna. They were very much worried, they said. Not a muscle on the face of the guru moved. 'Let him be for some time in that state,' said Shri Ramakrishna. 'He was pestering me so much for this.' At long last when Naren regained normal consciousness, he was summoned upstairs by the Master. 'So, did you have what you so keenly desired?' Shri Ramakrishna asked with a smile. 'But now it will be kept secure, locked in a strong safe and the key will be with me. The safe would be unlocked only when you have finished the task Ma wants you to perform. And then you will be bidding goodbye to the World.'

The guru had on an earlier occasion scolded Naren when he tried to test his powers of *samadhi* and had asked Kali to touch him. Kali had felt something like an electric current enter his body.

Even though this pursuit of *samadhi* and other spiritual practices on the part of the disciples were going on, the steady deterioration in the health of Shri Ramakrishna caused them a lot of worrying. Once when some of them were sitting around Ramakrishna with sullen faces, Shri Ramakrishna tenderly moved his emaciated hand on the heads and faces of Rakhal and Naren, who were sitting closest to him. Shri Ramakrishna asked: 'Do you know what I am seeing? I see God in every creature, in everything. He is the Executor. He is the person being executed and He is the cross of execution.' After saying this he slipped into the state of *samadhi*. When he became normal and opened his eyes, he made a pregnant uttarance: 'Now I don't feel any pain whatsoever. I am fully relieved.'

August 1886 had started with the Bengal sky overcast with dark clouds, the minds and hearts of the disciples were overcast with the dark shadows of death. Shri Ramakrishna's consumption of food had gone down very low. He talked mostly with signs. He had become quite emaciated. Yet the smile on his face and the gleam in his eyes had not left him. On 11th or 12th of August, he called Naren upstairs. He was sitting erect with the help of several bolsters. He asked Naren to sit on the bed right in front of him using gestures. Soon, thereafter, he went into the state of *samadhi*. Observing all this as Naren was, he experienced some powerful current emanating from the guru's being and penetrating his own self. He was getting charged, as it were. Suddenly he slipped into *samadhi*. When he came back to himself and opened his eyes, he found the eyes of Shri Ramakrishna overflowing with tears. He then spoke softly, 'Well Naren, I have given away to you everything I had. Now I have become a penniless fakir. You will achieve great things because of what I have given to you. After achieving that you'll go back to where you have come from.' And it took only a few years for this prophecy to come true.

In spite of all this, two incidents of this very period marked out Naren singularly. On one occasion while he was sitting with Shri Ramakrishna, the latter, recommending several things to Naren, said, 'You will look after the other disciples and give them all necessary assistance and guidance.' 'I won't do it,' was Naren's sulky reaction. 'Your very bones will make you do that,' was the reply that had come out of the mouth of Shri Ramakrishna, showing his full confidence in the ability of Naren.

The other incident was equally peculiar. Barely a couple of days before Shri Ramakrishna's departure from this world, Naren was standing in front of the guru's bed when a thought lurked up in his mind: 'The guru often said that he was Rama, he was Krishna, born again for the good of the world. If he says so when he is standing on the doorstep of death, then only I'll believe in him.' Hardly had the doubt arisen in his mind, the weak voice of the guru fell on Naren's ears. 'Naren, still doubting? I am that very Rama and I am that very Krishna, Ramakrishna, but not in your Vedantic sense,' Naren was dumbfounded. His doubts got dispelled.

It was August 15 of the year. In spite of his rapidly falling health because of the cancer and because of the ever decreasing intake of food, he had continued to mould his disciples. Without performing any ceremonial initiation into *sannyasa,* Shri Ramakrishna had rooted the idea of renunciation coupled with service to humanity, so firmly that no gusts of family ties, of social status, of comfortable life could sway them from that ideal. Yet they were human and were living so closely with Shri Ramakrishna that the fear of losing him had gripped them firmly.

But nature does not heed to anybody's feelings and leaves their bereaved lovers mourning. So also was the case with Shri Ramakrishna. He was lying in his bed. He was looking like a skeleton. And on that day, August 15, 1886, ever since morning he appeared to be sinking slowly. The disciples were sitting all around, or when tired of sitting stiff, would get up and stroll in the room with sullen faces. The doctors had given up all hopes. Balaram and Girish were summoned. Shashi could not control himself and started crying. The hearts of all present there were crying. Shri Ramakrishna's breathing had become abnormal. In such a physical condition, he had given no response when a bowl of his usual porridge was brought to him in the evening.

But a couple of hours after nightfall, he regained consciousness, spoke with an almost normal though weak voice and demanded something to eat. The bowl of porridge was soon brought there. With the help of bolsters, he sat upright in his bed and emptied the entire bowl of its contents. The disciples felt happy and relieved at this. He also said that he was feeling better and he started talking to the disciples in a very low voice. Naren suggested to him to rest and go to bed. It was to him only that the guru's final words were addressed. All of a sudden he uttered Kali three times and stretched himself on his bed. Thinking that the guru was resting and sleeping, Naren went down to retire.

Midnight had passed. The clock was slowly ticking. It was two minutes past 1.oo a.m. of the 16th August. All of a sudden a thrill seemed to pass through the body of Shri Ramakrishna. His eyes became half open with their pupils looking down on the nose tip. He wore his usual blissful smile. All the hair on his body stood on edge. He had passed into the state of *samadhi*. It was not the usual state of *samadhi* from which he returned. It was '*Mahasamadhi*'—the great *samadhi*—from which there was no return.

Not quite. Like old clothes he had discarded his body. So the question of his returning in the same bodily frame did not arise. But he did return.

On the afternoon of 16th August, his body was taken to the Kashipur cremation ground and amidst shouts 'Jai Shri Ramakrishna,' it was consumed by fire.

But within no time he showed up before his wife Sharadadevi, who was preparing to switch over to the life style of a traditional Hindu widow. He said, 'Don t change at all. I am not dead. I have simply gone from one room to another.' This happened more than once and the Holy Mother continued to wear the bangles he had got specially made for her, wear a sari with a small red border and had not got her hair removed.

Naren was moving with a companion in the garden of the Kashipur house a couple of days later. He had a clear vision of his guru. He was to have such visions later on also.

But for the time being, the guru was gone. And since the lease of the Kashipur house was to expire on the 31st of the month, where to go after renunciation, what to do and how to live?, were all questions.

A hundred problems at home were also waiting for Naren.

11

The Maṭh, Built on Ruins

The long illness of Shri Ramakrishna had prepared his disciples for his departure from the world, yet the void his death had created was unfathomable and the shock was not small. The disciples felt orphaned. They wanted to renounce the world, but where to go and what to do was the question facing them like a hungry tiger with mouth wide, open.

The lease of the Kashipur house was to expire on the 31st August, 1886. Though two or three days after the passing away of Shri Ramakrishna, the gatekeeper of the Kashipur house had tried to prevent Shri Sharadadevi's hackney carriage from leaving the place, the disciples continued to occupy the place until the end of the month. The place was full of the memories of their dear, revered guru. The devotees, as per custom, had collected ashes and bones from the Kashipur cremation grounds, placed them reverentially in a metal pot and started worshipping them. The disciples had a plan to bury these relics somewhere on the bank of the Ganga and put up a monument or a temple there. But this required a lot of money and the disciples had none.

Ramachandra Datta had a place on the outskirts of the city with some wide open space. He planned to bury the pot of relics there and build a small temple. He called the place 'Ramakrishna Yogodyana.' The disciples would not let him do that. There was a tussle. The Holy Mother Sharadadevi did not like this 'fight over the ashes,' as she called it, so soon after the passing away of her great husband. Naren intervened. Another similar pot was brought in. Some ashes were put into the pot, the pot was decorated with vermillion and flowers and was carried in a procession to the Ramakrishna Yogodayana of Ramachandra Datta. It was interred ceremoniously and soon thereafter a temple dedicated to Shri Ramakrishna was constructed. The other relics were, however, stored in another pot and it was secretly taken to Balaram's house.

As mentioned in the previous chapter, the very next day after the passing away of Shri Ramakrishna, Sharadadevi had a very clear vision of her husband, advising her to refrain from adopting the custom of a Hindu widow, because he was not dead but he had gone from one room to another room. This vision was repeated and then only Sharadadevi became bold enough to swim against the tide of custom. An year later when she went to live at Kamarpukur, her husband's native village, the village folks were very harsh in their critisicm of Sharadadevi.

Sharadadevi had gone on a pilgrimage to Kashi, Vrindavan, Mathura etc. She was accompanied by the wife of Balaram Bose and the wife of Mahendranath Gupta. Three young disciples of Shri Ramakrishna—Kali Yogin and Latu—had accompanied her. The other disciples were staying at the Kashipur house. They continued their meditation and other spiritual practices, sang *bhajans*, started worshipping the photograph of their guru and held philosophical and other discussions. But they were greatly perplexed at the stark fact facing them, that after August 31 of the year 1886, they would have to disband themselves. They had no idea at all about the future course of the rivers of their lives. All of them, without exception, had resolved to give up the world and become *sannyasins*. Their guru, a few weeks before his passing away, had given each one of them a piece of ochre cloth. He had also asked them to go out and beg for food like other *sannyasins*. Sharadadevi was the first to offer her contribution. And when they had returned with grains of different sorts, it was all mixed and cooked in one pot and Shri Ramakrishna was the first to have a grain of that holy *Prasada*. Excepting these two things, he had not made them perform the viraja homa—the fire sacrifice—performed by every novitiate joining the order of *sannyasins*.

Leaving aside the formalities, the frightening question facing the young men, who so eagerly cherished the ideal of renunciation, was where to go after leaving their parental homes and where to stay, what to do, what and how to eat and how to live. It was no use merely adding a dozen more ochre-clad beggars to the vast army of the ochre-clad *sannyasins* of various orders moving around the country from Badrinath to Rameshvaram and from Dwarka to Jagannath Puri. Naturally, they were all forced to go back home. Only but Gopala, the senior most amongst the disciples who had brought the pieces of the ochre cloth to Kashipur for distributing them to sadhus and which were distributed by Shri Ramakrishna to his own disciples with the remark, 'where will you get such enthusiastic and dedicated sadhus?' Others had nowhere to go to. Latu had been away, accompanying Shri Sharadadevi. Almost all the others were forced, very much against their will, to go back home. The group was disbanded and had got completely disheartened. The future was as dark as an *Ashadh*—july rain cloud, but without the benefit of rain.

Just then, Shri Ramakrishna made himself present before a well-to-do devotee of his, Suresh-or Surendra Mitra, who had been the backbone behind the Kashipur stay of Shri Ramakrishna. 'Don't you see the hardship my young disciples are facing? They want to renounce *samsara* and live like *sannyasins*. Provide a house for them and make other arrangements for them to live together.' Surendra dutifully obeyed. He called Naren who lived close by and told him of the blessed vision of his. He told Naren that whatsoever he was giving for the Kashipur house, he would continue to give for the maintenance of the group of disciples.

A cheap house had to be hunted for. And they got one in the Varahanagar area, a bit away from the city, on the bank of the holy Ganga. The house was one with a few rooms on the ground floor and a few on the first floor. However, a part of the terrace had caved in and the house that had been lying unoccupied for quite a few years was said to be a haunted one. The house was literally in ruins, that's why its rent was ten rupees a month. When the young disciples charged with enthusiasm, went to occupy it, no ghost ever crossed their way but they found that there were numerous reptiles like snakes and lizards to keep them company. They also found that the plaster on the walls had come off at many places and the broken doors and frames of a couple of windows put them in direct contact with the sun and the wind and the rain. But the young monks did not feel any hardship because of the dilapidated condition of the house. They were enthused that they were able to launch on a new path, although the newness was going to take a decade to emerge.

As mentioned earlier, Kali, Latu and Yogin had been on a pilgrimage with Shri Sharadama. Naturally, they joined the Varahanagar *Math* later on and since Yogin remained attached to Sharadama till he died at a young age, his presence at the *Math* was very limited. Tarak—Shivananda—had also gone on a pilgrimage after the passing away of Thakur and as soon as the *Math* was established, Naren sent a telegram and Tarak joined the *Math*. In spite of objections and hitches by parents Sharat and Shashi joined the *Math*. Their parents blamed Naren for robbing them of their brilliant sons. Gangadhar and Baburam also were among the founder members, though the wanderlust of Gangadhar was soon to drive him away to far off places. There were no ghosts in the *Math* but the young occupants called themselves 'devils'.

Unfortunately for him, as well as for his *gurubhais*, because of the legal and other problems at home, Naren had not been able to become a full time member of the *Math* from the beginning.

Very much against his will, he was forced to attend to the legal matters till the judgement of the case filed by the relatives for a claim on the house was delivered. Fortunately it was in favour of Naren's family. But so long as the matter was pending, he was often called upon to go to the attorney and to some witnesses. This kept him preoccupied against his will and so he had not become a full time resident at the *Math*. Some *gurubhais* had expressed their dissatisfaction at this. But Naren was just helpless. He could not leave the serious matter, hanging like a sword of Damocles, in the lurch. He joined later on.

The copper pot containing the relics of their guru, which they had kept hidden at Balaram's house was quietly brought into the *Math*. The young monks started worshipping it as well as a photograph of Ramakrishna. All others moved out and in of the *Math* for a short or a long time, but Shashi stuck there like a leech, never left the place until asked by Naren to go to Madras to take charge of the newly established centre there in 1897. Regularly, punctually and piously he carried out the ceremonial routine of worship in the morning and at vespers. And he had taken upon himself to offer *Prasada* to Thakur. Those earlier days were the days of permanent shortages and Shashi would often go a—begging, procure some rice, cook it, and after offering it to their Deity they would all share it and give out a sigh of satisfaction. Naren rightly selected the *sannyasa* name Ramakrishnananda for Shashi. He proved its appropriateness by his devoted service to Thakur in Madras later on.

Besides this *puja, bhajans* and meditation the group spent their time in reading and discussion. They read scriptures, philosophy, science, history, almost every serious thing. Besides the Hindu scriptures, they devoured the teachings of the Buddha and read the *Bible* also. A few of the monks had attended missionary schools and colleges and had come in contact with the life and teachings of Jesus, presented more or less from the missionary point of view. Here it was not so. Portions from the

'Gospels' were often compared with the teachings of the Hindu scriptures and in the light of their guru's teachings. Naren provided the leadership in all this; he was intellectually head and shoulders above the group and he was ordained by Thakur to do so. His razor-sharp intellect, his keen understanding and powerful memory were great assets to him. He was the first don of the new lyceum.

The teacher and the taught at the Varahanagar *Math* jumped up with joy at the invitation from the mother of Baburam to go to her village Antpur, in the Hoogly district nearby. It was nearing the last week of December, 1886. Except those like Latu, Yogin, Rakhal etc, who were away, Sharat, Shashi, Tarak, Kali, Sharadaprasanna, Niranjan and Gangadhar were in the group led by Naren. Baburam's mother was herself a devotee of Shri Ramakrishna and she was very happy to receive this group of young monks. The railway compartment the young *sannyasins* were travelling in on their way to Antpur was reverberating with devotional songs. The trip was not merely a pleasure trip for the nine young monks. It was turned into a spiritual retreat. Long hours of meditation, some reading and discussion occupied the youths. It was calm and serene, conducive to the spiritual task the young men were after. The cool and pure air of the village filled their lungs with vigour and the full meals served with maternal affection filled their tummies. They meditated in a group, sang spirituals in a group, discussed in a group and moved around in a group. The stay strengthened the bond of brotherhood.

One evening, after dinner, the group gathered in the open, lighted a fire to ward off the cold and started meditating. It was a long spiritual vigil and a rich one too. Then, Naren quietly launched upon the life story of Jesus. The central theme of his story was not the miracles Jesus is said to have performed, but the overflowing compassion and the great renunciation of Jesus. He knew the Gospels as well as any great devotee of Christ and, while narrating the story, he quoted from the Gospel according to St. Mathew. 'The foxes have holes and the birds have nests, but the Son of Man hath nowhere to rest his head.' Then he mentioned the journies undertaken by the apostles of Christ at great risk to their lives. He next invoked his brother monks to go the way of the apostles of Jesus, pledge themselves to renounce the world and serve mankind. All of them were so charged that they were all standing in a circle around the fire while pledging themselves so. And they called upon the holy fire and the stars above to be witnesses to their pledge. Then they discovered that it was 24th of December, the Christmas eve of the year and what other day would have been more propitious for the young *sannyasins'* vow of devotion and dedication?

With renewed vigour, the party returned to Varahanagar. Though the life was the same as they had lived previously, the Antpur change had injected a new vitality in them. They were now getting adjusted to their life without their great guru. His was a touch of a mother, always showering affection. And he had declared that Naren was an incarnation of Lord Shiva, the mighty God of fiery energy and manliness.

The flaming fire of knowledge ever burning in him, along with turning all the dross of ignorance and bigotry into ashes, would also stretch its seething tongue all around and many other things in the vicinity would get scalded. No fire fighter was born to quell Naren's fire. But Naren himself would come around and since his heart was full of genuine love for his *gurubhais*, he would apply some soothing balm of words, put in some humour and the cool breeze blowing from the Ganga would evoke a loud laughter from all the assembled *gurubhais*.

But along with the fire of knowledge, another fire was singeing in the heart of Naren. Was this *puja* of the picture of Shri Ramakrishna, the singing of *bhajans*, sometimes accompanied by dancing, sitting in meditation in a quiet corner and reading and group discussion, was that only the goal their Master had set for them? More particularly, for him, Naren? Shri Ramakrishna was a great seer and he had boldly declared that he, Naren, was destined to perform some great task of Ma. What was that task? How was he to perform it? And when? Naren knew no answers to these questions. The furies in him tormented him day and night. It was as if he was groping in a tunnel of darkness, 'blind darkness' in the words of the *Isha Upanishad*. Naren felt himself like the blinded Biblical Samson, entirely helpless, entirely clueless.

Naren prayed and prayed. God appeared to have turned deaf to his prayers. He turned to his Guru for guidance. The smiling image of Shri Ramakrishna bore his bewitching smile which appeared to be as enigmatic as the answers of the ancient Greek oracles. Should he plunge himself into the eternal Ganga and drown himself?

Yes, he should plunge, but not into the waters of the Ganga flowing by but plunge into the vast ocean of Bharat across the Howrah bridge. Suddenly, he heard a call from within, or was it from without? To leave the narrow precincts of the city said to have been founded by Job Charnok and get lost into the vast ocean of religions, of castes and creeds, of men and women, of poverty and riches, of princes and peasants, of languages and dialects, of all the diversity proclaiming the unity of Aryavarta. Reciting of books of history was one thing, the touch of reality was the real thing. Sharadananda has noted in the fifth part of the biography of his guru that his guru, the great seer that he was, had declared that, 'The day Naren comes in contact with pain and misery the pride of his character would melt into infinite compassion. Naren's strong faith in himself will turn into an instrument of re-establishing in discouraged souls the self-confidence and faith they have lost.' The freedom of Naren's conduct, which was based on great self-mastery would manifest itself, brilliantly in the eyes of others as a manifestation of the true freedom of his edge. The vast, suffering, poverty-striken mass of people was like a big forest of *arani* trees. Naren's sensitive heart was like a dry piece of the *arani* wood. The moment one was rubbed against the other, everything in his mind would go up in flames. The flames would burn away all that was dross, and the pure unalloyed gold in him would begin to shine. Just like the mythical monkey god Hanuman, the great devotee of Shri Rama, who had jumped over the sea to get news of the torment faced by Sita, Naren also wanted to do so.

A *sannyasin* cuts all bonds. Why should Naren be bound down by the *Math*? The fellow disciples at the *Math* were much closer to each other and to Naren than blood brothers. They were all capable of taking care of themselves. Each one of them could satisfy his own intellectual need and the journey of the spirit was, ultimately, a march in the single file. Each one of the disciples could and should go his own way. The guru had led them like that and had placed each one on the end of the jumping board from where each one had to jump himself.

So Naren decided that the life they were then leading at the Varahanagar *Math* was not the life meant for him. True it was that it was not a life of luxury. More often than not, it was difficult at the *Math* to satisfy their basic wants. Each inmate at the *Math*, for example wound a piece of ochre cloth around his body. And on a string in the verandah were hanging a full length dhoti and a bigger piece of the ochre cloth. Anyone going out of the *Math* on an errand to the city would use them. Shortages of all things did create problems, but that was not the driving force so far as Naren was concerned.

Mahendranath Gupta visited the *Math* quite often and spent quite some time there in the conpany of Naren and other young monks. He has recorded the discussion he had there, particularly with Naren. The level of the discussion was always befitting the height of both the intellectuals as well as their spiritiual depths. Yet at some places we see traces of Naren's discontent at the humdrum life at the *Math* and the desire to go out in search of the task he was destined to perform. The book of life was calling him to open it and read it, page by page, sentence by sentence and paragraph by paragraph. He would have first to see the book and then open it to read.

Narendra and the others at the *Math* had performed the *Viraja homa* and taken to the life of *sannyasins,* a la Hindu tradition. It was almost an injunction for a *sannyasin* to move out from place to place, to become a *parivrajaka.* Naren had not taken the name of Vivekananda then. He left Kolkata in the garb of a *sannyasin,* sticking to all the vows of a *sannyasin.* He was carrying no money, whatsoever. His only belongings were a *danda,* a thick, long staff, a *Kamandala,* a metal pot with a spout, and a couple of books, the *Gita* and the *Imitation of Christ.*

12

First Forays

Naren had by then taken the Monastic vows and taken the name, Vividishananda. But during his wanderings he had changed the name a couple of times, and, as testified by Lokmanya Tilak, at times, he moved without a name or no name, his odour from afar announced his arrival. For the sake of simplicity, we shall call him Vivekananda. Vivek in Sanskrit means discrimination and he certainly was very discriminating. His guru knew this well and had certified it.

Swami Vivekananda was the major domo of the Varahanagar *Math.* Vivekananda had laid down the routine to be followed, he had also decided the *arti* songs. And he himself led in singing them with a soulful voice. He would procure books, make his *gurubhais* read them and discuss them, himself leading and guiding. Scriptures were read and analysed. This was all a group activity but carried on within the narrow confines of the convent- *Math.* Each one of them desired self realisation. In order to achieve that Brahmananda-Rakhal-had gone to the holy banks of the Narmada and Akhandananda-Gangadhar-had set out for climbing the snow-capped Himalayas and crossing it over to penetrate into the monasteries of the Lamas in Tibet. Other young friends also, except of course, Ramakrishnananda, moved out and in. They visited various places of pilgrimage, far and near, met holy men there and talked to them. But this was more or less tradition. It did give them some joy, peace of mind, understanding and contacts. But in the heart of their hearts they remembered it very well that their guru wanted them to break new ground. Was not the guru himself a silent revolutionary?

Vivekananda was the most perplexed person. The guru had boldly prophesied that Naren was destined to do some great work of Ma. What was that work? Where to find it? And how? Ramakrishna, like the inscrutable sphinx, had not specified it and in his absence, who could guide the young troubled monk? Right from his early boyhood, he was frequently having two visions: in one he saw himself as Napoleon, conquering all land he sat his foot upon, ruling over it like a great monarch and dominating over everyone and everything around him. In another, he saw himself as a half clad *sadhu*, without any material possessions and standing on the Everest of renunciation, all the world falling at his feet. He had renounced the world and become a *sannyasin*, yet the dream of conquest had not left him. The conflict was seething in his mind, burning his viscera. Unfortunately for him, there was no *Bhairavi*, disembarking and walking straight to him as in the case of Shri Ramakrishna to cure him of his burning sensation. He was not so lucky.

He must go out and search for the 'task' he was destined to do as prophesied by his Master. He must take a plunge. If what Shri Ramakrishna had foretold were to come true, he would swim and find it out on the other shore. Or else, he would get drowned, sink like a big lump of lead.

One place which attracts all pious Hindus is Kashi, one of the seven cities, promising salvation. Vivekananda was not hankering after the traditional salvation, freedom from rebirth. He wanted to seek that which would make him free from the agony of the uncertainty of the mission he was destined to perform. Thriving as the city was in the time of the great Buddha more than 2500 years ago, the city is one of the oldest cities in the world much older than most other cities. Vishvanath, the Lord of the Universe, is the presiding deity. There are temples of numerous other gods and goddesses. There is the holy Ganga flowing by. The great Buddha had consecrated the place by preaching his first sermon there. Shankaracharya, the great propounder of the *Advaita* philosophy, had given it a touch of his own serenity. The traditional method of teaching the *Vedas*, the six *darshanas*, the great grammar of Panini was being followed in the *pathshalas* of the city. The streets of the city are still reverberating with the echoes of various *mantras* and *sutras*. Might not this probing in the past open the vistas of the future for Vivekananda? The monk himself was one score and four years of age. Might not a drop of the edifying Ganga remove the blanket of uncertainty covering his vision? Might not the Lord Shiva open His third eye and with a flaring ray of light lightup his path engulfed by darkness?

Vivekananda's trip to Kashi, undertaken in early 1888 and in the company of a *gurubhai* and a devoted friend, did not take him to his goal, but it gave him an opportunity to meet a learned *pandit* and see Bhaskarananda and Trilang Swami, two great spiritual leaders then known all over India. Kashi is a small mirror reflecting the whole of India, as people from the length and breadth of the country flock to Kashi for a pilgrimage. Kashi is thus a mini India, reflecting all the diversities of languages and sects and castes and social ranks and the underlying unity of spirit bringing them all to the holy city. The mental screen of Vivekananda was receiving all these impressions, storing them, sorting them.

Vivekananda learnt a lesson of courage there. One day while he was returning from a temple, a flock of monkeys was attracted towords him and it started pursuing him. This made the young Swami run. The monkeys also started running after him. An old *sadhu* coming from the opposite direction held the running Vivekananda by hand and gave him a lesson: 'Don't run away from evil; face it and fight it.' Vivekananda who was running out of breath, took this advice to heart, stopped, turned around and stood facing the monkeys following him. The simians following him also stood still, and, as if imitating him, turned about and went back. 'Face evil and fight it,' was the great lesson young Vivekananda learnt. The young monk's will to fight was strengthened.

He returned within two months to the *Math*. Might be, he wanted to try himself out, test his capacity to endure, to go with out friends. It might as well be his anxiety about the running of the *Math* in his absence, his care for his *gurubhais*.

While he was at the *Math*, he urged his *gurubhais* to go out of the *Math* to the villages nearby and do some preaching. It is not known to what extent this advice of his was followed by the band of monks at the Varahanagar *Math*. They were, probably, not sure of themselves. And without insisting on them to do his bidding Vivekananda again left the *Math* for Kashi. There Swami Vivekananda came in close contact with one Pramadadas Mitra, who was a great scholar of Sanskrit. Swamiji's desire for mastery over the great classical language came to be fulfilled at Kashi with the help of discussions with Babu Pramadadas and the rich collection of books on various subjects the Babu had. Swamiji became attached to Pramadadas who solved a number of queries of Vivekananda. So erudite was the Babu that Swamiji stayed with him for a few days and held discussions with Pramadada, and after leaving Kashi, he corresponded with Pramadadas and put forth his puzzles as the number of letters—33 in all—that the Swami wrote to him showed.

From Kashi, Swamiji went to Ayodhya, the place associated with the great hero of the *Ramayana*, Lord Rama, considered the 7th incarnation of Lord Vishnu, Vivekananda's heart was filled with joy there. From there Swamiji went to Lucknow, which was still preserving the graces of the rule of great *Nawabs*. The architecture of the Imamvada and mosques and palaces, which reflected a blending of the Muslim and the Hindu architectural styles fascinated Swamiji. From Lucknow, Swamiji proceeded to Agra to see the marble marvel, the Taj Mahal, and various architectural relics of the great Mughals, ruined palaces and forts, the great makabaras and mosques. At all the places, it was a journey in the past and the relics helped the strong imagination of the young monk to recreate the past in all its glories.

From 'Love sculpted in Marble,' Swamiji went to Vrindavan, the place of the unsculpted, immortal love of Radha and Krishna. Vrindavan is situated upstream on the Yamuna about 40 miles north and Swamiji walked down the distance. It was the August of 1888 and after the rains, Vivekananda might have found the walking pleasant. He might also be cherishing the desire to walk over the land hallowed by Shri Krishna. As he was nearing Vrindavan he saw a man reclining against the trunk of a tree and puffing his pipe with pleasure. Swamiji desired to have a couple of puffs. But the man, looking at Swamiji, respectfully said that he was a scavenger, an untouchable! The caste consciousness, ingrained in Swamiji's blood, made him march ahead, but only a few steps. Soon, his vow of *sannyasa* flared up in his mind: as a *sannyasin*, he was above all castes, and all persons, irrespective of their castes or creeds were equal to him. He soon returned, and very much against the will of the man with the pipe, took it from the man's hands and bringing it near his own mouth and cupping his hands, Swamiji enjoyed a couple of puffs. With the outgoing smoke from his nose and mouth, Swamiji drove away from his mind the traces of caste consciousness and started moving towards Vrindavan.

Swamiji's guru, Shri Ramakrishna had visited the place twenty years ago and was so seized by Radha-consciousness that he didn't want to leave the place. Ramakrishna had gone there in the company of Mathur Babu, the pillar of the Dakshineshvar temple, and he did not have to worry about anything. Vivekananda was a *Parivrajaka,* without any belonging, without any money, without anyone to look after any of his needs. He had placed himself in the arms of God. He had to beg for his daily bread. One day, he had been to the Govardhan hill, connected with the story of Shri Krishna's fight against the god Indra and coming out victorious in the end. Swamiji climbed the hill, went round the hill ceremoniously and sat for meditation. All of a sudden, it started raining. Swamiji had vowed not to beg his daily bread on the day. If someone were to offer food to him, then only he would eat. He was walking towards the town, bathing in the rain, wading through the muddy waters and hungry. He walked on and on. Suddenly he heard a cry, 'Swamiji Maharaj.' A man was calling him to oblige himself by accepting *Prasada,* food! Swamiji started running. The man with the food parcel also ran after Swamiji and at long last, he caught up with the latter. He who had given teeth to Swamiji, gave him something to munch also. And when Swamiji had finished eating, the man who had brought the *Prasada* disappeared.

At Vrindavan, Vivekananda had a nasty experience too. He went to the Radha Kunda-a small built-up pond-one afternoon when it was all quiet and there were no visitors. He washed his *kaupin,* the ochre piece of cloth covering his body, spread it on the bank for drying and went in for a dip in the Kunda. He was a good swimmer and the cool waters of the Kunda were found refreshing. When he came out of the Kunda after some time, he found his only covering i.e, his kaupin, stolen! It was taken away by some monkeys and they were sitting away on a tree nearby holding the *kaupin* and looking at Swamiji, repeating as it were the lila of Krishna, who had taken away the clothes of the *Gopis* bathing in the Yamuna. They probably wanted to know what move the naked *sannyasin* would take. Dejected completely, and ashamed to move about naked Swamiji started moving towards the jungle with the view of abandoning his life and complaining to Radha. All of a sudden a man manifested from nowhere and approached Swamiji with a new *kaupin* and some food.

Vivekananda accepted it thankfully as a grace of God and then, on going to the Radha Kund, he found his old kaupin lying there. The monkeys had abandoned it. Such are the ways of God, and of monkeys.

From Vrindavan, Vivekananda proceeded to Haradwar, at the foot of the Himalayas. On the way he stopped at the railway station of Hatharas. As the place is about 30 miles away, Swamiji, penniless as he was, might have walked down the distance from Mathura. It was a small station and as soon as the station master, one Sharat Chandra Gupta, saw the colossus like Swamiji, he was instinctively drawn to the monk. A glance at Swamiji made the station master understand that the monk had been hungry since long. He invited Swamiji for a meal. On seeing the station master's face, Swamiji read the former's feelings and asked with the simplicity of a child: 'Well, what fare will you serve?' In reply, Sharat Chandra recited a Persian couplet, saying, "O beloved, you have arrived at the most proper place. I'll cook something by cutting my heart and offer it to you!" After some time he heard the Swami reciting a bhajan conveying, "O my dear, rub ashes on your moonlike face and then come to me!" The station master went into his house, cast away his station master's uniform, applied ashes on his face and stood before Swamiji! And in a few days, the station master left his job, took to *sannyasa*, was initiated by Swamiji—he was among the first so initiated if not...the first—and joined Swamiji on his journey to the Himalayas. He had as yet not left service. He was on leave.

They arrived at Hrishikesh, where the Ganga, descending from the mighty Himalayas, enters the plains. Many *sannyasins* come to live there and when it is summer, many of them visit the holy shrines of Badrinath and Kedarnath and also visit Gangotri and Jamnotri, the sources of the Ganga and the Yamuna. The journey is quite hazardous, yet has been attracting a big number of pilgrims since times immemorial. Many ancient *rishis* and *sannyasins* have spent long periods in meditation in the caves of the mountain, unseen by people. But the desire of Vivekananda to retire into a cave and meditate could not be fulfilled. In spite of the murmuring waters of the Bhagirathi, the cool mountain breeze, the serene calm and the atmosphere throbbing with the spirit of the lakhs of *sannyasins* and saints who had lived there in the past, the station master fell so ill that he had to be taken back to Hatharas. He recovered there but Swamiji fell ill. On hearing this, the *gurubhais* feverishly appealed to him and he went back to the *Math* with his new disciple, Sharat Chandra. Sharat sent in his resignation and was ordained as a monk, with the name, Sadananda.

The home-coming of their dear leader towards the end of 1888 had filled the hearts of his *gurubhais* with delight. Almost a year long period of seminary studies started. His presence strengthened their love of *sannyasa* and made them look at the scriptures afresh. Many injunctions of the *Smriti*s were questionable: How right was it to prohibit the study of the *Vedas* by the *Shudra*s! Child marriage was another problem. Stone like rigidity of the caste system had stratified the Hindu society. Crossing the seas was absolutely forbidden. All such injunctions of the *Smriti*s might have been necessary at sometime in the past. But they were fetters today, checking all progress. Some of the young monks, who had come in contact with the Brahmo ways of thinking, who had read English and Sanskrit classics, who had also read some other Western thinkers, were, all taken aback. A society has to be progressive, but with such solid fetters, around the legs, no society can progress. A happy period of almost an year at the monastery thus passed away.

But there was a call from within and without, which would not let Vivekananda be at the *Math*. Vivekananda, who was going to earn the appelation, 'The king of Monks,' heard the king of mountains, the Himalayas, calling him. He had to listen to it, respect it and jump into the lap of the mighty mountain, where, very probably, the call of destiny, still just murmuring unclearly in his mind, might become clearly audible. So once more to the north-West, upstream the great Ganga, towards her snow-clad source.

His first halt was at Vaidyanath, a holy Shiva shrine in Bihar, just north West of Bengal. His next halt was going to be Kashi, where he wanted to meet the great scholar Pramadadas Mitra and put before the learned *Pandit* many problems he was facing while reading the ancient texts. But before he could do so, he was informed that his young gurubhai, Swami Yogananda was afflicted with small pox. With the view to nursing him Vivekananda ran to Prayag—Allahabad, standing on the confluence of the Ganga and the Yamuna. Because of careful and timely nursing and because of Thakur's grace, Yogananda soon recovered. Allahabad was a home to many Bengalis, working as officers in government service and they were all attracted by the talented young monk from Bengal. His genius overawed them. Swamiji heard there about Pavahari Baba literally meaning, 'one living on air' (without food), a saint of great repute living at Gazipur. Swamiji went there. The saint was living in a cave on the Ganga, avoided contact with people, would come to the opening of the cave and sit with his back facing the mouth of the cave for talking only to visitors he considered genuine seekers. Swamiji met the Baba several times. He was very keen to be the Baba's disciple and learn Hatha Yoga, a kind of Yoga laying great emphasis on bodily contortions. Ramakrishna appeared in a vision and prevented Vivekananda from taking to the Hatha Yoga path. Somehow, Vivekananda was a bit insistent about learning the Hatha Yoga. But his guru appeared again and prevented his great disciple from taking to the Hatha Yoga and set him once more, as it were, on his trail. This took place around January, 1890.

While at Gazipur, Swamiji came to learn that one of his younger *gurubhais,* Abhedananda was taken seriously ill at Kashi. Swamiji ran down to Kashi. He was living there at the house of Pramadadas, the great scholar. Fortunately, Abhedananda soon recovered. Then the garden of Pramadadas became Swamiji's *tapovan* for meditation. While there, the sad news of the death of

Balaram Bose, a great devotee of Shri Ramakrishna reached there. Swamiji was shocked to hear the news and the memory of the numerous occasions of great pleasure spent at Balaram's house on the occasions of their guru's visits welled up in his mind and Swamiji was moved to grief. Pramadadasa, according to whose line of thinking, a *sadhu* should be quite aloof from social relations and should be above joy and grief, was astonished at Swamiji's expression of grief. Swamiji said: 'Please don't talk like that. We are not dry sadhus without any feelings. Would all bonds of selfless love melt as soon as a person becomes a *sannyasin*? A *sannyasin* also has a heart.' Swamiji immediately left for Kolkata to be with the grieving family.

More bad news was waiting for him. Suresh or Surendra Mitra, the financial backbone of the *Math* was taken seriously ill and he succumbed to illness on the 25th of May, 1890. It was at Surendra's place that Vivekananda had first met Shri Ramakrishna. The financial difficulties of the *Math* increased manifold.

In the meanwhile Akhandananda had returned from his Himalayan sojourn and his *gurubhais* flocked around him to hear from him about his *yatra* to Kedarnath, Badrinath, Gangotri, Tibet etc. He narrated the hazards he had faced on the journey, the grace of Thakur that saved him time and again, the extremely cold climatic conditions and the great sublime beauty of some of the places he had visited. As stated earlier, Swamiji's mental ears again heard the high Himalayan peaks beckoning him. He proposed to Gangadhar: 'Let us both go to the Himalayas together,' and Gangadhar-Akhandananda, was ever willing. He wanted to go once more to the sublime snow-clad mountains. He also wanted to be with his great gurubhai, Naren, whom he loved and respected utmost.

13

In Search of His Mission

"I won't return from the Himalayas until I have acquired the spiritual power to transform someone's heart by a mere touch," these were the words, conveying his firm determination, uttered by Vivekananda before his *gurubhais* at the *Math*. And we see the same steel of firmness, when he went to Sharadama to offer his *pranams* before leaving. Taking the dust off her feet, Vivekananda said, "Ma, I have come for your blessings. I'm going out and won't return if I do not acquire real knowledge."

"Don't talk like that, Naren," Ma replied. She never used the monastic names of her sons. "Thakur has marked you out for some great work and you are destined to achieve it. And have you been to your own mother to bid her goodbye and seek her blessings?"

"Since you are the real mother, Ma, I am not going anywhere else," the young monk replied. This utterance of his clearly indicated how he had severed all family ties. His compassionate consideration for his own mother was to erupt a decade later and make him take some concrete steps for her welfare. But that was to be when he was to see himself on the doorstep of death.

The first halt of the two young monks, Vivekananda and Akhandananda was at Bhagalpur. They first stayed at the house of one Kumar Nityananda Sinha. The teacher of Mr. Sinha, Mr. Manmathnath Chaudhari, took the two young monks to his house. In a letter to a disciple of Vivekananda, written in 1906, Manmathnath later described the arrival and impact of Swamiji on his mind: 'One morning in August 1890, Swami Vivekananda, accompanied by Swami Akhandananda became my guests. Thinking them to be ordinary *sannyasins* like others, I did not take any notice of them and did not enter into any conversation with them. Some time after lunch, I started reading a book on Buddhism, written in English. Vivekananda who was sitting a few feet away asked me "What are you reading?" I mentioned the English title of the book and asked him if he knew English. "A little," he replied. Then I started talking to him about Buddhism. In no time I learnt that he was a thousand times more knowledgeable than I. He quoted from a number of books in English. Babu Mathuranath and I were simply amazed at the sweep of his knowledge.'

Manmathnath next brought out the number of *Upanishads* he had and placed some abstruse passages before the Swami who satisfied his host by explaining to him every passage without so much as touching any of the books. He was so impressed by Swamiji that he requested the latter to make Bhagalpur his permanent home. But Swamiji left the place quietly after spending a week there, when Manmathnath had gone out for some work. After spending a night at Vaidyanath, they reached Kashi.

Swamiji very much liked to stay there and spend long hours in discussing the ancient scriptures with Pramadadas, but the call of the Himalayas was ringing in the ears of both the *sannyasins* and while parting company, Swami Vivekananda said to Pramadadas, 'I'm leaving now. But when I return, I'll burst like a bomb on the society and the society shall follow me like a faithful dog.' So deep-rooted was Swamiji's faith in himself. But the 'bomb' had yet to collect its fire power.

At the insistence of Akhandananda, Swamiji went with him to Ayodhya, where the young monks met a mahant, well-versed in Sanskrit as well as in Persian. Swamiji saw a really pious person in him. From Ayodhya, both the monks moved to Nainital. After spending a fortnight there, they left for Almora on foot, since both the sadhus kept no money with them. On reaching Almora, Akhandananda took Swamiji to the orchard of one Ambadatta and he himself went to inform his gurubhai Sharadananda and another devotee Vaikunthanath, who were staying with Lala Badarisha. The Lala became greatly attached to Swamiji and Swamiji also took a great liking for the Lala. Badarisha served Swamiji and his *gurubhais* with great devotion. There Swamiji heard the sad news of the death of his sister. This set him thinking about the condition of the women of India and their amelioration. The news also made him seek soon the shelter of the Himalayas.

Along with his *gurubhais,* Swamiji moved to Gadhwal. Akhandananda began to suffer from bouts of severe cough and proceeding a step higher became impossible. The party left Karnaprayag. On the way down hill, while they were living in a chatti—a rest house—Vivekananda also fell ill. After resting there for a week, the party moved down to Rudraprayag. The snow-clad mountains, the deep and dark woods all around, and the murmuring rivulets, everything there presented an atmosphere for meditation. It was so serene that it looked as if time itself was standing still. The serene calm was contagious, and Swamiji's heart was filled with the high tide of spirituality. He liked to cling to the place and imbibe as much spiritual delight as he could, but the mountain God thought otherwise and wanted the young monk to fulfil his destiny and in order to do that Swamiji had to come down to the depressing plains and get himself completely merged into the vast ocean of men and women of India. He had to come in direct contact with the degradation the country was wallowing in. He would be able to conquer the spiritual Everest only after he dived deep into the ocean of misery his great nation had sunk into. A man with very sharp memory though he was, he seemed to forget the forecast of his guru. 'The very day Naren comes in contact with suffering and misery, the pride of his character will melt into a mood of limitless compassion. His mighty faith in himself will become an instrument to establish once more the faith in their own selves lost by the unhappy souls. And the freedom of Naren's conduct based on his mighty mastery of the self will brilliantly light into the eyes of others and manifest itself as the true liberty of his ego.' These are the words recorded by Swami Sharadananda in the last part of his great 'Life of Shri Ramakrishna' (the fifth part). Vivekananda's illness was an excuse to put in focus his life mission, Ma's great work, as Shri Ramakrishna had so succintly put it.

At Rudraprayag some government officers saw the ailing sadhus and administered some jungle drugs. This brought down the fever and when both Vivekananda and Akhandananda were able to move about a bit, the kind officers hired dundees—chairs for ferrying people up and down the mountains—and sent them down. Akhandananda fell ill again and they had to take him to Dehradun for treatment. The British civil surgeon diagnosed it as infection of the lungs and after treating him for a few days advised Akhandananda to be removed to plains. Swamiji asked him to go to Prayag, but Akhandananda went to nearby Meerut.

With his other *gurubhais* Swamiji went to the holy Hrishikesh, where the Ganga takes a U-turn. Swamiji and his companions were enamoured by the serenity of the place, associated with the names of so many *rishis* and saints and took shelter in a hut near a temple, a bit away from human habitation. But alas! Swamiji's desire to sit in quiet contemplation was soon shattered to pieces by the serious illness that attacked him. He started running high temperature and became delirious. The *gurubhais* were unnerved at this. Nothing in this world was dearer to them than Swamiji and he was taken seriously ill, and in a place where medical help was not available at all. A tribesman of the hills was sought for help. He gave Swamiji some wild root and this helped Swamiji revive. But they did the wise thing of going down towards the plains. And moving down to Haradwar and then to Kanakhal and then to Saharanpur, the party came to learn that Akhandananda had chosen to go to Meerut. With Brahmananda, who had joined them at Haradwar, the moving *Math*, as it were, came down to Meerut.

Akhandananda, to whom Swamiji was very dear, was taken aback at seeing the shattered health of his great gurubhai.

Swamiji spent five full months at Meerut, recuperating and then forbade his *gurubhais* from accompanying him, trailing him or meeting him. He had resolved to start the journey of his mission and he didn't want to be bothered by the illness of any of his *gurubhais,* nor he wanted any of his *gurubhais* to bother about his own health in case he fell ill. He did not want to be pampered by anyone. The presence of a gurubhai or *gurubhais* was also a sort of attachment, *maya,* and he firmly determined to cut himself off from all bonds. He left alone for Delhi the same day in January, 1891.

Hardly three decades had passed since Delhi had ceased to be the Mughal capital. The British had conquered the age old capital but had not started ruling from there. The British influence had started spreading its tentacles, yet the old Mughal charm had not become extinct. The Red Fort, the Qutub Minar, the ruins of the palaces of bygone Muslim rulers, the mosques and the makbaras and the quietly flowing Yamuna, who had preserved in her heart reflections of all the glorious and inglorious past, captivated Swamiji. He called himself Vividishananda but the sweet smell of an English speaking *sadhu* brought his fellow monks to him in a few days. He remonstrated with them and fled like a wild lion cub. Parting from his friends was a great delight to him.

Swamiji started his *pada-yatra*—walking on foot—from Delhi and reached Alwar, about a hundred miles south West in northern Rajasthan, then known as Rajputana. Chance or fate put him in immediate contact with the Divan, the Prime Minister, of the state. Needless to say that the Divan was greatly impressed by the majesty of Swamiji. The Divan thought that the young Swamiji was sent by God to teach the Maharaja a lesson. The Maharaja had cut himself off from his subjects and lived a lavish life, mainly in the company of his European friends. Seeing a brilliant and highly educated monk, the Maharaja asked Swamiji why he was living so. In reply, Swamiji asked the Maharaja why he was living such a lavish life, cut off from his subjects and neglecting his duties as a king. The people standing around stood aghast at the bluntness of Swamiji's question put to their Maharaja with the calmness of a sea. 'Because I like that way,' was the reply given by the Maharaja.

'And I do so because I like this way,' Swamiji said quietly.

They were all in the gorgeous house of the Divan. The walls of the drawing room were decorated with various paintings, one of which was that of the Maharaja. The Maharaja might have come under the influence of the founder of the Arya Samaj, Dayanand Saraswati. Swami Dayananda Saraswati was a contemporary of the guru of Vivekananda, had brought about the revival in the *Vedas*, had condemned all idol worships, believed in the uplift of women and had also taken the bold step of reconverting people to Hinduism. Might be under the influence of the Arya Samaj or having come under the influence of the missionaries, the Maharaja's next question was, 'why should we worship a lifeless idol?'

Swamiji asked someone to remove the picture of the Maharaja hanging on a wall and bring it before him. He had it placed on the floor. As soon as it was done so, he looked at the people around him, all of whom were the servants of the Maharaja, and asked them to spit on the picture. They were all shocked. The fear that Swamiji might lose his head because of his statement put in the presence of the very Maharaja, whose likeness was there in the picture, had gripped them. All of them stood tongue tied.

'Why don't you do what I say? This is a piece of paper only, come on, spit on it,' said Swamiji.

When this was repeated once more, someone had the courage to speak; 'Swamiji, it is the picture of our beloved Maharaja. We can't even dream of spitting on it. We respect our Maharaja. We respect his picture also.'

'You are right,' said Vivekananda, 'this piece of paper is only a likeness of him. Yet you exhibit the same respect for it as you do for your king, because it reminds you of him. A stone or wooden idol is not God, but it reminds us of God and His greatness. That's why we are worshiping the idol. No one worshipping an idol worships stone or wood. It reminds the devotee of God. That's why he worships the idol.' This opened the eyes of the Maharaja. He soon underwent a total change.

This was not the only encounter of Swamiji with a king or with a Divan. He was to accost a number of them in his long sojourn. But to him, the prince and the pauler were both alike. He was as much at home with an untouchable as with a learned Brahmin *pandit*. A royal palace with mahogany furniture and an unfurnished hut with its floor were equal to him. Castes and creeds, high and low social ranks, money and poverty made no difference to him. At Alwar, Swamiji had taken the bold step of accepting the invitation from a maulvi to dine at his place and thus had boldly shown that he practised what he preached—the equality of all mankind.

As Swamiji was to move southwards, he was to come in contact with the vast mass of men, a few living a lordly life but the vast majority seething in poverty brought about by the British. Without reading Dadabhai Naoroji's great book, 'Poverty and the Unbritish Rule in India,' Swamiji was to acquire the knowledge of the poverty of India directly with his own eyes. And all the various impressions his greatly receptive mind was gathering were going to help him resolve the many conflicts he was a prey to, the conflict between the desire to pursue independence and the desire to serve society, the desire to achieve the *Advaita samadhi* of the *Vedanta* and the desire to put the ideal of *Vedanta* into practice as pointed out by his guru, the desire to sit in a cave to meditate and the desire to ameliorate the poverty of the great nation! The vista that was to open before his mind's eye as he was to move from place to place and meet people of all strata of society was to hit him with a hundred lances of inequalities, of illiteracy, of stubborn sticking to outdated social practices, of hapless widows, of prejudices of caste and creed, emphasising minutest shades of differences and yet.... and yet exhibiting an undreamt of underlying unity. But as yet, he was probing his own mind as well as the outside world.

Leaving Alwar on 28th March, he came to Jaipur, where he came in contact with a great scholar of Panini's grammar and took advantage of him during his stay of about a fortnight there and then proceeded southwards to Ajmer, where he chanced to meet the great nationalist leader, Shyamji Varma and Harvilas Sarada, a great social reformer. After a short stay there, he proceeded to Mount Abu. The Jain temples there, about eight hundred years old, built by a Jain Prime Minister of Gujarat then, are landmarks in Indian architecture. They are the first extant temples or buildings where marble is used. Shah Jehan's 'Tear in Marble' came later. The Jain temples are unique for they represent the old traditional Indian architecture, without any trace of saracenic architecture. Swamiji was greatly attracted as much by the natural scenic beauty of the place as by the Jain temples. There he retired into a cave and spent some time in quiet meditation. It was there that he came in contact with the Maharaja of Khetdi, a princely kingdom, about ninety miles north of Jaipur. Ajit Sinhaji, the Maharaja of Khetdi, became greatly attached to Swamiji and from the hill station of Abu took Swamiji with him to Khetdi. His adoration and respect for Swamiji was simply boundless. He took Mantra initiation from Swamiji and thus accepted Swamiji as his guru. The Maharaja had no son and he prayed to Swamiji to bless him with an heir. Pleased as Swamiji was with the treatment meted out to him by the Maharaja, Swamiji showered his blessings wholeheartedly on the king.

From Khetdi, Swamiji proceeded southwards to Ahmedabad. He was spotted, while sitting under a tree opposite the exit gate of the railway station by Lal Shankar Trivedi, holding the office of a sub-judge. Swamiji stayed a week with him and spent his time in studying Jainism. Swamiji turned westward from there, to Saurashtra, then known as Kathiawad. The small peninsula had more then 200 states, some of them were very small and only a few of them were enjoying the first class status. He went by train to Wadhavan—now named Surendranagar—and from there walked down to Limbadi, 25 miles south. The long walk must have been quite tiring, so he sought a resting place and was directed by some Samaritan to a house on the outskirts of the town occupied by some sadhus. Swamiji took shelter there. He was welcomed and given a room. Soon, however, he came to overhear that, on seeing the brilliant face of young Vivekananda, the Mahant was telling the other sadhus: 'We are lucky to have such a celibate *sadhu* amongst us. We'll force him to break his vow of celibacy in order to achieve our objective.' Swamiji also heard the door of his room being closed and bolted from outside to prevent his escape. He had landed himself in a *Vama Margi Akhada*, a centre of a sect of sadhus who do such out of the way practices in the name of religion.

Next morning he saw, from the window, a young boy coming to deliver milk. The carefree boy was beckoned by Swamiji. He asked the boy to pick up a piece of a broken earthen pot and a piece of charcoal, lying in the compound, scribbled a few words on the piece and asked the boy who was observing Swamiji with a mixture of curiosity and awe, to deliver his great epistle to the king of the place. Fortunately for Swamiji, and the world, the message of a *sadhu* being in danger was immediately accepted by Yashvanta Sinhaji, the Thakor Saheb of Limbadi and Swamiji marched from the sadhus' prison to the Thakor Saheb's palace.

After meeting the Maharaja of Bhavnagar, one of the class one state of Saurashtra, and visiting a couple of places, Swamiji made his next halt at Junagadh, then ruled by a Nawab. There he was the guest of the Prime Minister of the state, Haridas Desai, who instantly recognised the potentialities of Swamiji, who professed great affection for the latter and whom Swamiji treated like his father, as is born out by the letters Swamiji wrote to him. Haridas Desai was a great administrator and before he was invited by the Nawab of Junagadh to become his Divan, he, Desai, had helped four other princely states in setting their houses in order, in coming out of debt and in modernising their administration.

The British government had appointed him as a member of two important commissions. After meeting Swamiji and hearing his story, when Mr. Desai had once been to Kolkata to attend the government commissions meeting, he had paid a visit to the house where Swamiji's widowed mother was living. Being moved very much by the condition in which the widow Bhuvaneshvaridevi was living, he had written a letter to Swamiji, expressing his agony at the condition of Swamiji's family and also asked Swamiji whether he had done the right thing in renouncing the world. In his reply of 29th January, 1894, written from Chicago, Swamiji says: 'If there is any being I loved in the whole world, it is my mother. Yet I believed, and still believe that without my giving up of the world, the message which Ramakrishna Paramahansa, my great Master, came to preach would not see the light, and where would those young men be who have stood as bulwarks against the surging waves of materialism and luxury of the day?' Beginning with this tragic note struck by the moving reference to the miserable condition of his mother and other members of the family, the heroic in Swamiji raised its head and Swamiji went on to tell the Divanji of the call of the great mission he had been destined to perform. Unfortunately, Desai Haridas did not live to see the triumphant return of Swamiji and the establishment of the Ramakrishna Mission in 1897. The strong bond with Desai had made Swamiji go to Desai's native place, Nadiad, Central Gujarat, and spend one or two days with the brothers and other family members of Desai. At Nadiad, Swamiji had met a great Gujarati Vedantic scholar, Manilal Dwivedi, who had sent two papers of his to the World Parliament of Religions, Chicago, attended by Swamiji in September 1893.

Junagadh stands on the lap of Mount Girnar, which is associated with Hindu, Buddha, Jain and Islam religions, representing, as it were, the synthesis of religions Swamiji's guru had preached. Swamiji had retired in a mountain cave for meditation and had returned fresh and invigorated.

The next place of Vivekananda's visit was Somnath dedicated to Lord Shiva since times immemorial. The thriving shrine was plundered by Mohammad of Ghazni and the idol was shattered to pieces. It was rebuilt, but attacked again and again by Islamic zealots. Queen Ahalyabai Holkar of Indore had piously put up a small temple for Somnath, a few feet away from the ruins. Thanks to the efforts of late Kanaiyalal Munshi, a leading advocate of Bombay, a Gujarati author of repute of the first half of the twentieth century, a follower of Mahatma Gandhi and a politician, reconstruction was undertaken on the very site on the sea where the original temple, ransacked by bigots stood, and reconstructed almost in the old style of architecture. The ruins must have moved Swamiji and filled his heart with great sadness. The ruins represented to him the fall of India and they must have forged Swamiji's will for an early revival of the grandeur that India was.

While at Somnath, Swamiji had met Rao, the King of Kuchchh. Kuchchh had two holy shrines, Koteshvar, which stands almost on the Tropic of Cancer, and Narayan Sarovar. On the way to both these places, there stands a temple dedicated to Goddess Ashapura, the family deity of the Rao and his clan, all Jadeja Rajputs. Swamiji visited all the shrines and went to Bhuj, the capital of the Kuchchh state and thanks to the note given to him by Haridas Desai, had become the guest of Moti Mehta, the Divan of the state.

Swamiji's dear gurubhai Swami Akhandananda was trailing Swamiji and moving from Khetdi to Ahmedabad, to Limbadi, to Junagadh, to Somnath, to Koteshvar and to Narayan Sarovar, like the puppy of a hound, at last caught up with Swamiji. Swamiji showered his affection on him but remonstrated with him for following the former. Akhandananda, who considered Swamiji as his elder brother, friend, philosopher and guide told Swamiji that he, Akhandananda, just could not control himself, that he was feeling like a lost lamb without Swamiji and now that he had seen Swamiji once more, he promised Swamiji that he would let the latter alone and would not cross Swamiji's path any more. He did break his promise though, by meeting Swamiji once more at Porbandar, the place of birth of Mahatma Gandhi.

Swamiji's visit to Porbandar proved to be a turning point in his life. Thanks to the recommendation of Desai, the Divan of Junagadh, Swamiji became the guest of Mr. Shankar Pandurang Pandit, a learned Maharashtrian, a great scholar of Sanskrit and a linguist, posted there as administrator by the government of Bombay Presidency. Swamiji lived with the Pandit for quite a few months derived maximum advantage of Pandit's library, discussed several issues with the Pandit, learnt French—Mr. Pandit knew French very well and had a number of French books with him—and surprised his *gurubhais* at the Varahanagar *Math* by penning them a letter in French. But the most important thing was his advice to Swamiji, "Swamiji, our people here don't have the capacity to grasp your great message. Why not go to the West? People there are very receptive. They will understand and appreciate your message." The germ of going to the West was planted in Swamiji's heart at Porbandar.

Swamiji had also been to Dwarka, one of the four main places of pilgrimage of the Hindus. A Greek sea captain, who had been roaming in his small boat about half a century after Christ, had passed by the place as mentioned in his great inimitable book, 'Periplus of the Erythrean Sea' and called it Baraka. The place is associated with the life and legend of Shri Krishna. Even Somnath is associated with the final scene of Shri Krishna's life, where the Yadava clan, in a state of great inebriety, invited a curse and, as a result, each member of the clan started fighting with the other, with the result that all of them were killed and, their leader, the great Krishna, saddened by the event, stretched himself on the ground a couple of furlongs away from the Somnath temple, covered himself top to toe and fell a prey to a hunter's arrow and breathed his last.

Swamiji's affection, for Haridas Desai was so great that it had taken him to Junagadh more than once. But now the call from within was driving him to move southwards and, as mentioned earlier, after spending a day or two with the brothers of Haridas Desai, Swamiji moved to nearby Vadodara then ruled by the great Gaikwad Sayajirao. A brilliant Bengali youth of twenty one, who was to return after a long stay in England, to Baroda(Vadodara) a year later was to earn a great name and fame. He was to leave the service of the Gaikwad, turn a revolutionary and later on, coming in contact with the teachings of Shri Ramakrishna and Swami Vivekananda, was to establish himself as a great spiritual power house. He was Shri Aurobindo.

From Baroda, Swamiji went to Khandava in the Central Provinces. He chanced to meet there one Haridas Chatterjee, a Bengali advocate, practising there. He was simply delighted to see a young Bengali *Sadhu*, with a lion like personality, encyclopaedic knowledge, penetrating intellect and sharp memory, and for Swamiji, it was a sort of home away from home. Swamiji had probably heard about the Parliament of Religions to be held at Chicago in 1893 from Chaganlal Pandya, an employee of the Junagadh state, but a scholar, hailing from Nadiad. He was sure to have spoken about Manilal Dwivedi, whom Swamiji had gone to see during his short stay at Nadiad. Haridas at Khandava was also a well read individual with varied interests. Talks with him encouraged Swamiji to go to Chicago and when Swamiji moved to Indore, the idea took a firm root and Swamiji expressed the desire saying that he would like to attend the Chicago Parliament but going there needed money, and he himself was a pennyless *sannyasin*. Haridas expressed his desire to collect money for the trip to America, but Swamiji refused and said that he first wanted to go to Rameshvaram and then only he would decide.

Swamiji's next place of halt was Mumbai-(Bombay then). He was there the guest of barrister Ramdas Chhabildas, who was the brother in law of Shyamji Krishna Varma, whom Swamiji had met at Ajmer. The barrister was a leading citizen and was the son of the great philanthrophist Chhabildas Lallubhai. While at Bombay, Swamiji had paid a visit to the Kanheri Caves, about 25 miles north of Mumbai, surrounded then by thick forests, with tigers and leopards roaming freely. From the top of the hill on which the caves are situated, the view was panaromic. A few miles north of the place, there was the old port mentioned in *Buddhist Jataka Tales* as Shurparak, now called Sopara. Swamiji might have seen in his vision the white fluttering sails of ships leaving the Shurparak harbour laden with cargo of various types. His resolve to bring back the glory of the past must have been steeled.

Swamiji left for Pune from Bombay. At the Victoria Terminus now Chhatrapati Shivaji Terminus, the barrister Ramdas, or someone deputed by him, must have accompanied Swamiji to buy his ticket and to see that he was properly seated in the train. And strangely enough, he was made to sit in the same compartment as Lokmanya Tilak was seated in, as recorded by Tilak himself. The two great sons of Mother India started talking. Swamiji did not reveal his name, but he could not hide his personality. Tilak did not need any secateur to cut through anything as the personality of Swamiji was seething through every pore of his body, every glance of his eyes, every word he spoke. He spent a few days with the great nationalist leader, went to the hill station Mahabaleshvar in Satara district, met the Thakor Saheb of Limbadi there once more, then proceeded to Kolhapur and then to Belgaum. At first he had become the guest of a Maharashtrian gentleman on whom Swamiji had a note by an officer of the Kolhapur State. When he saw his *sannyasin* guest smoking and chewing pan, betel leaf, he received a mild shock. Swamiji clarified to him that it was the renunciation of lucre and lust that mattered. After curing a Bengali gentleman here of his cynical attitude towards *sannyasins*, Swamiji moved southward to Bangalore. But only after convincing the Bengali gentleman at Belgaum of his concern for the brethren of his country when Swamiji came to learn there that someone had died of hunger in Kolkata.

At Bangalore, somehow, he came in contact with Sheshadri Iyer, the Divan of the State. The greatly impressed Divan took Swamiji to the Maharaja of Mysore, who immediately invited Swamiji to be his guest. That was the impact of Swamiji's personality. The Maharaja was stunned to hear Swamiji say that all officers and courtiers were alike, in reply to a question from the Maharaja. When they were alone, the Maharaja warned Swamiji that such outspokenness might invite danger to life and body. 'Would any true *sannyasin* be afraid to tell the truth even though he sees danger to his life, lurking in front of him?' said swamiji later on. When the Maharaja had come to learn about Swamiji's intention of going to America, the noble Maharaja had expressed his willingness to help Swamiji in all possible ways. 'Not now,' was the Swamiji's reply. But the Maharaja got Swamiji's message recorded and the precious thing is still preserved.

At the time of Swamiji's departure for Trichur, the Divan tried to put a wad of currency notes in the pocket of the coat Swamiji was wearing. Instead, Swamiji asked the Divan to buy only a railway ticket to Trichur. Bidding goodbye to the Divan, Swamiji arrived at Trichur. From there, he went southwards to Cochin, which was then the capital of a Princely State, and from there he went to Trivandrum then the capital of the Princely State of Travancore. He was not dressed as a *sannyasin* as in the south and his guide was a Muslim, so the sixteen year old son of Professor Sundaram took Swamiji to be a Muslim. Swamiji had shocked the pious professor by telling him that he, the professor, was a person without any faith, even though he spent a couple of hours in his daily worship. When professor Sundaram had doubted Swamiji's ability to address the august assembly at Chicago while he was refusing to deliver a public lecture the professor was eager to arrange, on the ground that the lecture would only invite ridicule. In reply to the professor's doubt, Swamiji had said, "If God wills it, I shall be the carrier of his voice and if I hold fast to my vows of truth and the life of a *sadhu*, God will surely give me the strength to speak there." The acorn of the orator was to burst forth into a giant oak on September 11, 1893. And that same professor was to write when Swamiji left the place after nine days, 'When Swamiji bade us goodbye we felt all light has gone out of our home.'

In the game of hockey or football, some time passing is resorted to and instead of aiming straight at the goal point, the ball goes crisscross. Similarly, Swamiji, who wanted to reach the southernmost point of India, went to Madurai in the northeast. There he chanced to meet Bhaskar Setupati, the King of Ramnad State. Swamiji had come across very few kings as cultured, as farseeing and as devoted as King Bhaskar. It was a love at first sight and he became a great devotee of Swamiji. King Bhaskar also insisted that Swamiji should proceed to America without any delay and showed his willingness to help Swamiji with money.

From Madurai, ruled over by the Goddess Meenakshi from her gorgeous temple, Swamiji proceeded to Rameshvaram, the southernmost sacred place, of the four holy places, of the Hindus. It stands where the Palk Straits and the Bay of Bengal meet the Gulf of Mannar and the Indian Ocean. King Rama is said to have crossed over to Sri Lanka from here with the help of a bridge constructed by Rama's army of monkeys by bringing boulders from around and thus filling up the sea. On his victorious return from Sri Lanka after vanquishing Ravana- who had forcibly taken away Sita, Rama's wife, Rama is said to have built the temple for Lord Shiva and the *lingam* was worshipped by both Rama and Sita.

From the holy Shiva shrine, Swamiji hopped over south-westwards to the southernmost tip of India, Kanyakumari, a shrine dedicated to the Goddess Parvati, but as a maiden. How very typical that Parvati, daughter of the Himalayas, chose the southernmost tip of India for her penance! But such things bind the vast country together. It may also, be mentioned here that Lord Rameshvara takes His daily bath with the waters of the Ganga. Invisible cultural links bind India. Like a tiny tot severed from his mother's hand, Swamiji ran to the temple of the Goddess. He worshipped the Goddess with his heart and soul. At Dwarka he had seen the Western tip of the motherland and now he was standing at the southern end. He had been to the Himalayas in the north. Traversing from Kolkata in the east Swamiji had seen the varied topography of the land, the fertile Gangetic plains, the snow-clad Himalayas, the sandy deserts of Rajasthan, the tempting mirage in the Rann of Kuchchh, the tossing waves from the far off West and South washing the feet of the deities at Dwarka and at Somnath, the undulating *ghats* of Maharashtra, the vast land, watered by the Ganga, the Yamuna, the Narmada, the Tapi, the Godavari, the Krishna and the Kaveri. He had seen temples standing defying invasions, deities being worshipped over centuries by millions and millions, abject poverty, pomp and pageantry of princes, self centred men rolling in wealth and scoffing at poverty, poor, hapless widows exhibiting their great wealth of faith, cruel divisions of caste and creed, illiteracy, twisting of ancient text by so called *pandits*.... he had seen man in his varied forms and states and he had also seen God in that man. Amelioration of the poverty of the country was the problem. It was through relieving people of their miseries that God was to be worshipped and realised. Shri Ramakrishna had said, 'Religion is not for empty bellies.' During all this sojourns and meeting and mixing with people, all his prejudices had worn off and his mind and spirit had acquired the clarity of the great undefiled Mansarovar reflecting every shape and colour of every cloud. The problem, as vast as the country itself, became clear to him. From dark midnight Swamiji had moved towards an early dawn.

Just as he had plunged into the vast sea of men and their problems when he had left his native place in 1890, so did he plunge into the shark infested ocean to the south and went swiming to the rock, quite at some distance and facing the temple, facing his vast motherland. The tossing waves did not deter him. He always liked challenges. He made it to the rock and sat there meditating, with his face looking north. From the tip of Kanyakumari, he saw the land spreading east and West, rising, as it were like an inverted pyramid. His eyes were seeing the coastlines but his mind's eyes opened up the great vista of the glorious past of the *Vedas* and the *Upanishads*, of the Buddhist monks traversing beyond the mountains and the seas and carrying with them the message of the great Buddha, the powerful Chandragupta defeating Selucus Nicator, the governor of parts of northern India, of Alexander the Great, the great emperor Ashok getting his edicts preaching of love and service inscribed in the various parts of the country, the oldest university of the world at Takshashila on the banks, of the mighty Sindhu, he also saw hordes of invaders entering the country via the Khyber Pass, plundering and overrunning the country, trying to disrupt the country's political, social and religious structures, razing down Hindu temples of worship, the Hindu society getting more and more contracted in its narrow shell and going downhill in all the spheres of life, the great Mughal emperor Akbar trying earnestly to bring about a synthesis, the tired, weather-bitten barks of the Portugese, followed by other hungry Europeans, followed soon by missionaries with the zeal for conversion, the vast Hindu society, losing contact with the outside world, taking false pride in its past and slipping more and more into mire. He also visualised saints like Nanak and Kabir trying to arrive at some synthesis, and he also visualised his guru in the clearest form, who had practised all the leading faiths and preached for respect, and equality and synthesis of all faiths. Yes, the sun had risen now. His doubts had got dispelled. The path of his destiny had become clear to him. He offered *pranams* to his ever smiling guru. With the resolve to go West to preach *Vedanta* and to bring money to relieve the miseries of the people of his country Swamiji rose from the rock to plunge back into the heaving waters of the mighty ocean to come back to the Mother Goddess, the Guardian, of the country. He had gathered his pearl.

To go to America and the West, to preach *Vedanta* and raise funds for the betterment of his people, that was his firm resolve. And India should accept the twin ideal of renunciation and service.

14

Preparing for Departure

Swimming from the tiny tip of a hidden finger of the mighty Poseidon, Vivekananda, who landed back on the mainland at Kanyakumari, had undergone an immense internal transformation. The cauldron of uncertainty seething within him had subsided and it had turned into a light guiding his path. He now wanted to share his views with others, wanted to share his light with others, wanted to have a band of helpers. From Kanyakumari, he rushed to Madras, on foot. On the way, at Pondicherry, he had met an orthodox *pandit,* who quoted from the scriptures to declare emphatically that going over the seas was totally forbidden. Vivekananda left him to cling to his antiquated belief and moved northwards to Madras, now called Chennai.

The city of Madras gave Swamiji a great gift of a band of young disciples, devoted and dedicated, highly educated and ready to do anything Vivekananda would bid them to do. Shingarvelu Mudaliar was a professor of science at the local Christian College. He was very critical of the traditional Hindu religion, leaning towards Christianity and was a bit agnostic. He underwent such a transformation that Swamiji said, "Caesar said, I came, I saw, I conquered." But Kidi, as Swamiji called Prof. Shingarvelu Mudaliar, came, he saw and he was conquered. Later on he became the first editor of the *Brahmavadin,* the first magazine disseminating Swamiji's teachings and the teachings of *Vedanta*. Still later on he had taken the vows of *sannyasa* and joined the newly established Ramakrishna Order. Another Madras disciple attached to Swamiji was Alasinga Perumal.

These young men were enamoured of Swamiji and were ever ready to do everything at his bidding. Since Vivekananda had spoken to them about going to America, they started collecting money for his journey and for other expenses. But going to America was till then Swamiji's own desire. Orders must come from the higher-up. Since there were no such orders till then, Swamiji told his devoted band of followers to distribute the money they had collected amongst the poor; being a *sannyasin* he himself could not keep a pie with him. The disciples must have been disheartened because collecting funds for the Swamiji's foreign trip must have been a big uphill task for them. But they obeyed their guru's bidding and did as they were directed. Swamiji had prayed to Jagadamba and sought her guidance and help. He had turned himself into a tiny tot of that Universal Mother. He used to sit longer in meditation. He was now a changed man, charged with his mission. The band of devotees around him was attracting more and more talented youths of Madras.

Some one living in Hyderabad, the capital of the big state of the Nizams then, came to hear of Swamiji and sent him an invitation. A big crowd had gathered at the railway station to welcome the young monk. The great significance of his visit there was that, while addressing the students of a college there, Swamiji spoke about 'My Mission to the West.' The choice of this topic indicates two things: his determination to go to the West and the purpose behind the proposed visit. No record of the lecture exists, so we do not know whether there was any reference to the World Parliament of Religions. He is quite likely to have mentioned it. When he left for Madras, the crowd at the railway station was much bigger and shouts of 'Vivekananda ki Jai' rent the air. This was the one and only public lecture delivered by him before embarking for America.

He had spoken publicly about his mission to the West. But did his mission have the backing of Jagadamba? He had asked his Madras disciple who had moved from door to door and raised an amount of about 600 rupees to be distributed to the poor people, simply because his desire to go to America had attracted no response from the divine Mother. But his uncertainty did not last long. He had a distinct vision of Shri Ramakrishna walking upon the waters of the sea and beckoning Naren to follow him to the other side. Yet he hesitated. The vision was repeated. He was now on firmer grounds. Yet he was hesitant and to do away with all doubts, he immediately wrote a letter to the Holy Mother Sharadamani Devi, begging her blessings for the leap he was taking. The reply was received by him almost by return post. But, on getting her son Naren's letter, Ma herself was a bit uncertain and worried about her son's well-being in far away lands. But Shri Ramakrishna appeared post haste and removed all her doubts and worries. She soon conveyed her blessings to Naren, wishing him all success in his mission, about the outcome of which Naren knew little and she knew less. On reading the letter, Swamiji felt Ma's affectionate hand caressing his head and back.

It was now March of 1893. Swamiji started his preparations in right ernest. All of a sudden Jagmohanlal, the secretary of the Maharaja of Khetdi, came to Swamiji in Madras with the happy tidings that because of Swamiji's blessings the Maharaja was fortunate to have an heir and that the Maharaja had requested him to go to Khetdi and bless the newborn prince and then leave for America. Maharaja Ajit Sinhji would help by making all arrangements. It was a journey of about 1,500 kilometres, involving two changes, one at Bombay and another one at Ahmadabad. From Ahmadabad, it was a meter guage train, chugging out a bit slowly. It was the age of steam engines and at every watering station, the train would halt for twenty to thirty minutes.

The Maharaja of Khetdi was simply delighted to see Swamiji, whom he considered to be his guru, his benefactor. The Maharaja got the new born prince to be brought before Swamiji who showered his blessings on the heir apparent. Swamiji's presence there, in spite of the hectic preparations of Swamiji for his long sea voyage, greatly enthused the Maharaja.

There was an air of festivity all over the place. All in the kingdom were happy and were showering gifts on the new born prince. Parties were being held. The Maharaja was also holding various types of functions. But the function of a musical soiree arranged by the Maharaja proved to be a turning point in the life of Swamiji.

Swamiji had studied *Vedanta*, preaching equality of all, had smoked an untouchable's pipe, had stayed with Hindus and Muslims alike, had seen no difference between high and low, caste and creed, race and sex, nevertheless he had a lesson to learn. And, wonder of wonders, it was taught to him by a nautch girl at Khetdi. Though initiated by Swamiji, the Maharaja was a man of the world and loved all the pleasures of the world. He had a programme of music arranged in the evening. The singer was a professional nautch girl, considered as good as prostitutes by the society, from whom decent people just keep themselves away at least publicly. Courtiers had assembled, the sarangi was being tuned and the tablas, percussion instruments like drums, were being adjusted. Just before the start of the soiree, the Maharaja sent words to Swamiji, who was in an adjacent room, to come to listen to the music. The Maharaja might have by then known of Swamiji's love for and mastery over music. When the messenger delivered the message, Swamiji thundered, "Go and tell your Maharaja, such *jalasas* are taboo for a *sannyasin*." His voice was so loud that every member of the audience heard it. The nautch girl also had heard it. The hidden insult to her and to her whole tribe must have touched her to the quick, but at the social rung where she was, she had to bear it. She could not respond by words. And yet, she wanted to draw Swamiji's attention to the gaping wound in her heart the words of Swamiji had caused. She indicated to the *sarangivala* to pick up the tune of the song she started singing. The song she started singing was no ordinary one. It is an immortal lyric by the great saint poet Surdas, praying to God to overlook the devotee's sins of commission and begging for His compassion.

'O Lord, take not my shortcomings to heart.
Equanimity is Your name, if You wish, ferry me across.
A piece of iron (in the form of an idol) is worshipped by one,
Another such piece has fallen into the hands of a butcher,
The philosopher's stone, without discrimination, turns both into gold.
One stream is called a river, another one, a gutter,
When they meet and mix up, they are named the purifying divine river (Ganga)....'

No sooner did Swamiji hear the refrain, than he dashed into the large hall where the programme was going on, his pride was humbled, and he took his seat respectfully folding his hands towards the singer for obliterating the sense of high and low from his mind. He well might have remembered his great guru bowing down to the prostitutes as forms of Ma Kali. After a few days Swamiji left for Bombay.

Jagmohanlal, the secretary to the king, accompanied Swamiji to Bombay. On the way at the Abu Road Station, where the train halted for a long time, Swamiji got off the train to stroll on the platform. And his eyes caught sight of two of his *gurubhais*, Rakhal (Swami Brahmananda) and Hari (Swami Turiyananda). All the three were delighted. Swamiji spoke to them of his visit to the U.S.A., to attend the World Parliament of Religions. The fire of Swamiji's firm resolve was radiating all over. 'Haribhai,' Swamiji said to young Swami Turiyananda, thumping his fist on his chest, 'this Parliament is meeting for this.' What a prophetic expression! The simple person that he was, Swamiji had no idea of the hurdles in his way to the Parliament. But he had faith in God's compassion that would make a dumb talk and a lame cross a mountain.

Ajit Sinhji's respect and love had lengthened the stay of Swamiji at Khetdi, and though the Rajasthan heat in May was unbearable, Swamiji could not and would not displease the Maharaja. As Swamiji had to rush to Bombay, the only sad thing was that he could not make a stop over at Nadiad to meet the brothers of Haridasbhai, the Divan of Junagadh. Swamiji was being accompanied by Jagmohanlal. It was a first class train journey to Bombay and thanks to his Maharaja, Jagmohanlal had purchased a first class boat ticket for Swamiji. Jagmohanlal also got a couple of robes of ochre silk and such other things made for Swamiji.

The name of the boat was Peninsular, owned by the famous 'P' and 'O' Liners. On May 31, 1893, the steamer lifted anchor and started moving south to Colombo. It was very strange that instead of going via the Suez Canal and the Mediteranean Sea and touching some port or ports of Europe, such a roundabout route was preferred. But God's ways are strange.

From Colombo Swamiji's boat carried him to Penang to Singapore, to a couple of ports in China and then to the Japanese port of Nagasaki. He was very much impressed by the progress made by Japan. Thence he sailed across the Pacific. On the ship he had another great and noble son of India as fellow traveller. He was Jamshedji Tata, the pioneer of industry in India. Both were sailing in the same boat, the boat streamed her way to America, the boat determinedly going towards the amelioration of their motherland.

The steamer docked at Vancouver, some day in mid July, 1893. Swamiji landed in America.

15

A Peep into America

Almost four hundred years before Swami Vivekananda had set his foot on the Western coast of America, Columbus had set his foot somewhere in the east, believing mistakenly that he had landed on Indian soil. He was followed by several other European conquistadors. Hoardes of people from various countries of Europe followed. They fought amongst themselves, but mainly fought against the hapless, innocent natives of the country, who neither had invited the European intruders, nor done any harm to the invaders. Open thuggery was practised by the European settlers. Civilizations were wiped out. The Europeans fought amongst themselves for the loot and plunder of the vast, untapped natural resources of the enormous mass of land spread almost from pole to pole. After the landing of the May Flower and hordes of Irish settlers rushing to America whenever the potato crop failed, the British or Anglo-saxon influence was predominant almost all over the North America up to Mexico, where the climate was warmer and was found more congenial by the Iberians. Almost all over South America the Iberian influence predominated, but again, at the cost of native Americans. The Maya, the Aztec and the Inca civilizations were simply annihilated. All American prosperity stands on this foundation of plunder, merciless killings and destruction of civilizations.

But, after the defeat of the French and after the war of American Independence, the British influence became more pronounced in the U.S.A. Thanks to the ships with their cargo of the black men and women enslaved from Africa, labour was cheap, cost almost nothing, and agricultural production of food grains and cotton went up. This was given a giant push by the various inventions of the industrial age, which brought about great changes in all the walks of life. Production of goods had increased by leaps and bounds. New discoveries made transportation quicker and safer and a steamship could carry as much ware as could be carried by ten sailing ships. Moreover, the infighting of the kingdoms of Europe was absent in the newly discovered land. This led to an unimaginably rapid stride in prosperity. The idea of the phenominal growth, for example, might be had from the growth of population of Chicago from 338 in 1833 to over one million in 1890. The wealth of America was simply bursting at its seams.

Upto the end of the eighteenth century and the early years of the nineteenth century, covetousness was the governing motive. The Harvard University was established very early. By 1700 two more universities also had started functioning. Pursuit of art and culture was as far away from them as from the Bourgeois's Gentilhomme of Moliere. The first gleam of light is seen in Longfellow (1807-1882), Emerson (1803-1882), Whitman (1810-1892) and Thoreau (1837-1862). Later on Harvard had Eliot, William James and John Wright. Translations of the *Gita* and a few other spiritual classics of ancient India had reached America. This Indian influence was clearly evident in the moulding and writings of Thoreau, Emerson and Whitman. Thoreau's criticism of the absolutely uncalled for attack on Mexico that led to the annexation of Texas and his refusal to be recruited was like the Satyagraha of Gandhiji, that came about half a century later, and had, like Gandhiji, led him to prison.

Sir William Jones, a high judicial officer of the East India Company in the last quarter of the eighteenth century, had translated *Shakuntalam*, the great drama of Kalidasa, and had opened the gates to Sanskrit classics. Some French scholar had translated the Gita into French and Thoreau had most probably read it. Emmerson's famous poem Brahma appeared in 1856, reverberating with the Upanishadic philosophy. Quite a few lines in the poem appear to be translated from verses in the *Gita*. Miss Greenstidel, a young lady of twenty-two, who lived in Detroit and saw Swamiji in February 1894, had come in contact with the *Gita*, probably the beautiful translation by Edvin Arnold, titled 'The song Celestial.' The shattering of faith in the *Bible*, caused by Darwin's Theory of Evolution, had given rise to Christian Science of Mary Baker, Theosophy of Alcott and quite a few such sects. The American mind, towards the last quarter of the nineteenth century had thus become absorbent although it must be clearly stated that the influence of Emerson, Whitman and Thoreau had hardly touched even the surface of the vast strata of American society. All conditions led towards the development of utilitarian attitude in life, towards pragmatism.

The sudden increase in wealth brought about by the industrial revolution, vast unexploited land, extremely cheap farm labour provided by the slaves, absence of rivalry as in European nations, rapid spread of educational facilities, made some people think of celebrating the discovery of the new world by Columbus in 1493. They decided to do something great to commemorate the 'Discovery' by Columbus. The choice for the celebration fell on the newly developed Chicago because it was more or less in the centre of the country, it was a junction of many railroads, it had nice waterfront on the Lake Michigan, but more probably because it had promised the target amount of money. Amidst these solely money minded people who cared only for profits, there were a few individuals like Charles Bonney, who thought of giving a touch of culture to the proposed World Fair. They conceived, deliberated and then planned, to have conferences to discuss various aspects of life. One of the conferences they had thought of was the World Parliament of Religions. It, indeed, was a great idea and Mr. Bonney had seriously felt that bringing together thinkers of all great religions on one platform would lead to religious harmony. His proposal was accepted by the Organising Committee, but quite a few of them, like Barrows, thought that it would provide an excellent forum to prove to the world, the superiority of the Christian religion. After all, were not various Christian missions sending out armies of missionaries to the various heathen countries to convert people there to Christianity and thus promise them heaven after death? The Chicago Parliament, they thought, would establish beyond doubt the superiority of the religion founded by the only son of God. Before and since the birth of Jesus, Christian God, seemed to have practised birth control.

When the World Fair was held at Paris during 1888-89, to celebrate the centenary of the French Revolution electricity had made its appearance. Means of transportation had improved noticeably and many new discoveries like the camera, for example, had given a new turn to life. Europe considered herself to have reached its zenith. The sun did not set on the British Empire, and other European countries like Portugal, France, Germany, Holland etc., all had carved out their empires in different parts of Asia and Africa and were exploiting them. Naturally, floating as France—as well as Europe—was on this great wave of enthusiasm, the Paris World Fair was a great success.

Only four years had passed to the Paris World Fair, but progress in engineering, in transportation, in the use and spread of electricity had taken many leaps by 1893 and added to all this was the American megalomania, to do something bigger. The Chicago World Fair had this background. The quadri-centennial celebration of the discovery of the continent provided the driving force and Bonney's proposal to hold cultural conferences gave the whole thing a distinctive form. They had started making preparations for the event since 1890 with great enthusiasm and skill. The great Gujarati scholar, Manilal Dwivedi, whom Swamiji, had met at Nadiad, was one of the advisers of the Parliament of Religions. He had not been able to go to Chicago but he had sent two papers to be read there. He was a great scholar of *Vedanta*.

The organising committee had sent out letters to the heads of various religions and sects, giving them information about the Parliament of Religions and inviting them to remain present themselves or send delegates on their behalf. Pratap Majoomdar of the Brahmo Samaj and Virchand Gandhi, a Jain, had got themselves formally enrolled as delegates. Pratap was a senior leader of the Brahmo Samaj and in that capacity had visited Britain and America earlier. Pratap considered himself next to Keshub Sen, who, alas, was no more! Along with the late Keshub, he had visited Shri Ramakrishna a number of times, but, might be, he did not cherish the same regard for the Paramhansa that Keshub did. And he also knew Swami Vivekananda from the latter's premonastic days, when, as young Naren, he had joined the Brahmo Samaj, taken part enthusiastically in all the proceedings and had also joined the choir of the Samaj and soon become its leading member. Neither Mr. Majoomdar, nor his 'Naren' had any idea that they would be meeting in Chicago. And Majoomdar had not dreamt that the young Naren, who was hardly known to anyone beyond the tiny circle of Shri Ramakrishna's disciples, would prove his guru's prophesy about his being 'eighteen times brighter than Keshub' true and few would refer to him, Pratap Majoomdar. Virchard Gandhi represented Jainism who was in no way related to Mahatma Gandhi.

But that Naren of old, Swami Vivekananda now, had many hurdles to cross. He found out that he was too early for the Parliament, which was to start on September 11, whereas he had arrived in mid July, almost two months early. When he had approached the Theosophy People for help, they had asked him to first join the Theosophy Group. On his refusal to do so and on finding him in dire circumstances, the reaction of the august Theosophy was, 'let the devil die.' But the Devil was destined not to die but become immortal and outshine the entire Theosophy establishment.

16

Lost and Found

The boat carrying Swami Vivekananda had touched Vancouver in July 1893. And with it, Swamiji's stars seemed to look the other way.

All through out his wanderings in India from I888 onwards, Swamiji had travelled the lightest, since he was not carrying an extra pair of clothes, he had no need of a steel trunk or a leather bag. Nor he carried any bedding with him. Nor he kept any money or traveller's cheques with him. It was a unique node of travel. But while embarking at Bombay, Jagmohanlal, the secretary of the Maharaja of Khetdi, had loaded him with extra silken clothes, a cabin trunk and also with some cash. As a *sannyasin* he could move about in India without any cash on his person. He just couldn't start begging immediately on landing in America, and even if he did so, the response might probably be of being kicked out or being handed over to the police. So, very much against his will and inclination, Swamiji had to take care of his possessions and of money.

Swamiji's troubles had started quite a few days before he disembarked at Vancouver. Neither Swamiji himself nor his well wisher and provider had taken into consideration the necessity of woollen clothes in the cold climatic zone Swamiji was setting his foot on. Even before the boat anchored at Vancouver, the cold breeze from the north reminded Swamiji of his days in the Himalayas. And the big trunk he was carrying needed the help of a coolie. And from that moment fleecing started. Dollars which appeared very big in India seemed to disappear like mice running into their holes. And it was a three day journey to Chicago. The railway ticket, food on the way, every thing appeared to cut big holes in Swamiji's pocket.

On arriving at Chicago, he had to seek shelter in a hotel. His purse was getting thinner and thinner. Though not quite unmindful of it, Swamiji went to visit the World Fair and was enamoured of it. It was a huge lay out and visiting various stalls was a tiring business but the display by various industries and countries was simply impressive. Everything that was exhibited there reflected something new and was represented in a novel manner. All that was so different from what he was used to see at home. He enjoyed this sight-seeing for about a week and then went to the office of the Fair to make enquiry about the Parliament of Religions. The answer he received shocked him to the very bones. He had arrived there in July and the Parliament of Religions was scheduled to meet in September, more than a month and a half later. The worse part of the reply was that he would not be admitted as a delegate to the Parliament, because no religion or no sect had deputed him to represent itself at the Parliament by officially sending his name. The worst part of it was, the time to enrol as a delegate was already over. So, 'Sorry. Next Person please' was the reception Swamiji got.

It is not at all easy to imagine the shock Swamiji, though a sannyasi, must have experienced at that reply. He must have been completely shaken out of his wits. Neither the well-wishers living in different places in India, who had spoken to him about the Parliament of Religions, nor the educated young enthusiasts of Madras, nor anybody he had spoken to about the Chicago gathering knew about the exact dates of the meeting of the Parliament, with the result that Swamiji had landed almost two months ahead of the meeting of the august assembly. The result was felt by his poor purse getting slimmer and slimmer by the hour like the Barbie doll. And what was still worse was the fact that no one in his circle knew that participation at a conference needed being sponsored or delegated by some recognised body. Swamiji must have felt extremely dejected and miserable and let down. The reality that he faced in Chicago must have shocked him out of wits. Sister Nivedita, the Irish disciple of Swamiji, has aptly compared this affair with the unplanned and unorganised Hindu Religion.

Swamiji must have felt benumbed at the reply. He had told his friends and wellwishers in India that he was going to America to participate in the Parliament of Religions. And here, at Chicago, he was being debarred from entering even. What to do next? Where to Go? He did not have enough money, probably, for a ticket to India. The ground under his feet was shaking. At Kanyakumari, he had thought of preaching *Vedanta* to Americans and seek monetary assistance from them to relieve the miseries of the poverty stricken people of his country. The Chicago Parliament would have served the purpose of introducing him. And now that door was bolted. He was himself in need of assistance.

Even though he was a *sannyasin*, above pleasure and pain, yet the very awkward situation he had found himself in, the terrific impact of the refusal from the Parliament office, his lack of proper clothing and his being followed by hooligans because of his attire looking odd to the Americans, the high cost of living there and his own poor financial condition, all this was quite likely to raise his blood pressure and make him chickenhearted. But, it must be remembered that he had a strong conviction before he had left his country, which had made him utter the words, 'This Parliament is meeting for this,' and thump his chest while uttering this. In the innermost being he must have felt that. But in Chicago he must have felt highly dejected. However, his deep faith came to his help. The first thing to do, he felt, was to move out of Chicago, a costly place made costlier because of the World Fair. He came to learn that Boston was cheaper, so he decided to go to Boston.

Leaving everything to Mother Kali, Vivekananda got into an east bound train for Boston, seven hundred miles away. On the train, he met a middle aged lady, Kate Sanborn. Some say, she had met the Swami earlier. Whatever it might be, she showed some interest in Vivekananda. The colour of his skin, his strange ochre coloured robe, his turban, everything was strange and attractive in a way. But, most probably, the eyes of Swamiji, revealing his personality, might have drawn the attention of Kate. It was a pretty long Journey, and they soon started talking. This conversation gave her a greater insight into the Swami's personality. And she invited him to be her guest. Swaniji found in her a sympathetic listner, the first American to do so.

In his first letter (of August 20, 1893) to his dear Madras disciple Alasinga, written from Breezy Meadows, Swamiji has written, 'Just now I am living as the guest of an old lady in a village near Boston. I have an advantage in living with her, in saving for some time my expenditure of one dollar a day and she has the advantage of inviting her friends over here and showing them a curio from India.' Thus he poked fun at his own self. In the long letter, among other things, he asks Alasinga to arrange to send him some money, but there is no mention of the refusal of the Parliament authorities to him, no despair, no plan of action. Swamiji exhibits a masterly self control by avoiding any reference to the unpleasant welcome he had received at the Parliament Office. This shows Swamiji's fortitude. In spite of being turned away from entering the Parliament of Religions, Vivekananda did not want to leave the country, like a routed and demoralised army. Did he have any inkling in the heart of his hearts that somehow or other, he would be able to gatecrash into the Columbus Hall and fulfil his guru's prophesy?

Although he had a nasty experience in Boston of being followed by a crowd of people following him on account of his strange attire and had to run to save himself from being molested by the hoolgans, with his coming over to Breezy Meadows, a new breeze had started blowing. Kathy Sanborn was a woman of culture and social standing and she introduced Swamiji to a few persons of prominence in the area. Swamiji talked to various groups at Katherine's or at a few other places. He was also invited to deliver a couple of lectures, and notices of these talks and lectures appeared in local newspapers. Swamiji got a woollen suit for himself made, even though it depleted his poor purse. This change in clothes made it a bit easy for him to move about freely.

But the small breeze turned into the pleasant Malaya winds when he was led to meet Professor John Henry Wright. Professor Wright was an eminent classical scholar, teaching Greek literature and philosophy at the Harvard University and known all over America for his erudition. It being vacation at the university, he had gone to Breezy Meadows with the members of his family for a quiet life. Somehow, Swamiji came to be invited by him, not for a formal cup of tea or coffee, or just lunch or dinner but for a weekend. Vivekananda went to Professor Wright's cottage on some Friday afternoon and stayed there for a couple of nights.

Thanks to Sister Gargi (Marie Louise Burke), we have come to know the impact of Swamiji's, visit there on the Wright family and the way professor Wright opened the door of the Parliament of Religions for Swami Vivekananda. Apparently, it was a chance meeting, but it appears to have been arranged by destiny. In one of her volumes titled, 'Swami Vivekananda in America: New Discoveries', Sister Gargi has placed before the World the letter Mrs. Mary Tapan Wright wrote to her mother about the visit of Swami Vivekananda to her home. Every word of her letter throbs with the vivacity, the joy, the feeling of how she felt at the sudden and unexepted impact of Swamiji on her entire being. She tells her mother of the friar like vow of poverty imposed by Swamiji on himself, his encyclopaedic knowledge, his mastery over the English language, his sharp memory, his wit, his charming personality, his ability to adjust and so on. The long letter running into four pages throbs with the impact Swamiji had on her and on her husband.

Professor Wright did not write a letter to his mother about Swamiji, but he wrote a letter to the organisers of the Parliament of Religions some of whom he knew intimately, conveying to them that Swamiji's knowledge was deeper and vaster than that of most of our learned Professors put together and, he recommended that, though Vivekananda was not sponsored by any organisation, it would be in the fitness of things to accept him as a deligate. And to Swamiji he had uttered the famous words: 'To ask you for any credentials, Swamiji, is like asking the sun for his right to shine.' And the sun of *Vedanta* was to shine in all its glory. But a small cloud was to come in its way.

Though a *sannyasin*, he must have felt chagrin and annoyance on his way to Boston from Chicago. And being a *sannyasin*, on his return journey to Chicago, Swamiji must have heaved a sigh of relief. Professor Wright had given Vivekananda a letter of introduction to some of his friend. The *sannyasin* who had conquered all desire, lost the note of the Professor on the way and, worse still, arrived at the Chicago station late at night. He thought it better to rest for the night at the railway station and enter the city next morning. Not being possible at all to sleep on the platform as in India, he retired to a goods wagon—the Americans call it a 'box car'—and spent the night in it. When he got up next morning, his clothes had caught the dirt from the floor of the wagon: and he appeared a bit worried, a bit uncertain and a bit more dirty. He couldn't help it.

He started walking on the road outside the railway station with his bag in one of his hands and knocked at a few houses one after another for providing him some rest and some assistance. But his strange attire, turned stranger by the night in the railway wagon, his haggard looks, and the colour of his skin also, made every door he knocked get closed with a big bang, at times with a few insults being hurled at him. 'The guest is God'; this old Upanishadic saying was not known to the Americans. After performing this exercise of knocking at several doors and failing to get any response, and after walking with his luggage in his hands for some time, Swamiji got tired and placing his bag by a lamp post, submitted himself to Mother Kali, He was lost once again.

But by the grace of the Mother he was soon found. He had hardly thumped his bag on the footpath and stood with his hands on a lamppost, when a window on the other side of the road, facing him opened, showing the face of a middle aged woman. She caught sight of Swamiji. With his quaint dress, a bit dishevelled and dirtied by his night in the 'box car,' his stately figure and a face like one chiselled by Michaelangelo, looking a bit worried and yet holding his calm, this well-to-do lady, Mrs. George Hale, was immediately attracted. Curiosity, but more than that the Samaritan spirit, brought her out of her house, and made her cross over to where Vivekananda was standing like a lamb that had lost its way. A lady with an attractive and graceful personality stood facing Swamiji. Strangely enough, the first question that came out of her mouth was, 'Sir, are you a delegate to the Parliament of Religions?' Swamiji gave an affirmative reply and narrated his difficulties briefly. The kind Mrs. Hale immediately invited Swamiji to her home. Swamiji was alloted a room, and after he had got freshened up, she offered him breakfast. Then she herself accompanied Vivekananda to the venue of the Parliament. In Mrs. Hale Swamiji found a mother and always addressed her so in all his correspondence to her or to her daughters.

At the office of the Parliament, Swamiji gave Professor Wright's letter of reference and the lost lamb found the pen. This happened, probably, on the 10th of September. Swamiji was properly accomodated and after his usual meditation, must have slept soundly. And before the setting of the sun next day, the organisers of the Parliament of Religions, the various delegates representing different religions and religious sects, the vast audience in the Columbus Hall and the world at large, everyone was to find that what was lost was not a lamb but a majestic lion, awe inspiring and commanding respect.

17

The Hour of Glory

September 11, 1893, 10.00 a.m. The Columbus Hall was full of people. No seat was vacant. Several people were occupying the aisles. A bell started ringing. The ringing filled the Hall. And exactly at the first stroke, the various delegates with serene faces and wearing different costumes, led by Cardinal Gibbons entered the hall and walking down the aisle took their seats on the simply decorated big dais. The cardinal was the president. All eyes in the hall were glued on the delegates slowly moving towards the dais and each one taking his/her seat.

The proceedings started with a small Biblical prayer. Then there was a brief welcome address. The next step was self introduction by the visiting dignitaries. Each one, whose name was called out, rose from his seat, walked to the front and read out from some papers. Each one was applauded. That was politeness. That was courtsey. The archbishop of the Greek Church, Pratap or Nagarkar, a Confucian from China and a Buddhist had spoken. They received usual applause. Vivekananda, who was watching all this, was taken aback when he was told to speak. He begged for postponement more than once. At the post lunch session, his name was announced without consulting him. The young Indian Monk was stunned, but only for a moment. He closed his eyes, as if he were praying, and he was certainly praying to his guru and Sarasvati, the Goddess of learning. Then he got up from his seat in the front row, stepped ahead and commenced: 'Sisters and Brothers of

America,' he uttered while addressing the audience. And these words of Swamiji evoked a thunderous applause from the audience. They felt instinctively that the words came from the speaker's heart. The great hall reverberated for a couple of minutes with the clappings. The audience felt a new life giving breeze blowing.

The attire of Swamiji with his long red robe, an ochre sash at the waist and yellow turban on his head was no doubt arresting. Equally arresting was the black hair flowing down from under his turban, his wheatish complexion, his typical features and his calm posture; much more arresting, however, was Swamiji's spell-binding voice. But, probably, still more arresting was the personal appeal in his words touching the chord of the heart of every member in the audience. The speakers they had heard so far came, probably, a bit pompously and read out from a text prepared a few weeks or a few months ago. It was dull and lifeless and formal. Here was Swamiji, standing up a bit reluctantly, holding no file or papers in his hand and speaking extempore. The five words he had spoken were not stale, they carried the fresh fragrance of his heart. They had burst forth like a flower bursting from a bud.

Swamiji's brief address differed fundamentally from the addresses delivered by the speakers who had preceded him. Each one of them had spoken about the god of his sect or of his religion. Swamiji's god was universal, embracing everyone in His loving arms. In the fewest of words, Swamiji had given a thorough introduction of the Hindu religion, the Eternal Religion, pin-pointing its spirit of tolerance and respect for other religions. Quoting a verse from a great Sanskrit hymn, Swamiji said that all religions or sects were like different rivers going along different paths but meeting ultimately the same ocean. There is only one God, he said. And the concluding remarks of the Swami were: 'And I fervently hope that the bell that tolled this morning in honour of this convention may be the death-knell of all fanaticism, of all persecutions with the sword or with the pen, and of all uncharitable feelings between persons wending their way to the same goal.' A message of love uttered after thousands of years.

And there was a thunderous applause, not the terrific thunder of Jove,[2] but of sincere delight that had filled up every heart in the Columbus Hall. It lasted for over two minutes. People, mainly ladies, sitting in the back rows rushed forward to have a *Darshan*—closer look, at this evangelist of religious tolerance and preacher of universal love, speaking not about the god of his single sect or religion, but of an all embracing God, exuding love and compassion. A new chapter in the spiritual history of the world was being opened.

Seeing the women reaching towards Swamiji, a lady had this to say, 'Well, my lad, if you can resist this onslaught, you are indeed a God.' And during his long stay in the West, Swamiji stuck to his vow of continence and never fell a prey to lust.

The words spoken by Swamiji had this penetrating appeal because as the Great French savant Romain Rolland has put it, 'Swamiji's speech was the tongue of flame'. And the flame was not a burning one but enlightening, ennobling, purifying. Every member of the audience was enwrapped by the apostolic flame. Leading American newspapers like *The New York Herald* and the *Boston Evening Transcript* declared that Swamiji was a great favourite of the Parliament. His fame spread far and wide. The readings from lifeless scrolls by the other speakers would stand no comparison with what Vivekananda had spoken extempore. One of his American disciples, compared Swamiji's voice to that of a finely tuned musical instrument. This voice had become the carrier of the great message of universal love and the message was coming from the heart of one whose great Master had

---

2 Jove is another name of Greek God Jupiter.

inhaled the essence of all religions, who breathed love and brotherhood and who was a man of the highest realisation. Vivekananda declared that he was merely a conduit of his great guru's teachings.

Besides Vivekananda, there were Pratap Majoomdar, representing the Brahmo Samaj, there was Nagarkar from Bombay, one Mr.Gandhi from Gujarat representing Jainism and one Chakravarti accompanying Dr. Annie Besant, the leader of the Theosophical Society. Majoomdar and Mrs. Besant were well-known figures, known in India and abroad, but a totally unknown identity so far, Vivekananda, outshone them all completely. He proved true his Master's prophesy, 'If Keshub has the power of one sun, Naren has that of eighteen suns!' Pratap could not bear this humiliation at being left far behind by a choirboy of yester year. His jealousy took a vicious turn. Could he foresee that the reformist zeal of the Brahmo Samaj would be a short lived affair? Did all this lead him to join the band of Christian missionaries in spewing venom against Vivekananda? But it had proved to be an exercise of casting a handful of dust against the sun.

The small, unpremeditated lecture of Swamiji was delivered with the aim of giving a brief outline of Hinduism, 'Sanatana Dharma,' Eternal Religion as it is called. But it went much further than that. The real Hinduism which had almost got fragmented into numerous tiny sects was resurrected again. The resurrecting, really speaking, was done by Shri Ramakrishna, but Vivekananda was destined to become the mouthpiece of his great guru in spreading the message of tolerance, of respect and acceptance of all religions. Later on, Mahatma Gandhi was to include prayers from all religions in his daily prayer. By this revelation of the true spirit of the Mother of all religions, Vivekananda silenced dogmatic preachers and idol breakers, people who believed that truth about God was their sole monopoly and also hit hard at the zealot proselitisers. This had not gone unnoticed and someone who was able to see the truth in what Vivekananda had revealed did say that it was futile to send an army of missionaries to the land of Vivekananda. It had also evoked the reaction of attack on Swamiji by the missionaries. But he himsef had proved more than a match for them.

The first speech delivered by Swamiji at the Parliament of Religions on September 11, brought about a total change in his life. From an obscure, unknown, vagrant, wandering, uninvited and undeputed monk he became a famous sannyasin, commanding respect and honour from people. He rose to the status of a world teacher. Professor Wright had not compared him for nothing with the sun whose right to shine could not be questioned. And the small dark cloud of ignorance on the part of the people was removed the moment Swamiji's spiritual splendour manifested itself at the opening session of the Parliament of Religions. There was nothing that could eclipse the radiance emanating from that great apostle.

But Swamiji did not care for name or fame. His heart was bleeding for the millions of poor and deprived countrymen of his. It is said that having been placed on the pinnacle of glory, when Swamiji went at night to his bed for sleeping, he could not climb up onto the comfortable bed but cried out in anguish for his suffering countrymen. The purpose of his visit to America, the land of riches, was to preach *Vedanta* to the Americans and raise money for the upliftment of the impoverished people of India. He had never intended to be famous. But fame had come hunting him and, if not at the first few words he had spoken, at the end of his first small *Upanishad* like address, he was raised to the Everest of glory. His words had stirred the hearts of his listeners in the Columbus Hall. When the newspapers carried them in print the next day, they echoed in the ears of lakhs of readers. And they reverberated into the ears of Romain Rolland three and a half decades later. Swamiji's words were the descendants of the 'word' spoken of by St. John, the 'word' that was in the beginning.

Except for the chance meeting at the Abu Road railway station with his *gurubhais*, Swami Brahmananda and Swami Turiyananda, Swamiji had not conveyed a word to any other of his *gurubhais* about his trip to America. Even Brahmananda and Turiyananda, very likely, did not understand then the full significance of the Parliament of Religions. Nor was there any time for Vivekananda to pass on any information about the Parliament, about which he also knew very little.

In the first letter to his *gurubhai* Sharat (Sharadananda) from the U.S.A, dated 29th May, 1894, about ten months after his arrival there he shared neither his worries nor his glorious success with them. Like a true *sannyasin*, he looked at downs and ups with equanimity. As he did not lose his heart over one, he did not feel elated by another. Vivekananda was not famous like Annie Besant or Majoomdar in India. It took almost an year for Swamiji's home town, Kolkata, to organise a function honouring the great success of one of her sons.

The very first speech of Swamiji at the Parliament of Religions was unique in more ways than one. The Archbishop of Canterbury, the head of the Church of England, had declined the invitation to the Parliament stating in his letter that he did not consider other non Christian religions equal to Christianity and it would be below his dignity to sit on the same stage as was to be occupied by the representatives of other inferior religions. The Khalifa of Turkey, who was considered the Head of Islam also did not condescend to attend the Parliament on the same ground. The introductory lecture of Vivekananda was like the lance of Achilles, penetrating the sheaths of exclusiveness, self imposed superiority and 'holier than thou' attitude exhibited by both the religious leaders and by many Christian missionaries. Hinduism and Budhism, the two great religions of India, had gone out of India to far away lands, but never with a sword, never with an exclusive attitude, never with a superiority complex.

Since the publication of Darwin's Theory of Evolution a number of educated people in the West had lost their reverence for the *Bible*. Galileo had hit the first nail and a crack had appeared on the body of Christianity. With every progressive step in physical science the crack was getting wider and wider. Darwin's theory was a big blow, as it hit hard at Genesis. But Darwin was luckier than Galileo who was forced to disown what he had seen through his telescope and what he was propounding. Times having changed, Christian authorities could not do anything to Darwin, although it might be stated that even today, in some of the states in the U.S.A., schools are forbidden from teaching the Theory of Evolution. Barring this obstinacy to accept all religions as equal, the Americans, one might say the Westerners, were all riding on the wave of modern science and were in search of something new that would convince the intellect and yet uplift the spirit. The message given by Swamiji was exactly the thing. It was so different from what was being dinned into their ears. It had shaken them up from their false sense of superiority. Swamiji's message had opened the doors of their intellects and hearts wide open. It had razed to the ground the castle of prejudice so cleverly built by the churches that sent out armies of missionaries for the 'salvation' of 'heathens' of Asia and Africa.

Swamiji showed to them in crystal clear terms how hollow was their claim of superiority. As a matter of fact, later on at the Parliament, Vivekananda was to hit a hammer blow to the Christian tenet that everyone was born in sin and because of the so called original sin, even a new born infant dying immediately after birth, could not go to heaven. Quoting from an *Upanishad*, he had said, 'Ye children of immortality, to call you sinners is a sin!' Those words had a great appeal on his audience who felt relieved of the feeling of guilt of the original sin. Vivekananda purged the minds of his listeners of the fear of purgatory, of hell. His stress on inclusiveness, respect for and acceptance of all faiths, and the catholicity implicit in the idea appealed to the vast concourse of men and women in the Columbus Hall and the much vaster number of readers of the newspapers that carried the report of the proceedings of the Parliament the next morning. It was something so different from what was being dinned into their ears day in and day out. Their shell of artificial superiority crumbled and their eyes having been cleared of the dross of myopic beliefs, were able to see the truth about religions, about mankind.

Vivekananda's first address had established him as the hero of the Parliament of Religions and people were to learn more of his profundity, his encyclopaedic range, his ready-wittedness and his ability to thrust and pierce and parry as the Parliament proceeded.

In the days following, Vivekananda spoke about a dozen times. His main lectures were as follows: (1) Why we Disagree, (2) Religion is not the Crying Need of India, (3) Orthodox Hinduism and Vedantic Philosophy, (4) The Modern Religions of India, (5) The Essence of the Hindu Religion, (6) Buddhism, The Fulfilment of Hinduism. Besides those lectures, he also spoke on four or more occasions.

The thrust of his argument was always the same. He would put forth new arguments and illustrate his thesis with parables, but the refrain was always the same, his firm conviction of a boundless, universal religion, going beyond space and time. Men might be different, but mankind was one and it had to be united spiritually. 'We are all,' he said, 'like the frog in the well who could not even imagine the limitlessness of the ocean. An individual worshipping a totem, an individual worshipping an idol, the one worshipping a symbol and the one sitting in quiet meditation and thinking of the Infinite Absolute were,' he said, 'on different stages of evolution. The difference was in the distance from the goal. The ultimate goal for each one was one and the same.'

This approach propounded by Swami Vivekananda shook the very foundation of the towers of religions standing on the belief of superiority, on the belief of only their religion being right and others' being wrong, being of no consequence. It also hit hard at the 'pious' act of proselitisation. 'The Christian is not to become a Hindu or a Buddhist, nor a Hindu or a Buddhist to become a Christian. But each must assimilate the spirit of the others and yet preserve his individuality and grow according to his own law of growth. (Address at the Final Session, September 27, 1893, The Complete Works of Swami Vivekananda vol. 1, p. 24). Many of his listeners in the Columbus Hall and a number of readers of the newspapers that carried his unique message, people who had an open mind, found this idea of equality of all religions very appealing.

'Buddhism was,' according to him, 'The Fulfilment of Hinduism.' Delivering a lecture on the subject on 26th September, 1893, Swamiji had made the startling statement, 'I am not a Buddhist, as you have heard and yet I am.' In the beginning of his lecture on the subject, while it was announced that he would criticise Buddhism, he had said, 'How can I criticise him whom I worship as God incarnate on earth.' He then compared the relationship between the Hindu (Vedic) religion and Buddhism with the relationship between Judaism and Christianity, and pointing to the sharp contrast between the relationships of the two, he said, 'Jesus Christ was a Jew and Shakya Muni was a Hindu. The Jews rejected Jesus Christ, nay, crucified him, and the Hindus have accepted Shakya Muni as God and worshipped him.' The contrast between the two is a very marked one, hinting at the spirit of toleration pervading the Indian ethos. Swamiji did neither make a mention of this spirit of reverence nor did he mention the intolerance of Judaism, prevalent two thousand years ago. But for this attitude of intolerance, the Jews might have escaped persecution by Christians all over Europe leading to genocide by Hitler and the great exodus.

In his paper on Hinduism, read on the 19th of September, 1893, Swamiji pointed out the varied hues of the rainbow by saying, 'From the high spiritual height of the *Vedanta* Philosophy, of which the latest discoveries of science seem like echoes, to the low ideas of idolatry with its multifarious mythology, the agnosticism of the Buddhists, and the athcism of the Jains, each and all have a place in the Hindu religion.' He then put the question, "Where is the common centre to which all these widely diverging radii converge? Where is the common basis upon which all these seemingly hopeless contradictions rest?" In answering this question, one might say, Swamiji made a reference to science and said, 'science is nothing but the finding of unity.....Physics would stop when it would be able to fulfil its services in discovering one energy of which all the others are manifestations, and the science of religion become perfect when it would discover Him who is the one life in a Universe of death, Him who is the constant basis of an ever-changing world.... By the law of association, the material image calls up the mental idea and vice versa. That is why a Hindu worships an external symbol while he worships.... He knows as well as you do that the image is not God, is not omnipresent'... "External worship," say the scriptures, is the lowest stage; struggling to rise high, mental prayer is the next stage but the highest stage is when God had been realised.' The emphasis, as is evident, is on realisation and not external forms of worship.

Elaborating his thesis further, he said, 'Unity in diversity is the plan of nature, and the Hindu has recognised it. Every other religion lays down some fixed dogmas, and tries to force the society to adopt them.... The Hindus have discovered that the absolute can only be realised or thought of, or stated through the relative and the images, crosses and crescents are simply so many symbols—so many pegs to hang the spiritual ideas on.'

Towards the end of his great paper, Swamiji put forth some hints for a universal religion.

Swamiji's final address at the concluding session of the Parliament of Religions, delivered on 27th Sept., 1893, echoes and emphasises unity in diversity. He conveyed his sincere thanks as he only could. He began by thanking those noble souls whose large hearts and love of truth first dreamed this wonderful dream and then realised it. He was not at all satirical but he was sincere in saying, 'A few jarring notes were heard from time to time in this harmony. My special thanks to them, for they have, by their striking contrast, made general harmony the sweeter.'

His concluding words are most marvellous, hinting as they are at the narrowness of some exclusivists and end with his prophetic statement. 'It has been proved to the world that holiness, purity and charity are not the exclusive possessions of any church in the world, and that every system has produced men and women of the most exalted character. In the face of this evidence, if anybody dreams of the exclusive survival of his own religion and the distraction of others, I pity him from the bottom of my heart, and point out to him that upon the banner of every religion will soon be written, in spite of resistance: "Help and not Fight," "Assimilation and not Destruction," "Harmony and Peace and not Dissension."

As stated earlier, Vivekananda was only reflecting what he had learnt from his Master, who was a living symbol of harmony, love and assimilation.

Apart from Mervin Shell, Chairman of the Science section of the Parliament, even Barrows had to admit the resounding success of Swamiji and Annie Besant also had to join the chorus.

18

Three Years in the West

Success did not, could not, go to Vivekananda's head. Being a *Sannyasin,* he was above praise and blame, success and failure. But in order to be with his own self, he had to retire from the din and bustle of the Fair and the Parliament. He went naturally to the house of Mary Hale, who had taken him under her shelter on his arrival from Boston, helped him feel at home and then led him to the Parliament. It was but natural for Vivekananda to respond to the maternal care of Mrs. Hale by addressing her as 'Mother.' 541, Dearborn Avenue, Chicago, was his American address for a pretty long time and any mail from India would first reach there and thence it would be redirected to him wherever, the wandering monk would be moving.

A new chapter in his life was now opened. From total obscurity until 11th September, he was now standing in glorious brightness, radiating his great spiritual light all around. Many were to bathe in that light and a lucky few were to follow him and become his disciples.

It was a new chapter for America and the Western world also. As Diana Eck has stated in her article on the occasion of the Centenary of the Parliament of 1893, in that year in Chicago there were Christian churches only. Now, in 1993 there are several mosques, Buddhist temples, Hindu temples and of course, a Centre of the Ramakrishna *Math.* She had also pointed out that various universities have introduced courses in comparative religions and comparative philosophies. And there has been, literally, a flood of Swamis, and yogis, some of whom have exploited the gullible over there by preaching instant *samadhi*, levitation etc.

Externally, at least, Swamiji was caught in a conflict. He was moving in the land of riches, with wealth surrounding him and tempting him but he believed in total renunciation. It was not any vanity that had made him utter at the Abu Road station in front of his *gurubhais*, 'This Parliament is meant for me'. His mission was dictated by destiny. Had not his guru declared, 'Naren would one day shake the world?' The world was 'shaken', but 'Ma's work' he was destined to do was still waiting for him.

But before he could launch up on his mission, American snobbery, as Romain Rolland has put it, threw itself upon him, and, in its first flush threatened to smother him with luxury and vanities. The first impact of the wealthy West had dazzled him but further and closer impacts were opening the seamy side of the Western life style before him and his earlier impression started fading. He found himself surrounded by the narrowness of sectarian fanaticism and the horrible ignorance, one may say, deliberately cultivated, partly by geographical isolation and partly by the wealth acquired by robbing its natural inheritors, and the 'I care a hang'—the isolationist—attitude grown out of being out of the periodic fights amongst the European states for maintaining the 'balance of power' and the race for imperial supremacy.

All this he came to learn after he accepted the offer of a lecture bureau for a lecture tour of the country. The simple Swami was soon to find out the typical way of keeping the lion's share of the income from the Swami's lectures by the bureau to itself and offering a pittance to him. He had toured the *eastern* part of the U.S.A. the mid-West, Chicago, Des Moines, Iowa, Minneapolis, Detroit, New York, Boston, Cambridge, Baltimore, Washington, etc. At the earliest opportunity he managed to free himself from the clutches of the exploiting lecture bureau and started moving on his own.

But at several places his fame was preceded by the vile and vicious prejudice of some intolerant missionaries who believed in the superiority of their religion. Vivekananda was a heathen. He was an idol worshipper. He had broken the rules of the caste system by taking to *sannyasa,* though he was a '*shudra;*' he was regularly eating beef, forbidden for all Hindus. Even his character was attacked. And yet, as Sister Christine has mentioned, he quietly overcame this onslaught and people started flocking in increasing numbers to hear him speak. At times, the *kshatriya* (warrior) in him rose up and pricked nails in the balloon of their Christianity: 'With all your brag and boasting, where has your Christianity succeeded without the sword? Yours is the religion preached in the name of luxury. It is all hypocricy that I have heard in this country. All this prosperity, all this from Christ! Those who call upon Christ care for nothing but to amass riches! Christ would not find a stone on which to lay his head among you... You are not Christians. Return to Christ!'

Very hard hitting words these. But he just could not tolerate the hypocricy, 'Name of Rama on the tongue, a knife in the armpit,' as an Indian saying goes. Once he got so terribly furious at the hypocricy of his audience in Boston that instead of speaking on the topic fixed for the evening-he was to speak on his guru Shri Ramakrishna, the subject dearest to him—he was so repulsed by the sight of the audience that he brusquely changed the topic. He would not open the doors of his heart where Ramakrishna was dwelling before such cunning foxes and cruel wolves. The reaction of the audience could well be imagined. Hundreds walked out of the hall noisily and the Press also did not spare him either. Some clergymen seized such opportunities, followed him like hounds and poured vitriolic scorn on him. As stated earlier, they spread spicy stories. One such story was that Swamiji had wronged an ex-employee of the Governor of Michigan. The Governor's wife issued a denial. But very often such denials go unnoticed. The missionaries in India also seized the opportunity to hit Swamiji in his absence as hard as possible and the Brahmo Samajists, under the leadership of Pratap, joined the chorus. A few of the Brahmo leaders had never looked kindly upon the influence of Shri Ramakrishna on their leader Keshub. Particularly after Keshub being forced out of the Brahmo Samaj, some of the lesser men who took over the leadership broke away completely from Shri Ramakrishna and their jealousy at the stupendous success of his beloved disciple, which had completely eclipsed the reformist Brahmo Samaj and the traditional Hindu sects, had felt great heart-burns. Pratap had joined the chorus of the missionaries. The theosophists also had felt that Swamiji had taken the wind out of their sail.

This uncalled for attacks on Swamiji drew the attention of people to seek the reason of the attacks. By and by people learnt of the great success of Swamiji at the Chicago Parliament which had caused jealousy among his Brahmo compatriots and the fear of becoming jobless among the missionaries. Moreover, the letters that Swamiji wrote from America to his disciples in Madras, to the Maharaja of Khetdi, to the Divan of Junagadh and lastly to his *gurubhais* made the picture quite clear. And so, on September 5, 1894, almost one year after his thumping success at the Parliament, Kolkata organised a public function honouring her great son in absentia. More details of Swamiji's achievements in America were mentioned at the function and thus the people of his motherland came to learn of his achievements.

But by that time, Swamiji had spread the message of *Vedanta* far and wide. Astonishing as it might sound, he had refrained from speaking about his guru as well as from the zeal of converting people to Hinduism. As a matter of fact, he did not believe in conversion. His philosophy did not call for such conversion. After spending a few days of quiet rest and affectionate family life at the Hales, Swamiji first went to a couple of places like Des Moines, to the West and South of Chicago, and later on, in February, 1894, moved to Detroit, east of Chicago. He was to give there a series of lectures at the Unitarian Church. The local press, under pressure from local Missionaries opposed to Vivekananda tried to dissuade the people by whatever foul means they could resort to.

Kurt Fried Richs, Chairman of the *Vedanta Centre,* Wiesbaden (Germany) has given an interesting example in his article, Swami Vivekananda, The Apostle of *Vedanta* in Swami *Vivekananda, Hundred years since Chicago, A Comemopative volume* (Ramakrishna *Math* and Ramakrishna Mission, *Belur,* 12th January, 1994,p.123).

In Detroit he was invited by a private circle—a group of *pandits,* psychologists, clergymen, medical doctors and scientists who wanted to test him. They asked him to... There was no further discussion. They could not utter a word in his august presence.

Yet, the fame of Vive Kananda, as many in America spelt his name, had spread far and wide from his appearance at the Chicago Parliament five months ago, and people had flocked to hear him. One Mrs. Mary Funke, in her early twenties, was a person with a searching mind and was running from pulpit to pulpit to hear visiting religious dignitaries, to quench the thirst of her heart. She spoke to a friend of hers, one Miss Christine Greenstidel, about the arrival of 'Vivekananda, the Hindu monk, whose fame had reached there before him.' Miss Greenstidel was also feeling dissatisfied at the fare offered by the Church, was trying to read anything she could lay her hands on in order to satisfy her quest, and had read Edwin Arnold's translation of the *Gita,* 'The Song Celestial.' She was impressed by the Gita but how much of the teaching of the Gita was digested by her was a question. When Mary spoke to her about the series of lectures at the Unitarian Church by 'Vive Kananda,' she was a bit sceptical. But ultimately she accompanied her friend to the Unitarian Church. And then, her restlessness was stilled forever. Unknowingly, she did something 'which would change the whole course of my life and be of such stupendous import that it could not be measured by previous standards...Surely, never in our countless incarnations had we taken a step so momentous!' For, 'before we had listened five minutes, we knew that we had found the touchstone for which we had searched so long! 'These are the words Miss Greenstidel has written in her 'Reminiscences'. And against this one, there must have been many more persons who underwent transformation in their personalities a bit more or less. Greenstidel turned into Sister Christine and followed Swamiji to India to serve her. Miss Christine.—he enduringly called her his 'violet,'—was not as garrulous as Nivedita, but was a quiet worker, pouring her heart and soul into service. Swamiji treated her like a daughter and helped her in more ways than one. His numerous—71 in all—letters to her show the immeasurable depth of Swamiji's heart, his affection for the gem that Christine was and the extent to which he was ready to help her. She very much desired to come to India and be near Swamiji. Swamiji got passage money for her. And while she was on her way, he fell seriously ill. So he made arrangements with Nivedita so that Christine took the next boat home. So caring was Swamiji for her. She was a rare find. His health had improved and Christine stayed on in India. But the same Vivekananda had refused Mary Funke to go to India and serve him. 'Your duty is to serve your husband and your family,' he had told her.

Many others had got caught into Swamiji's net, Miss S. E. Waldo Sister Haridasi, Miss Josephine McLeod, Sara Bull, The Leggetts and many others. He had met them at different places, and in different circumstances. But each one of them was spell-bound and followed Swamiji physically as well as mentally and spiritually.

The theme of Swamiji's classes and lectures was *Vedanta*, the undercurrent of all Hinduism. He had stated what he firmly believed that he was amongst the children of the son of Mary. He had studied the *Bible* and always carried with him a copy of the great book, 'The Imitation of Christ.' His mastery of the *Bible* enabled him to establish contact with his listeners and also to reply to his Missionary critics.

After freeing himself from the noose of the lecture bureau, he had to face another trouble from the 'rich and the cultured' who tried to have Vivekananda exclusively to themselves. They would gather in their salons, where entry was strictly by invitation, and the elite gathering there would listen to Swamiji, probably with a glass of wine in their hands. Swamiji was totally opposed to this exclusiveness. His message of freedom from bondage was not for few. It was for all mankind. He fled from this club of leisurely spiritual people and found a cheap, hardly furnished room away from the Park Avenue, in New York. His lectures and talks were open to all and people started flocking in, filling up the entire room, some people were sitting on the table, some on the wash basin, others were standing, crowded in the room and still others standing on the staircase steps to hear Vivekananda speak, if not to have a glance of him. The simple room in which the Swami lectured to his audiences, a couple of times a day, also served as his living room and his bedroom as well. No fees were charged. Some people would contribute something and Swamiji would manage to pay the rent and buy some victuals to cook for himself. It was the life of a *tyagi*.

His references to India, her past glory, and the sucking of her blood by the Britishers leading to her impoverishment were not the main subjects of his lectures, yet his few references attracted criticism branding him a patriot. He was, no doubt, a lover of his motherland and his craving for her independence was no less than that of his other contemporaries like Tilak or Surendranath Bannerji. But he did not aim at mere political freedom. He aimed at the liberation of the spirit, because of the spiritual weakness, India had fallen a prey to foreign invasions. The Muslim hordes who had invaded India had made India their home and so there was no economic exploitation. It was the 'gift' of the European invaders. In spite of all this the spiritual fire had not completely died down. An almost illiterate villager, completely shielded from the onslaught of Western education and thinking, Shri Ramakrishna, with his Herculean effort, had rekindled it and Vivekananda, and his other *gurubhais*, were the carriers of the rekindled torch. With his formal education, his study of history and his knowledge of world affairs, he just could not help keeping himself away from the political goings on. As a matter of fact, before he left Kolkata for his wanderings, a police officer known to him had invited 'Naren' to dinner and tried to arrest him. But Naren had proved too strong for him. According to a report dug out by the 'Amrit Bazar Patrika', a well-known nationalist newspaper, the British police was keeping a record of his track from place to place in India. Yet, he had to stand up and say that he was not a patriot, in the narrow sense of the term, a person fighting only for the political freedom of his country. He was leading the fight for the salvation of the country's soul.

The incessant speaking posed a big problem. His worries about what to speak at the next meeting were put to an end by some mysterious happening. He would go to bed, praying for help and, all of a sudden, by midnight, his mind would be filled up with the ideas for his talk next morning. In this way he lectured on '*Raja Yoga*.' We are thankful to Miss Waldo for putting it down as dictated by Swamiji. The great psychologist William James was keenly interested in '*Raja Yoga*' and, might be, this interest of the great psychologist of the day made him write his book on 'The Varieties of Religious Experience.' Later on, Tolstoy also was interested by it. The interest was natural because Swamiji had expounded very logically and systematically, the principles of the Absolute. It was a perfectly scientific approach.

Swamiji got a nice change when he was invited to Greenacre, a lovely little place in Maine, one of the north-eastern states in the U.S. The place reminded him of the ancient *ashrama*s of the *rishi*s in quiet woods. There was a tall pine tree with its branches casting shadows all around. Swamiji chose the foot of the pine tree as his seat. He used to sit there cross-legged, on the ground, in the Indian fashion, and his listeners also squatted on the ground. Swamiji was a true *Brahmanishtha Shrotriya* like the ancient sages and exactly like them, he taught spiritual truths to the small number of devout listeners. The place became an ancient Indian *Ashrama* in modern America and the pine came to be known as 'Swamiji 's Pine.'

Swamiji's life was very hectic. He was running from place to place, giving lectures, conducting classes, solving the doubts of his listeners, receiving people, consoling them, writing letters and, most often, cooking for himself and for a visitor or two. At times he would be eating out also. This irregularity in food, eating different things and cooked in a way different from what he was used to, irregularity in the style of living and the extremely cold winters affected his health. He needed a change very badly. It came his way in the summer of 1895.

One of his disciples had a house in an idylic situation. It was a house on one of the small islands in the Thousand Island Park, situated on the river, St. Lawrence, carrying the waters of the lakes to the Atlantic. The place stands just where the Lake Ontario narrows down to become the St. Lawrence river. It is an isolated quiet place like an *ashrama* of the ancient Indian *rishi*s. The lady who owned the house got a special room constructed for Swamiji. Only a dozen disciples had followed him there— 'fit though few!' The teaching commenced on 24th of June 1895 and lasted up to August 12.

On the first day, Swamiji entered the room where the disciples were seated, with a copy of the *Bible* in his hands. He began by reading St. John's Gospel: 'In the beginning was the word. And the word was with God. And the word was God....' It was a select audience, eager to imbibe. The serene and calm atmosphere of the place, the placid waters of the river, the long summer days with many hours of sunshine and the sincerity of the group to imbibe and assimilate, everything was very conducive.

But for the effort of Miss Waldo, we would not have come to know what had transpired at the Thousand Island Park retreat. Very appropriately, she has called the talks of Swamiji, 'Inspired Talks.' Most of the dozen people who were there were meeting for the first time, yet they lived with the spirit of 'sisterhood.' Swamiji was in the most relaxed mood. There were no visitors, no callers. Although it was all in a room in a house, the atmosphere was like an ancient *ashrama*. It was an *Upanishad* in the literal sense of the term. And Swamiji was opening the realms of *Vedanta* before them. All who were there became transformed, charged with the great spark of spirituality. In her 'Reminicences' of Swamiji, Sister Christine has given a vivid account of the retreat at the Thousand Island Park.

Marie Louise, whom Romain Roland called 'tumultuous' took the vows of *sannyasa* with the name, Abhayananda the Fearless. She came originally from France and had become an American citizen. She was well known in the Socialist circles of New York. Leon Landsberg, a migratory Jew from Russia, was a very intelligent journalist of New York. He was so overpowered by Swamiji's talks and the treatise on'*Raja Yoga*,' that he also was initiated into *sannyasa* by Swamiji and given the name, 'Kripananda.' Both these *sannyasins* carried on the work of Swamiji in and around New York ceaselessly. Mention must be made of Mrs. Ole Bull, who later on donated generously to the work of Vivekananda, in establishing the headquarters of Ramakrishna Order at Belur—Kolkata. The Leggetts also were very great friends and their quiet farm house, Ridgley Manor, in the Catskil Mountains, near the Hudson river, was a second home to Swamiji. The descendants of the couple graciously donated the house on the Hudson, in the north of New York, to the Mission in 1993, where a branch of the Order has been started.

The account of the persons Swamiji won over would not be complete without the mention of J.J.Goodwin. He was the only shorthand writer to satisfy Swamiji. What was more the fact that, he soon left his job, stopped accepting money from Swamiji and became the faithful recorder of every word that Swamiji spoke until death in India cut him off untimely in 1897. His death had moved Swamiji greatly. He was caught by Swamiji in his net in America.

Soon after leaving the Thousand Island Park, Swamiji had sailed from New York to Marseilles for going to Paris. He was greatly influenced by the meteoric rise of Napoleon and he visited the Corsican's grave. The Louvre also had a special attraction for him. After spending a few days in Paris, he went to Kiel in Germany, to meet Paul Deussen, the great Indologist of the time. Deussen had invited Swamiji. But the two or three days Swamiji spent with him did not quench the thirst of the German Indologist. So enamoured was he that he followed Swamiji to England, where Swamiji was going to meet the great Sanskrit scholar Max Muller.

On setting his foot in Europe and after meeting people like Deussen, Max Muller, Sturdy, Miss Margaret Noble and others, Swamiji could easily note the difference between the New World and the old. The new world was enthusiastic but lacking in depth, would cheer with loud claps, gather around in big numbers, but all through out people there would be calculating the material benefits they would be able to reap out of the whole performance. In the old world of Europe, things were entirely different. People here would at first be cool and reserved, but when they would accept a message, they would do so with all their heart; they would be very conservative in showering praises, but once they did so, they would do it with perfect conviction. And, last but not the least, people in Europe could rise beyond material gains here and now and peep into distant past and dream of future. There probably was some historical reason for the difference; the hungry and the persecuted who went to America were first concerned with a shelter and bread. Vast lands were waiting there for occupation, for cultivation and for mining. Stories of gold-rushes and cowboys attracted more and more people. And almost all of them hunted for lucre.

An hour's visit to a church on Sundays and some contribution at the end was enough for salvation. Living was turning from simple to complex but was not accompanied by hard thinking. As a matter of fact, with the army of slaves up to the end of the sixth decade of the nineteenth century, untapped vast lands and resources undreamt of in Europe, benefits being brought about by new scientific discoveries and inventions, everything led to the moulding of the American way of life and philosophy. Whether God was in his heaven or not, all was well with the American World. The few universities that had come into existence still looked to the ancient seats of learning in Europe.

Mr. E. T. Sturdy of London had played an important role in calling Swamiji to England. This is clear from Vivekananda's letters to Sturdy, written in April and May 1895. Swamiji's correspondence with Sturdy shows an upward shooting graph in these earlier days. As the correspondence points out, Mr. Sturdy had invited Swamiji to be his guest. His wife, however, did not appear to share the same respect for the Hindu philosophy and its outstanding exponent of the day, Swami Vivekananda. Her coldness towards him, her indifferent treatment of him, the same simple fare she served him three times a day for many days and the constant frown on her face have all been mentioned by the Swami in a letter (NO.XLVI, from New York dated Nov.1899 - Vol.-VII, p.p. 515-519). Though Sturdy played an important role in putting Swamiji in close contact with England, the relationship soured later on.

But the case with Swamiji's relationship with England and her people was just the opposite. When he had landed in England in the summer of 1895, he was harbouring in his heart great hatred. The obvious reason for this feeling in his heart was the subjugation imposed by the English on his motherland. But after visiting England twice, during 1895 and 1896, and then returning to India, he had told his friends of the transformation he had undergone, 'There is none among you who loves the English people more than I do.'

After a happy summer, he went back to America. He had established a *Vedanta Centre* in New York and his two American *Sannyasin* disciples had kept the fire burning. It was the first centre of the Ramakrishna Order to come formally into existence. The Varahanagar *Math* had moved to Alambazar but it had no formal constitution, no registration no lectures to the public. This was to come later on, after his return to India in 1897.

He broke new grounds in America by meeting Nicholas Tesla, the leading physicist and a great inventor of the day. It was the first meeting between a scientist and a spiritual leader and was very fruitful. Tesla was interested to learn how close the ancient *Vedanta* was to modern science. New discoveries in physics and genetic biology were to bring them closer in the next (the twentieth) century. Swami Vivekananda also met in New York two leading scientists of Europe, Helmholtz and Lord Kelvin (then known as Sir William Thompson). These meetings indicated in crystal clear terms that Vivekananda was the first religious thinker bold enough to meet scientists and was the first such person as was ready to have his philosophic beliefs tested by modern scientists. Religion and philosophy have gone together in India and Swamiji was not a person to shun away from science. Their marriage would be a blessing to mankind. In the century that followed Vivekananda meeting such eminent luminaries in the field of science, science has moved far away from its entirely materialistic base.

After his return from England in November 1895, Swamiji put his New York work on solid foundations. He 'discovered' Goodwin during this period. Swamiji referred to him as 'my faithful Goodwin'. The world owes a debt of deep gratitude to him for presenting almost all of Swamiji's lectures and talks except on '*Raja Yoga*. As noted by Kripananda, the American disciple initiated by Swamiji, because of Swamiji 'the demand for *Vedanta* literature is fast growing and books by Max Muller, Colebrook, Deussen etc., are in great demand. The names of Shankaracharya and Ramanuja have become current coins.' In this letter sent for publication in the 'Brahmavadin,' a journal started by the Madras devotees of Swamiji, Kripananda further warns: 'The time is now ripe for Indians to claim Swamiji as their own'.

Swamiji had started lecturing in the hall of the Metaphysical Society of Brooklyn and the 'People's Church' of New York after his return from England. The crowds of people thronging to hear him moved to the 'Madison Square Garden,' a hall which could accomodate 1500 people. There he spoke on the '*Bhakti Yoga*,' 'The Real and Apparent Forms of Man', and last but not the least, on 'My Master.' After two and a half years' stay in the West, this was for the first time that Vivekananda was speaking about his guru. He felt very reticent about it and considered himself totally incapable of talking about the great Guru of his, though he had furnished some important information to Max Muller in England about Ramakrishna whose small monograph is the first biography of Shri Ramakrishna written in English. More than three decades later Romain Rolland was to pen his monumental work.

A reporter of the famous New York journal '*The New York Herald*' met Swamiji for an interview. His eyes were opened wide to see about one hundred and sixty people listening intently to Swamiji talk on 'Karma Yoga.' He paid a very glowing tribute to the genius of Swamiji.

Swamiji also gave a series of talks on the '*Bhakti Yoga*,' the '*Jnana Yoga*' and the Philosophy of the 'Sankhaya' and the '*Vedanta*.' His last lecture at the Madison Square Garden was on

'My Master,' delivered on February 24, 1896. And on that very day his *gurubhais* and disciples in India were celebrating the Guru's birthday in India with great devotion.

Swamiji had created a great impact on American minds. Mrs. Mary Funke has given us a detailed account of Swamiji's third visit to Detroit later on. Rabi Louis Grosman, who was in charge of the temple of Beth L, where Swamiji's last public programme was arranged was amazed at seeing the huge crowd inside and outside the temple and felt that there would be pandemonium. His fears were, however, belied and Swamiji was heard with rapt attention. His lectures at the gathering of teachers and students of philosophy were so greatly applauded and found so appealing that the authorities of the Harvard University offered him the Chair of Eastern Philosophy. But Swamiji's concept of a classroom knew no walls, no prequalification's for admissions. He politely turned down the offer. A similar offer was made to him by another Ivy League University, the Columbia University, New York. The difference here was that of the subject Swamiji would be teaching. He was offered a chair of Sanskrit studies. Accepting of any such job in return of salary was against his vow as a *sannyasin*. But both these incidents show the powerful impact the personality of Swamiji had made on the brilliant minds of America of the period. Some of the topics he discussed in detail in these lectures were the influence of Indian Philosophy on the ancient Greek Philosophy, the relationship between the dualist and the nondualist (*Dvaita* and *Advaita*) schools of thinking, Brahma etc. In his references to the Sankhya and Yoga he pointed out how deep were the roots of psychology in India, and how very precise and scientific was the approach.

When Swamiji had disembarked at Vancouver in July 1893, shivering a bit in his silken robes, there was no one to welcome him. When he moved to Chicago from Vancouver, he faced a worse fate. The reception there was much cooler. The strange alien visitor, who was not sent as a delegate by any religious organisation was simply made to turn about, as the date of enrolment of delegates had also passed. Moreover, he was too early for the Parliament of Religions. From an obscure, unknown, unwanted wandering monk, Swamiji's very first address at the Parliament had put him upon the pinnacle of fame. Since then he had moved around various places in the U.S.A., addressed many crowded gatherings, spoken to small select groups and conducted various classes. In spite of strong opposition by a section of the Christian missionaries, wherever he went, people thronged to hear his message of love, of synthesis of religions, of the preachings of the great Indian sages and many of his listeners soon became his devotees and a few became his disciples also. He had thus demolished the wall of isolation America had built around. And he had made a flood of new ideas flow into the minds of men. His message of God being one, all religions being different paths leading to the same goal, acceptance of all religions and reverence for them had made a tremendous appeal. He had also established a *Vedanta Centre* in New York. All this he had done singlehanded. He had no powerful organisation to back him up. As a matter of fact, he was put to such a penurious situation in the beginning that but for the gracious opening of the door of the Parliament for him at the instance of Prof. Wright, he would have been starved and as mentioned in the *Bible*, he would have had no stone to lay his head on. But his Guru's prophesy had to come true. What his inner voice had made him say to his *gurubhais* at the Abu Road Station in May, 1893, had to come true.

But Swamiji had to pay the price for all this. His constant running, incessant working, total irregularity in food, the mental and emotional strain caused by the abuses hurled at him by the missionaries were gnowing at his innards and though he was looking more or less the same Bengali athlete, of a dozen years ago, his energies were sapping and he desired to go back home, be with his old friends, wear his ochre clothes once more, walk bare foot and swim in the Ganga. In February 1896, he stopped giving public lectures and founded the *Vedanta* Society in New York with Francis Leggett as chairman. The sole aim of the Society was to spread the message of *Vedanta.* As he had said in one of his lectures at the Parliament of Religions in 1893, he did not at all want anybody to convert from one religion to another. Proselitising was not his creed. *Vedanta* is based on the *Upanishads* and they are entirely non-sectarian in character. People of all faiths were invited to become members of the *Vedanta Centre*. Tolerance, respect for all religions and acceptance of all of them were, and are the basic principles of the *Vedanta*. In a letter to Mr. Sturdy, Swamiji had written, 'I want to serve dry and obstruse philosophy, but after mixing it in the ' delicious sherbet of love, making it attractive by cooking in the Yoga-kitchen and making it tasty with hard labour.' One of the ideas of Swamiji behind the establishment of the *Vedanta Centre* was to harmonise different religions. He wanted the east and the West to join hands and march together with the *Vedanta* drum guiding their steps.

From Professor John Herry Wright in Boston and the members of the Hale family in Chicago, to the Leggett family, Mrs. Ole Bull, Miss Waldo, Mrs. Funke and Madame Calve, Swamiji had made many friends and well-wishers. He had helped Madam Calve, the leading opera singer of the age, to come out of the shock and grief that had overtaken her. Swamiji had also helped, as discovered by Sister Gargi (Marie Louise Burke), Mr. Rockefeller establigh his foundation for charity.

All this hectic and hard life had affected Vivekananda's health. In his famous poem, 'My Play is Done', Swamiji had written

'Oh! I am sick of this unending farce; these shows,
they please no more;
This ever running, never reaching, nor even a
distant glimpse of shore' ---

Swamiji seems to have hinted at the feeling of tiredness he was suffering from. Another of his great poem, 'The Song of the *Sannyasin*,' was also written around this time.

The two Americans, initiated in *Sannyasa* by Swamiji, were there and were doing good work. Miss Waldo, whom Swamiji had given the name of Haridasi, was also there, but there was a demand for an Indian *Sannyasin*. Swamiji wrote to his gurubhai Sharadananda to come over immediately. But it took sometime, and he met Swamiji later on in England.

Swamiji had stopped giving lectures and talks from the end of February, 1896 and he had sailed for England on 15th April, 1896, bidding goodbye to the Statue of Liberty, standing facing the New York Harbour.

His arrival in London was preceded by the arrival of Swami Sharadananda. The two gurubhai's met after a lapse of several years. It was a unique meeting, full of affection, full of respect, full of memories. Swamiji came to learn about the Alambazaar *Math*, about his other *gurubhais*, about the Holy Mother Shri Sharadadevi and various other devotees of Thakur. Swami Sharadananda on his part learnt many things about the work in America and in England, about the friends who had proved of great help, about the devotees who had flocked around Swamiji and he also spoke of those few who had become his disciples. Sharadananda's heart was filled with great joy to learn that the message of their Guru had spread far and wide and was doing so farther and wider.

Sharadananda had no experience of giving lectures, so he felt quite hesitant to do so in England. Like a hard task master, Vivekananda trained his gurubhai and one day he simply announced that Swami Sharadananda would address the audience on the day. A few days later, Sharadananda crossed the Atlantic and on reaching New York, took over the work there, making it a great success.

Soon after setting his foot in London, Swamiji had started giving lectures on '*Jnana Yoga*', 'The Necessity of Religion', 'The Absolute and Manifestation,' 'Practical *Vedanta*' etc. Goodwin took them all down in shorthand, and so they are available as spoken by Swamiji.

At the end of one of his lectures, applauded by the audience, a grey-haired old man stood up and said, 'Sir, you have given a great lecture and I offer my sincere thanks to you for it. But you haven't said anything new to us. Swamiji roared in reply, 'Sir, I have told you only the "Truth" and nothing but the "Truth." And this truth is as old as the mountains, the rivers, mankind, nature, and God Himself. If I have been able to put it in a way to make you think and act accordingly, am I not doing a good thing?' 'Hear,' 'hear', burst out the audience. Swamiji said that he had found the truth because it was already there in his heart. 'No sect will give it to yourself, it is lying there in your own heart. You have to give it to Different people give different names to it. They all ask you to believe a certain thing. Listen carefully. That precious pearl is lying within your own self. And that is the truth: "Thou Art That."'

He spoke about Shri Ramakrishna. And in speaking about his Guru, he forgot himself completely and boldly proclaimed, 'I am what I am only because of him. Whatever is beautiful, true and eternal in me or in my speech has all come from his speech, his heart, his soul.'

Indian students in England at that time went to him for guidance, which he gave very willingly. On 18th July, 1896, Swamiji addressed a gathering of Indians living in Great Britain and Ireland, held under the auspices of the London Hindu Association. Prince Ranji, who later on ascended the throne of the Nawanagar state in Saurashtra and came to be known as the Jam Saheb, was honoured by the Indian Majlis of the Cambridge University for his brilliant performance in cricket. The Majlis had invited Swamiji on the occasion and he had 'responded to the toast of India amidst loud and deafening cheers.' This function was held on 21st November of the same year (C.W. Vol, IX, P. 541).

Swamiji felt very happy to meet Professor Max Muller once more. This meeting with the old Professor 'who so loved Indian culture' took Swamiji back to the age of ancient *rishis* like the great sage Vashishtha. The Professor's monograph, 'Ramakrishna, His Life and Sayings,' owes much to Swamiji.

In a very touching letter to his American friend Francis Leggett, written on 6th July, 1896, Swamiji wrote, "The work is growing silently yet surely in England...all great work is slow...yet that is the very reason why it is bound to work....My power of work is immensely increasing and becoming immensely effective. Some days I get into a sort of an ecstasy..." The entire letter reflects the exalted spiritual state of Swamiji's mind.

Swamiji then crossed the British Channel and went over to the continent of Europe. At Florence in Italy, he chanced to see his great American well-wishers, the Hales of Chicago, and both the parties were delighted at the unexpected meeting in a third country. Swamiji had also paid a visit to Rome and was greatly delighted to see the ancient city, standing through ages. However, he did not like the pomp and show at some religious ceremony in a church. Swamiji also visited Switzerland, had a dip in the waters of Lake Geneva, saw an old monastery, and was delighted to see the snow-clad Mont Blanc and other glaciers. He found the atmosphere there fit for meditation. He went to Germany and after seeing Berlin and other cities, he went to see the old, India loving *Pandit* Paul Deussen. They were both delighted to meet each other. Deussen had accompanied Swamiji to England, in order to be with Swamiji, whose encyclopaedic knowledge, whose dedication to spiritual life like the *rishis* of old, Deussen had read about in the Indian scriptures he was so assiduously studying, and Swamiji's love for mankind had made a permanent mark on Deussen. He met Max Muller once more and he also met Edward Carpenter, Fredrick Myers and Canon Wilberforce, the leading intellectuals of the time.

Swamiji's lectures in London in the October and November of the year were simply great. He spoke on "*Maya* and *Brahma*, '*Maya* and *Mukti*' and other Vedantic topics. The subjects were quite abstruse and alien to the audience, but Swamiji had a knack of putting things in a crystal clear language before his foreign audience. A second edition of '*Raja Yoga*' had to be brought out.

The work in London had increased very much and his gurubhai Abhedananda was summoned by him. Abhedananda proved to be a great success. Later on he moved to America, where he worked for a number of years.

All the while Swamiji was yearning to go back to India. The work in the West had taken the sap out of him and, at times, he remarked, 'my work is over.' Swamiji was presented with a scroll of honour in a big hall in the Picadili locality of London on December 13, 1896. The hall was overflowing with people. Abhedananda was present at the meeting. He had already made his mark and people were looking forward to him to carry on the work of *Vedanta*, whose solid foundation was laid by Swami Vivekananda.

Swamiji left London on 16th December, 1896, in company of the Sevier couple. Mr. Goodwin was to reach Naples by sea, from where Swamiji and the Seviers were to catch the steam boat for India.

Swamiji was returning to his motherland after winning laurels. It was the homecoming of a dear son of India, who had earned a great name for himself and for his motherland. A hero was returning home.

19

The Return of the Triumphant

Before going to Naples, Swamiji and the Seviers visited Milan, Florence and Rome. Basically, it was a pleasure tour which at times took the form of a pilgrimage. Swamiji was not an ordinary tourist. Rome, the eternal city, had its own attractions. The ancient Roman emperors, Pompeii, Julius Ceasar, Nero and their big Roman empire, Rome, as the heart of Christianity and saints like St. Francis of Assisi, Dante and the great Renaissance, the Sistine Chapel, St. Peter's Basilica and St. Paul's Cathedral had their our attraction were not merely tourist spots for Swamiji. He was moved to see the great Leornardo Da Vinci's painting, *The Last Supper,* depicting a turning point in the life of Christ. He, however, did not like the pompous show of religiosity at St. Paul's Cathedral. He was very happy to meet in Florence, by chance, as mentioned earlier, the Hales of Chicago, who had taken him under their wing, guided him to the Parliament of Religions and showered affection on him. The Hales also were equally delighted.

A very strange incident took place. A disciple of his brought to him a small image of the Sistine Madonna and requested him to bless it. But in all humility, Vivekananda refused to do so and very reverentially touched the feet of the Holy Child. When Swamiji was in Switzerland, he had shown the same respect to the Madonna; his party was moving in the Alps and he spotted a small chapel, perched somewhere on the quiet mountain side. Swamiji gathered some flowers from nearby bushes and placing them in the hands of Mrs. Sevier, requested her to go to the chapel and place them at the holy feet of the Madonna, saying, 'She also is the Mother.' The sincerity of the expression had moved Mrs. Sevier. These two incidents, one in Switzerland and the other in Italy, mark out Swamiji as the bridge between the East and the West, between various religions. All religions are to be accepted, none is to be rejected or run down.

Swamiji visited the Catacombs, the ruins of Pompeii and other such ruins, he had come to know about from his deep knowledge of Roman history, but he was feeling homesick, was eager to meet his *gurubhais* and his other disciples and friends, he was eagerly waiting to bow down at the lotus feet of the Holy Mother, Shri Sharadadevi, he was eagerly waiting for changing over from the Western dress the cold climate had forced upon him to the *sannyasin*'s single ochre cloth and, was waiting with equal eagerness to move barefeet and touch the mother earth. A pinch of dust of the motherland was worth much more than the conquests of all the continents. He felt very happy to get into the boat at Naples, join the waiting Goodwin and sail eastwards.

The pilgrim's heart was not merely full of the longing for home. It was also full of the rich harvest he had reaped single-handedly, during his stay of three and a half years in the West. His appearance in the World Parliament of Religions at Chicago was meteoric, but after that he had run in all directions in the U.S.A., in spite of granite-like opposition from the Missionaries, had sowed the seeds of *Vedanta*, of oneness of the Absolute, Indestructible, Indivisible God, of acceptance of all religions as various paths leading to that God, of love and respect for all men and all religions. He was able to initiate three Americans into *sannyasa*, make a few take the vow of continence, change the course of life of several people as in the case of the opera singer Madame Calve, and influence scholars like William James, Professor Wright, Paul Deussen, Miss Greenstidel, Miss Margaret Noble, Miss Waldo, the Seviers, Mr Sturdy and quite a few others. The Seviers had left their home lock, stock and barrel and were accompanying him to India. A few others were to follow later on for shorter or longer durations and two were to arrive later and make India their home. And the faithful Goodwin had embarked at Southampton and, as it were, was piloting the boat to Naples for Vivekananda and the Seviers to get into. They did so on 30th December, 1896, and the boat left anchor and sailed eastward.

On the last night of the year Vivekananda had a very astonishing dream. In the dream he saw an old bearded man who told him, 'Mark this place very carefully. I am one of the Therapeutic Essenes who lived here more than two thousand years ago. The great truth and ideas which we preached were presented to the world as teachings of Jesus of Nazareth. But such a person was never born. When this place is dug up in the future, various proofs attesting what I told you will come to light.'

Vivekananda suddenly woke up. It was midnight then. He strode out of his cabin and asked a sailor passing by, where the boat was at the time. Swamiji got the reply that the island of Crete was fifty miles away and the boat had just passed by the isle.

The word 'Thera' means the 'head of a group of Buddhist monks and-'peutic' is derived from the Sanskrit word 'Putra', which means 'son'. Jesus, it is said, was a follower of the 'Essen' religion or a religious sect. A dream like this could not be accepted as a historical proof about the basic facts of a religion. However, an article published in 'the Statesman,' a prestigious newspaper of Kolkata, a few years after the passing away of Swamiji, did mention that some excavation on the island of Crete, which is quite close to Asia Minor, revealed some artefacts throwing light on the birth of Christianity. A dream like this did not affect Swamiji's great regard for Christ. 'If I were living in Palestine when Christ walked on this earth, I would have washed his feet not with my tears but with the blood of my heart,' Swamiji had remarked once on seeing a painting of Jesus.

After the boat left Aden for Colombo, a strange incident took place. Two missionaries started behaving arrogantly and abusing the Hindu religion. When they could not listen to the arguments of Swamiji and see reason, but continued to show total disrespect to the Hindu religion, Swamiji caught hold of the collar of one of them and said, 'One more insulting word for my religion and I would throw you into the sea! ' A threat of force worked where all reasonable arguments had failed.

As the boat was moving southeast towards Colombo, Swamiji's heart started pounding. When he had left the shores of India on 31st May, 1893, he was an unknown, obscure, and penniless monk, totally ignorant of what name and fame he would achieve in a few months and how he would scatter the seeds of *Vedanta* in the West. Ramakrishna's prophesy of Naren 'possessing eighteen times the energy that Keshub Sen possessed' and, 'Naren will perform Ma's great work' also had come true. Naren had spread the message of *Vedanta* far and wide and had drawn the attention of the Western world to the real greatness of India. He had also exposed the hollowness of the myth of Christianity being the only 'true and great' religion. But his contribution to India was that he had awakened the giant from the stupor of a millennium, he had made the English-educated people of his country realise the grandeur of their motherland and his battle cry was the redeeming of the poverty of millions of his countrymen. In a stunning letter to his gurubhai, Gangadhar Swami Akhandananda, he had courageously added two little phrases to an ancient Upanishadic invocation which asked people to treat parents as gods, a guest as a god and a teacher as a god; 'treat the poor, downtrodden as gods, treat the illiterate as gods,' in order to serve them. Removal of poverty, untouchability, and illiteracy were the new *mantras* given by him.

The eagle was returning to its nest, tired and sick. But the great spiritual treasure he was bringing with him would not let him rest. The message of hope, awakening, and greatness of the spirit would not let him rest. As the boat was approaching the Malabar coast and the coast of Sri Lanka, his spirits revived. The rest for a fortnight on the ship and the cool, salty sea breeze helped him regain his energy. His odyssey of four years was coming to an end. His original idea in the earlier part of 1893 for going to the West was 'to get thirty crore rupees' for the removal of the poverty of India. He had certainly 'failed' in that mission. But the 'wealth' he was bringing with him was to make all India proud of him. His success in the West had given him unquestioned authority. He had established his kingdom in the hearts of men, an everlasting kingdom.

Surging as were the waters of the Indian Ocean, carrying Swamiji's steamer to Colombo, equally surging was the tide of joyfulness in the well-wishers, his disciples and the vast mass of men in the subcontinent to welcome their Deliverer back home. The recognition of Swamiji's success had been very slow, but then it had been very sure and was coming from the heart. The days of the conquest of land and of empire-building were over and the greatest of Indian emperor, Ashok the Great, had risen in the eyes of people after he had abandoned arms. Swamiji was no gun-totting cowboy or gold-digger, coloniser, or a builder of an empire. And yet he was the king of a much greater domain. Like Christ, he ruled over the hearts of men. He had conquered the heart of India and innumerable sons and daughters of the motherland were eagerly waiting to welcome their Deliverer. He had set the caged spirit of the country free and the birdlings were chirping their song of loving welcome. Swamiji had no idea of the enthusiasm, the news of his arrival had generated. Boundless was the joy and enthusiasm of Swamiji's *gurubhais* and Niranjanananda and Sadananda had dashed to Colombo to receive the uncrowned abbot of their *Math*.

As the boat carrying Swamiji sighted the palm-lined shore of Sri Lanka his heart buoyed up. Soon the skyline of Colombo became visible and, immediately thereafter, the dock where the steamer was to anchor. It was the 15th of January, three days after the thirty fourth birthday of Swamiji. The din from the shore was audible from some distance. A sea of men was there on the dock, with flags and garlands, waiting to welcome their great victorious leader coming home after about four years. Shouts of 'Vivekananda ki Jai' and the like were filling the sky. As soon as the boat came to a halt and the gate was opened for disembarkation, Niranjanananda rushed into the steamer and embraced his elder brother, Naren, now famous the world over as Swami Vivekananda. The shouts of welcome rent the sky. It was unprecedented. Swamiji was, as it were, bathed in flowers and garlands. The heart of India appeared to have moved south. Throngs and throngs of people flung themselves upon Swamiji to touch his feet. His path was strewn with flowers. There was sprinkling of rose water and of *Gangajal*. It took quite some time for Swamiji to leave the dock area and get into the waiting carriage. So high was the tide of the enthusiastic welcome.

The road was bedecked with festoons of flowers and Swamiji was taken to the Cinnamon Garden where a big, decorated *mandap* was erected. He was given a scroll of honour during his welcome. Swamiji's modest reply was, 'The honour showered upon a begging *sannyasin*, like me, reflects the spirituality of the people of the country.' He also clarified that he was not a political leader, a military general or a billionaire, but he was a penniless *sannyasin*. The enthusiastic welcome was not given to him as an individual, but to the spiritual idea behind him.

Swamiji delivered two public lectures in Colombo which were very well attended. He spoke about a 'universal religion' based on the Veda teachings. He moved to Kandy, where he was given a public reception. After a brief reply, he moved over to Anuradhapura, the ancient Buddhist place of pilgrimage. He was standing under the old tree while lecturing to a crowd of more than two thousand people. Some orthodox Buddhist monks, however, exhibited their narrow, sectarian, unBuddhist nature by blowing conches and beating drums. Swamiji bore it all patiently and advised his listeners to develop the spirit of tolerance for all religions and said that 'people might give any name but God is only one.'

From Anuradhapura, Swamiji and his party went to Jafna, 120 miles in the north, the means of transport being bullock carts. It was an experience for the Saviers. But the wide open sky, the somewhat cool January sun and the evergreen forests on both the sides of the trek, with their numerous birds filling the air with different cries, and above all this, the company of the spiritual giant, Swamiji, filling the time with his stories from ancient mythology made the four day journey a pleasant experience.

He addressed a crowd of about fifteen thousand people on his favourite theme, the *Vedanta*, for about an hour and the audience listened to it spellbound. Mr. Sevier, being requested to address, rose and spoke about why they had chosen to accept the Hindu religion and come over to India with Swamiji.

From Jafna the party took a boat to reach Pamban, about 125 kilometres West. Swamiji was given a royal welcome there, by Bhaskar Setupati, the Raja of the Ramnad State. The Raja had come in close contact with Swamiji during his wanderings in the country in 1893. As soon as Swamiji came out of the royal boat sent by the Raja, a tumultous shout of welcome rent the air. In a specially constructed, decorated *mandap*, Swamiji was given an address of welcome. In his emotionally charged reply, Swamiji thankfully mentioned the name of the Raja as one who was very keen on Swamiji's going to the West.

When the function was over, the royal carriage was kept ready to take Swamiji to the King's palace. But the king ordered to unfasten the horses and he started pulling Swamiji's carriage. Other volunteers also joined the king in pulling the carriage. It was an honour to do so. The carriage, thus pulled, went round the main roads of the town and was ultimately taken to the royal palace.

On the next day, Swamiji went to the gigantic temple of Rameshvaram and in his first public address on the Indian soil, Swamiji gave the clarion call: worship Lord Shiva in the poor, the weak and the suffering. This message so penetrated the heart of the Raja of Ramnad that on the very next day he satisfied thousands of poor people by giving them food articles and clothes.

From there, his northward journey started. He visited Ramnad, Manamadurai Madurai and Trichinapalli and reached Kumbhakonam. The story of welcoming shouts, falling at Swamiji's feet, profuse garlanding, mass processions and mass meetings in honour of the great triumph of a son of their mother India, addresses of welcome followed by Swamiji's replies became a regular routine. People would crowd the place, where he would be staying at all odd hours, to seek his blessings, to have his *darshan* and to touch his feet. His health, already run down by the assiduous work in the West undertaken by him for three and a half years, found it difficult to cope up with this onslaught of incessant chain of visitors from early morning to night. The train he was travelling by was not to stop at a small station. The town people were eager to have the Swami's *darshan*. They found out a way. They all lay down on the rails and the engine driver of the train carrying Swamiji noticed that the rails, for about half a mile, were covered by human beings. He brought the train to a halt, people on the rails stood up, shouted Swamiji's 'Jai,' Swamiji came out of the train compartment and gave *darshan* to the people and blessed them. The train could travel further only after that. All this was very exhausting and Swamiji had an idea of the madness he would be facing in Madras. Therefore, he rested for three days at Kumbhakonam before going to Madras (now called Chennai).

The city of Madras had got frenzied to welcome Swamiji. The main thoroughfares were decorated with festoons of flowers and green mango leaves. As many as seventeen arches were erected along the road Swamiji's carriage was to pass through and numerous posters and placards with writings like, 'Welcome, Messenger of Peace,' 'Long Live Revered Swami Vivekananda,' 'Awakened India Bows Down To You.'..etc., were displayed prominently. Local newspapers vied with one another in showering welcome to Swamiji. The heart of every Madrasi was overflowing with love and respect for Swamiji.

It was the morning of 6th February, 1897. Thousands of people had thronged at the railway station to welcome their dear hero, who had raised the head of Mother India high once more. The Madras disciples were more fortunate than Swamiji's *gurubhais* at Kolkata, because at Swamiji's instance and guidance and help the first journal *Brahmavadin* had been started from Madras. From thousands of miles away, Swamiji was providing all possible financial help and guidance to the inexperienced but highly enthusiastic Madras disciples.

Swamiji satisfied Madras by staying there for full nine days and, besides the reply to the public reception given to him, he had delivered five public lectures, setting the tone of the work he intended to do and its direction also. The subjects of the Madras lectures were: (1) *'My Plan of Campaign,* (2) *Vedanta in its Application to Indian Life,* (3) *The Sages of India,* (4) *The Work Before Us,* (5) *The Future of India*. Besides these five public lectures, he was invited to preside over the annual meeting of 'Chennapuri Annadana Samajam,' where he had spoken on *charity,* as befitting the occasion.

After initial formalities, Vivekananda boldly declared, 'I had a message from India to the West and boldly I gave it to the American and the English people.' With the same boldness, Swamiji pointed to the false propaganda by the Theosophists that they had 'helped' him in America and England. 'I have to tell you plainly that every word of it is wrong, every word of it is untrue.' Swamiji then told his audience about the strong opposition he had to face from the Christian Missionaries, mentioning the lies they hurled at him. He also mentioned how jealousy made

Pratap Majumdar of the Brahmo Samaj join the chorus of abuse initiated by the Missionaries and the Theosophists. Of course, he did not mention Pratap by name. Madras was—and is—the headquarters of Theosophy. In this way, he exposed all those who had tried their best to tarnish his image. But it had all amounted to just throwing dust at the sun.

But he soon turned to his theme, 'My Plan of Campaign.' A *sannyasin* and campaign are two contradictory terms. Vivekananda, however, was no ordinary *sannyasin* and a campaign was the need of the times—*Yuga Dharma* as they put it in Sanskrit. 'I have a message for the world which I will deliver without fear and without care for the future,' proclaimed Swamiji courageously. Social reform movement was going on all over India and Swamiji pointed out that 'I am a greater reformer than any one of them (the reformers in the country, particularly in Bengal and in Madras Presidency), but he said, 'I do not believe in reforms, I believe in growth.... This wonderful national machine has worked through ages, this wonderful river of national life is flowing before us. Who knows and who dares to say whether it is good and how shall it move?...Ay children, to try to remedy evil is not the true way,....The history of the world teaches us that wherever there have been fanatical reforms, the only result has been that they have defeated their own purpose.' Swamiji had seen the failure of the zeal of the Brahmo reformers and so he had come to the conclusion that no effective change could take place in a society by thrusting a zealous revolutionary change upon it. He believed in evolution.

Speaking about the opposition of the religious reformers to idol worship, he said, 'If such Ramakrishna Paramhansas are produced by idol worship, what will you have, the reformer's creed or any number of idols?.'

Swamiji then enunciated his plan of 'campaign.' 'My plan is to follow the ideas of the great ancient Masters...In India religious life forms the centre, "the keynote" of the whole music of national life, and if any nation attempts to throw off its national vitality— the direction which has become its own through the transmission of centuries—that nation dies if it succeeds in the attempt.'

Romain Rolland, who had seen nationalism at its worst in Europe, who had seen the entire continent of Europe fall a prey to the havoc caused by narrow nationalism, was not quite tolerant of any shadow of nationalism visible or audible in the energising message of Vivekananda and showed his displeasure at the desperate efforts of Gandhi to make religious spirit dominate political action (p.221, *The Life of Vivekananda*), probably failed to understand the Gandhian approach to life on the one hand, and the spirit of nationalism both Vivekananda and Gandhi wanted to awaken in a people lying dormant for about a thousand years. The sinews of India had to be strengthened. Even though Vivekananda's objective was spiritual awakening, he had kept himself away from politics. Shri Sharadama was to say later on, around 1910, when all Bengal was gripped by the fervent opposition to the partition of Bengal, 'even my Naren would have been behind the bars today.' Very few knew Naren as well as she did. Swamiji's emphasis, however, was on 'an upheaval of the spirit.'

'My plan', Swamiji said, 'is to start institutions in India, to train our young men as preachers of the truths of our scriptures in India and outside.' Why this emphasis? He further said, 'Everything else will be ready, but strong, vigorous, believing young men, sincere to the backbone, are wanted.' 'A hundred such and the world becomes revolutionised.' Mark the words: He wanted to revolutionise not merely India, but the entire world, and on the lines of the *Upanishads*. His was not a political revolution. It was a spiritual revolution. And, in order to succeed, he asked his listeners to make their nerves strong. 'What we want is muscles of iron and nerves of steel..... It is a man-making religion that we want. It is man-making theories that we want. It is man-making education all round that we want.... Give up these weakening mysticisms and be strong. Go back to your *Upanishads*—the shining, the strengthening, the bright philosophy—and part from all these mysterious things, all these weakening things, all these weakening things.'

He then added: ...'I believe in patriotism, and I also have my own ideal of patriotism.... First, feel from the heart. What is in the intellect or reason?.... Do you feel that millions are starving today, and millions have been starving for ages? Do you feel that ignorance has come over the land as a dark cloud?'... Swamiji's patriotism did not mean only freedom from political subjugation. It meant economic improvement of the masses, removal of all barriers of the caste system, educational improvement of the people. Gandhi had picked up the cue and he had admitted a Muslim family and the family of an untouchable to his *ashrama,* had initiated movement for the upliftment of the scheduled castes and scheduled tribes, had strived for the Hindu-Muslim unity and had drawn up a revolutionary plan of education, while carrying on his fight for freedom. And the basic principle of his fight was love and his weapons were truth and non-violence. Swami Vivekananda had coined the word *Daridranarayana*—God in the Poor—and Gandhi had made it a current coin. The seed laid by Swamiji sprouted and came to fructify in Gandhiji.

This was the bugle blown by Swamiji to wake up the dormant nation. And his electrifying words did shake up the dormant mass of men and women. It took a few years for the Rip Wan' Winkle to come out of the stupor of ages. But when, eight years later, Lord Curzon partitioned Bengal, the youths who joined the Anushilan Movement and such other movements, swore by Vivekananda. The Koalpada *Ashrama* and the home of Sharadadevi at Jairamvati were under constant vigil by the British police. A few young men who had been drawn to the cult of violence underwent change and had later joined the Ramakrishna Order. In this way, in both war and peace, the youth of India had taken refuge in Swamiji.

In his second lecture on the subject of '*Vedanta* and Indian Life', Swamiji scales sublimity. The subject was dearest to his heart and the Madras audience was very receptive. After pointing to the multiplicity of beliefs and practices in the Hindu religion, Swamiji says, 'All our sects agree that we all believe in the scriptures—the *Vedas*...The *Vedas* are divided into two portions—the *Karma Kanda* and the *Jnana Kanda*---The *Janana Kanda*, as embodying the spiritual teachings of the *Vedas* known as the *Upanishads* and the *Vedanta*, has always been cited as the highest authority by all our teachers, philosophers and writers, whether dualist or qualified monist or monist.' After some elaboration, Swamiji jumps upon the *Upanishads* and either quotes from one or the other *Upanishad* or translates some great passages from the great writings. And then he thunders: 'Strength, strength is what the *Upanishads* speak to me from every page... stand up and be strong. Ay, it is the only literature in the world where you find the word "Abhih," "fearless," used again and again; in no other scripture in the world is this adjective applied either to God or to man.... The *Upanishads* are the great mine of strength. Therein lies strength enough to invigorate the whole world, the whole world can be vivified, made strong, energised through them.'

This was the trumpet call Swamiji gave to the entire nation and thereby made the nation aware of freedom, not in the narrow political sense, but he talked of physical, mental and spiritual freedom. '*Upanishads,*' he emphatically declared, 'do not talk of salvation, but of freedom.' Like the traditional *pandits* and *sannyasins*, he did not put *dvaitism* against *advaitism*, but, following his guru, he said that *dvaitism*, qualified *advaitism* and *advaitism* were steps for one to climb and go higher and higher. Pointing to the divided and disorganised Hindu society, Swamiji said, 'we are hopelessly disorganised mobs, immensely selfish, fighting each other for centuries as to whether a certain mark is to be put on our forehead this way or that way.... We cannot expect anything high from a race whose whole brain energy has been occupied in such wonderfully beautiful problems and researches.' This was how he whipped the absurd customs of the society. 'Centuries and centuries, a thousand years of crushing tyranny of castes and kings and foreigners and your own people have taken out all your strength', he lashed.

'What is the remedy, then? Strength, strength is what we want. And the first step in getting strength is to uphold the *Upanishads*, and believe—"I am the Soul"... "I am the Omnipotent, I am the Omniscient. "This great message, must come out, must remain not only in the forest, not only in the cave, but must come out at the bar and the bench, in the pulpit and in the cottage of the poor man, with the fisherman who is catching fish, and with students who are studying." In short, he wanted everyone to inherit the great message of the *Upanishads* and live by it.

In his next lecture on 'The Sages of India,' there is again the theme of harmony: 'He, the great preacher of harmony, the greatest teacher of harmony, Lord Shri Krishna! The characteristic of Ramanuja was, 'the opening of the door of spirituality to everyone.' He then talked of Chaitanya and then mentioning his guru, Shri Ramakrishna, he said that Shri Ramakrishna had 'the great head of Shankara and 'the large heart of Chaitanya.'

'The Work Before us' and "The Future of India,' the two other lectures Swamiji delivered at Madras are very similar in their tone and emphasis. Briefly tracing the history of India, Swamiji emphasised on the absence of military conquests by 'India, and on spreading the message of love and harmony in many of the neighbouring countries.' At the same time, he never failed to point out the isolationism, the rigidity of the hierarchical caste system, refusal to learn from other nations and the sense of false pride which brought about the downfall of the country. Naturally, he wanted all these evil customs to go, he exhorted his countrymen to go back to the *Upanishads* and establish contacts with other nations and to learn from them.

In spite of his poor health, Swamiji had chosen to stay for 9 days in Madras, give five public lectures to huge crowds and meet an incessant chain of visitors, because in this way he was reciprocating what Madras had done for him prior to his departure to America. The frenzy of the people could be measured by the addresses Swamiji was presented there. All of them were not from the city of Madras itself, but they numbered two dozens. The Maharaja of Khetdi, a good friend of the Swamiji, had sent one, and several professors of the Harward University in the U.S.A. had also sent one. It was signed by William James, Professor Wright and others. The spectacle of their dear Swamiji, after winning international laurel, back amongst them was too great to be imagined by non Indians. In spite of his frail health, Swamiji had exerted himself quite a lot. So, instead of going by train, Swamiji preferred a boat. He left Madras on 15th February. The quiet, undisturbed voyage of a couple of days and the cool sea breeze would help him get back some energy. He very much desired to go to the Himalayas and breathe the cool, dry mountain air.

Landing at the Khidirpur docks and catching a special train, specially arranged for him, when Swamiji arrived at the Sealdah station, the shouts of 'Jai' rent the air. The number of garlands offered to him was simply unimaginable. And the mass of men on the railway platform was so milling that Swamiji and the party could go out of the station with great difficulty. An open Victoria, well decorated and bedecked with flowers was kept ready and Swamiji and the Seviers got into it. The horses were unyoked and young people started pulling the carriage with great enthusiasm. In front of the carriage was a band party and a group of people singing *kirtan*s and dancing. An informal reception was arranged at the Ripon College. The formal one was to take place a week later. No royalty was ever welcomed with this enthusiasm, with this affection. It was the triumphant homecoming of the son of Kolkata and all Kolkata, it seemed, had gone mad. Swamiji and the Seviers were taken to the bungalow of one Gopallal Seal in the Kashipur area. Though Swamiji stayed at the bungalow during the daytime, he rushed to spend the nights with his dear *gurubhais* at the Alambazar *Math*.

The day of February 28, 1897 was marked as a red letter day in the calendar of Kolkata, because five thousand people had assembled to honour their fellow citizen who had raised the head of India high amongst the assembly of the religious leaders of the world, thousands of miles away. The story of the thunderous applause at the very beginning of Swamiji's first short speech, followed by the rush of the back benchers to the front with a more thunderous clapping when he had finished that short *Upanishad* like speech of his, had taken quite some time to reach his home town. But once it had reached, people's hearts were flared up by national pride and awakening of national consciousness. The meeting was attended by Rajas, *Pandits*, and leading luminaries from all walks of life, by several *sannyasins* and even by a few Europeans. An address was presented to Swamiji and when Swamiji stood up to reply, the assembled people felt that the angel of modern India was speaking. There was a strong sentiment of nationalism in his reply, delivered as it were like Demosthenes. He spoke with great feeling about the Renaissance of India. He exhorted his countrymen to cast away all weakness, all inertia and go back to the rich spiritual inheritance left by the forefathers. 'Religion,' he said, 'is not external practice, but internal purity, tolerance and breaking of all barriers that divide.' This heroic speech made a powerful impact on the audience.

A couple of days later, it was the birth anniversary of Shri Ramakrishna. As per the custom, they celebrated it at the Kali Temple, the place of his *sadhana,* at Dakshineshvar. The celebration this time had an added significance in the fact that, the main apostle of Shri Ramakrishna had returned home only a few days ago, winning laurels in the countries of the white rulers! This was no mean achievement for the people, who were taught to consider the white people as superior.

A huge crowd had assembled at the Kali Temple to pay their obeisance to the Goddess, to her great devotee Shri Ramakrishna and to his great disciple Swami Vivekananda. Swamiji was filled with devotion as he went round all the old familiar places so closely associated with Shri Ramakrishna and so deeply engraved in his own memory. He was returning there after a lapse of seven years. He prostrated himself before the idol of the Universal Mother, Kali, paid obeisance to the other deities, visited Shri Ramakrishna's room, went to the Panchavati, where he had performed his *sadhana* and old memories welled up in his mind. He showed each one of the places to his foreign guests, narrating many old incidents and explaining everything in detail. He considered such celebrations necessary for keeping the lamp of spirituality burning in the masses who would find the Absolute Truth too difficult to comprehend.

A few days afterwards, he gave a public lecture in Kolkata on 'The *vedanta* in all its phases.' He had given a lucid exposition of his subject, which was so dear to his heart. '*Vedanta,*' he said, 'was the diadem of all philosophies. The Hindus should call themselves *Vedantins* first and Hindus next.' He also asked the audience to go back to the *Upanishads* and emphatically said that all activities and all movements of our life life must be based on the sublime teachings of the *Upanishads*.

'The nights he spent with his *gurubhais* at the Alambazar *Math* were very refreshing. He gave them an account of his experiences in the West, sometimes touching, sometimes hilarious. In a letter to a gurubhai in the winter of 1894, he had written that the cold was so intense that he feared his nose would fall off and pugnacious also in his references to the vile attacks by the missionaries, a bit resentful while talking about the Theosophists and Pratap, and appreciative of many people like Professor Wright, William James, Max Muller, Deussen, etc.

His days began quite early and ended very late, leaving him hardly any privacy or any time that could be called his own. Incessant chain of visitors, most of them unknown, flocked around him to seek quick solutions to their problems, easy answers to their questions, or just to satisfy their curiosity. Quite a few pestered him and sought his help in their causes, some of which were odious. A few *pandits* and youths went to him not to seek his guidance but to show their knowledge and draw him into arguments. But those sophists were soon floored by him. When a *pandit* in Madras had approached Swamiji and put a question in Sanskrit, Swamiji, replying in chaste Sanskrit, asked the *pandit* first to correct two grammatical errors in the question he had put to Swamiji.

All this pressure of hectic work coupled with the warm, moisture-laden air of Kolkata affected the already feeble health of Swamiji and he was advised to move to cool, dry air and away from the madding crowds. The only relieving feature was the addition of a few young men to the *Math*.

Swamiji went to Darjeeling in the Himalayas, along with the Seviers, Goodwin, a couple of his *gurubhais* as well as with Girish Ghosh. But a few days passed and he had to run down to Kolkata, to meet his friend, the Raja of Khetdi, who was proceeding to England and, who very much desired to take Swamiji with him. Swamiji came down to Kolkata to meet his dear friend but he was too ill to undertake the long voyage. He was advised complete rest by doctors. So, after seeing Ajit Sinh, the Raja of Khetdi, Swamiji once more went back to Darjeeling, to peep at the snow-clad peaks.

20

Weaving the Web

Vivekananda had started going out of the dilapidated *Math* in 1888 and finally his wanderlust had dragged him out of the capital of the British Indian Empire, taken him to the Himalayas, the sacred places of the Hindus, the ruined cities of the Muslim rulers—big and small, to zealots and to the noble-hearted, to the palaces of royalties, to the huts of the poor and to the roofless ones, great savants, illiterate people, nationalist leaders, philanthropists, the miserly, people with deep understanding, the progressives moving with the times, and the narrow minded traditionalists who would not budge even a millimetre from the beliefs and customs of a hoary past, people talking different languages and dialects of the country, talking in Sanskrit, Persian English and even French. He had seen the wounds and scars of his country, that had penetrated to the very bones. He had also seen the spiritual unity of the country, the blood that had been keeping the country still alive.

The desire to lift his brethren out of the wringing poverty and to spread the message of *Vedanta* in the West had taken him out of the country to far away America. In spite of all odds against him, he had burst forth like a rocket, flaring the entire horizon with its blinding light, and all of a sudden, from a mere nobody, he had become world famous.

He had not been successful in bringing money from America for the removal of the poverty of his countrymen. But the effect of his bursting forth at Chicago had electrified India, had rejuvenated India and had hastened the pace of her renaissance.

His was not at all a restricted political mission, yet his all-life-embracing approach had germinated various beds—social, educational, religious, spiritual, political etc., in the vast garden of India. But these were all side effects. His guru had once given a great *mantra*, *Shiva Jnane Jeevaseva,* realise God through the service of living beings. He wanted to put that *mantra* into practice.

In his letters addressed to his *gurubhais* individually or jointly, he had been hinting at the work to be done. We see the hinting right from his letter to Shashi—Ramakrishnananda—written from Chicago on 19th March, 1894. But in his letter addressed to all the members of the Alambazar *Math* from 'Reading in England' on 27th April, 1896, (C.W, VII, PP 491-498) Swamiji began by asserting his authority. He (Ramakrishna) gave me the charge of you all..... Hence I jot down the following hints,' says Swamiji. Then he began by laying down rules for the *Math*. In an earlier letter to his gurubhai Akhandananda, who had launched upon some activity of service to the deprived, Swamiji had showered praises on his gurubhai for the work he was doing and had hinted on the importance of such work. Since the *sannyasins* of a *Math* could not undertake any such activity, an institution, other than the *Math*, had to be established. In his letter to his gurubhai Akhandananda, written from the U.S.A. in March or April, 1894 (C.W.,VI.pp 287-88), Swamiji clearly injuncts, 'Go from door to door amongst the poor and lower classes of the town of Khetdi and teach them religion.... The poor, the ignorant, the afflicted—let them be your God. Know that service to them alone is the highest religion.'

If not to the mission, this is a direct reference to missionary activities. Such hints are seen in his letters to Shashi (Ramakrishnanda), of 19-03-1894, Rakhal (Brahmananda), of 1895, all his *gurubhais* (27-04-1896) etc. In different letters, he had asked his *gurubhais* not to remain confined within the four walls of the *Math*, singing *bhajans* and sitting in meditation, and worshipping the picture of Shri Ramakrishna. Now that he was back in India, the first thing he wanted to do was to have an organization, rather to have two organizations, one was the *Math*, where novices are trained and initiated into *Sannyasa* and absorbed in the Ramakrishna movement. And the other organization he wanted to raise, was the Ramakrishna Mission, to put into practice the *Vedanta* that had remained so far confined to the secluded Maths or caves. 'All are *Brahman*,' as preached by the *Vedanta*, 'all have to be served like Brahman, particularly those who have been deprived, dispossessed and kept out of bounds by the caste-ridden society.' Even while he was busy, receiving welcome addresses and replying to them, even while landing at Colombo he was surrounded by worshipping masses, and even though he was internally completely worn out, he would not rest untill the two institutions, so dear to his heart, took shape.

So he had arranged a meeting of all the disciples and devotees of Shri Ramakrishna to be called on May 1, 1897, at the house of late Balaram Basu. From the cool air of Darjeeling, Swamiji came down to the stifling heat of Kolkata. And when he proposed regular foundation of the Ramakrishna *Math*, with its rules and regulations and the proposal to get it registered so as to give it a legal status, it was wholeheartedly applauded.

But when he proposed the establishment of the Ramakrishna Mission, the response was quite different. Was it not an imitation of the Christian Missionaries? Would not the missionary activities bind the *sannyasins* with another kind of fetters? If the *sannyasins* keep themselves engaged in such activities, where would they find time for prayers and meditation? Do such service activities have any scriptural sanction? Would not these activities divert the minds of the *sannyasins* from seeking salvation? Had Ramakrishna ever enjoined such work?

These objections touched Vivekananda to the quick and he got excited. He asked, "How do you know that all these ideas do not fit into Gurudeva's thinking?... Do you want to imprison Shri Ramakrishna, who was the living idol of infinite moods, into the confines of your ideas... I'll break down all such boundaries and spread his ideas all over the world. He had never asked me to confine myself to the worship of his picture... He taught us many high ideals; we should practise them and preach them to mankind..."

..... "I have experienced Gurudeva's grace many a time in my life. I believe it is he, who, is standing behind me and inspiring me to do all these things... Ramakrishna was much greater than what his disciples think him to be... His grace could produce lakhs of Vivekanandas this very moment! But if he desires to have his work done through me, I must submit myself to his desire.'

The proposal was then accepted, but all present there did not do so whole-heartedly. A few days afterwards, a gurubhai remarked that the mission activities did not fit in with the preachings of Gurudeva, and such activities would divert the minds of the disciples from spiritual practices and devotion to various activities, and as a result, the *sannyasins* would become oriented to outside work preventing them from their *sadhana*. Swamiji started replying at first in a lighter vein, but soon flared up and said, "Do you all think you understand Shri Ramakrishna more than I do? You all believe knowledge to be absolutely dry and that it can be acquired through the dry path and that all delicate and noble emotions of the heart have to be butchered? Your devotion, really, is nothing but a loud expression of feeling; such devotion will make man a coward.... Who cares for your devotion and salvation? Who cares for scriptural injunctions? If I am able to awaken my countrymen rolling in *tamas* and inspire them to accept the path of *karma yoga*, I am prepared to go a thousand times to hell even. I am not a follower of Ramakrishna or of anyone else. I am the follower of him, who puts my plan into practice. I am neither a slave of Ramakrishna nor of anyone else. I am the slave of that person who does not care for salvation and helps and serves others."

While uttering these words, his body had started trembling and his voice had got choked, so terrific was the surge of feeling in him. Tears started flowing from his eyes. With lightning speed he got up from the meeting hall and swiftly retired to his room. A hush descended on the audience. His *gurubhais* started worrying. They felt remorse for their criticism. They were worried. Some time passed by. Then a couple of Swamiji's *gurubhais* made bold to get up and go to the room of Swamiji. They were awe struck at the sight. Swamiji was sitting crosslegged on the floor. His eyes were half closed. He was meditating. His whole body appeared charged with his deep feeling. Tears were running down from his half-closed eyes. No one dared to disturb him from his *samadhi*. An entire hour passed by. Then Swamiji himself rejoined his companions. Nobody dared to break the silence. Swamiji himself began speaking in a quiet tone. "When a persron gets absorbed in devotion, his or her heart and nerves become so subtle and delicate that the person cannot bear even the touch of flowers!.....I cannot think of Shri Ramakrishna or talk about him without being sentimental... I am trying hard to put my mind into steel shackles of knowledge, because my task for my country has not been over as yet...I have a lot of work to do. I am Shri Ramakrishna's slave and he has assigned me a lot of work. So long as I don't perform it, he would not let me rest.... "

This was enough for his *gurubhais*. They all understood the great milling effort of Vivekananda in suppressing his devotion and accept the path of knowledge. The chapter was not closed and they tried to provide some change to Swamiji and arranged for him to go out for a stroll. Swamiji regained his normalcy at night.

The motto that Swamiji had chosen for the Mission was very telling: 'For the salvation of the self, for the good of the world'. The way of the salvation of the self lies through the service of the world. And the world includes all living beings, all life. All emphasis was on service only.

Swamiji had seen the necessity of having a proper building for the *Math*. His *gurubhais* were moving like kittens from place to place. He was a farsighted man and he found a piece of fifteen acres of land at Belur, on the other side of the river, almost opposite to the Kali Temple complex at Dakshineshvar. Thanks to the help of an American disciple of the Swami, the land was purchased and in order to be near the construction site, the *Math* from Alambazar was shifted to the house of Nilambar Mukherji, closeby to the land they had purchased.

Swamiji's poor health forced him to retire to the Himalayas. Along with his foreign friends, he went to Almora, where very soon, later on, the *Advaita Ashrama*, so dear to the Seviers, took shape. In a letter to his American sister, Mary Hale, Swamiji had clearly expressed his poor health condition and said that, he would not live longer than four or five years. Unfortunately, this tragic prophecy was to come true. At Almora, Swamiji met a Muslim gentleman, who bowed down to the former very reverentially and became his disciple. He was a Muslim and Swamiji appropriately initiated him as 'Mahammadananda. Swamiji kept moving northwards to Amritsar, Lahore, Muree and Srinagar in Kashmir.

Swamiji had undertaken two trips to Kashmir. His second trip of 1898 was a very memorable one. He was being accompanied by Sister Nivedita and a couple of American Friends, Mrs. Ole Bull and Miss Macleod. They were moving in a separate houseboat. The destination, ultimately, was the mountain cave of Amarnath which is so snow-bound that the *yatra* takes place every year only for a month or so, around August, when the snows along the high mountain path have melted. Inside the cave, there is no stone idol or *lingam*, natural or established by some people. The *lingam* is a natural formation of snow. The way to the cave is extremely hazardous. One has to cross hills and dales and many rivulets carrying ice cold water, and the precipitous path along the side of mountain summits is extremely risky.

The *Advaita* Vedantin in Swamiji had been subdued by the devotion to Shiva and Kali, the God and The Goddess of the dance of destruction, of death. Swamiji's great poem, '*Kali, the Mother,*' was written on one of these days. He was so possessed by Kali that he saw the terrific form of the Goddess face to face. A horrible vision of Kali came to him one evening, and gripped by it he immediately started writing down the poem:

The flash of lurid light
Reveals on every side
A thousand, thousand shades
Of death begrimed and black -
Scattering plagues and sorrows,
Dancing mad with joy.
Come, Mother, Come.

These lines clearly indicate that he was invoking death. Speaking to Sister Nivedita, who was accompanying him on his pilgrimage, Swamiji asked her to 'Meditate on Death, to worship the "Terrible". Life and death are inseparable. One should not run away from Death. One has to accept Death, the Terrible.

He took bath in the five ice cold rivulets—the *Pancha Taranis,* before entering the cave of the Immortal God, Amarnath. He sat in meditation facing the snow *lingam.* When he came out, Nivedita's sharp eye noticed that he was totally transformed. He was no longer himself. A paroxysm of Shiva worship seemed to have gripped his entire being. Nivedita was shaken to the very bones at this sight. She was overwhelmed at the idea of 'God in the earthquake' or 'God in a volcano,' as she has so pointedly put it in 'The Master as I saw Him.' Romain Rolland's sharp eye points out the difference between the attitudes of Shri Ramakrishna and Swami Vivekananda very vividly. 'Ramakrishna bowed his head and kissed the Divine foot which trampled on his heart. Vivekananda, head erect, looked death in the eye, and his sombre joy of action rejoiced in it. He ran to hurl himself 'upon the point of the sword." (The Life of Vivekananda,

Footnote, P.143). Swamiji had said, 'I have hugged the form of Death...Shiva himself has entered into my brain.'

We get an account of this trip from Nivedita's great book. 'The Master as I Saw Him.' We also have reminiscences of the two American ladies, who accompanied Swamiji.

He was invited to deliver lectures at various places. His lecture at Lahore on *Vedanta* was a very inspiring one. One Tirtha Ram, a professor at a local college, was so moved that he left service, became a *sannyasin* and came to be known as Swami Ram Tirtha. All this strain was telling upon the health of Swamiji and was taking away any advantage the dry climate might have given in bringing him around. And although he was wandering, his heart was set on the construction work going on at Belur.

Before returning to Kolkata, an affectionate call from the Maharaja of Khetdi took him to Khetdi. An interesting incident happened at Alwar. During his earlier wanderings, seven years ago, as an unknown *sannyasin*, a poor old widow had taken kindly to him and had served him a meal of oven-fresh millet chapati. Swamiji surprised his hosts at Alwar by expressing a desire to be taken to the hut of the old widow for a similar meal. The old dame was overjoyed and served the Swamiji the hot millet chapati with whatever dal or vegetable she could procure. She considered herself blessed. On his part, Swamiji treated her with filial respect and at the time of his departure he slipped a hundred rupee note in the hand of the simple old devotee. After going around a few places in Rajasthan, Swamiji and his party returned to Kolkata.

The construction work on the new premises was progressing. It was not going to be merely a place of residence of sadhus. An academy for training young novices was to be constructed. A temple dedicated to Shri Ramakrishna, free from all sectarianism and universal in character had to be put up. There had to be guest houses for visitors, there had to be a library befitting the ideal of the *Math* and the Mission, keeping its windows open to all the winds of the world. The *Math* was consecrated on December 8, 1898.

But before the building of the new *Math* could come up, the activity of providing relief to the famine striken people started. Soon after the establishment of the *Math* and the Mission on May 1, 1898, Swami Akhandananda, instead of accompanying Swami Vivekananda and his party to the hills, chose to go to Murshidabad, the Nawab's capital once, and to the battlefield of Plassey, where Robert Clive had defeated the Nawab's army by all foul means. He was carrying two rupees with him to pay for railway fare, ferry charges etc. One late evening he arrived at a place called Dadpur and, there being no place for him to go to at that late hour, he slept on a stone platform in front of a shop. Out of the amount of two rupees he had with him at the start of the journey a few days ago, now he had four annas, one quarter of one rupee, left with him.

Next morning he got up quite early and after attending to other matters of personal hygiene, had a dip into the waters of the Ganga flowing near by. After saying his prayers, while he was returning from the river bank towards the village, he saw a poorly clad lean, and emaciated Muslim girl of about fourteen years weeping loudly. When Akhandananda asked her why she was crying, amidst sobs, she pointed to a broken earthen pot and said, 'Baba, this was the only pot in our hut for carrying water from the Ganga and storing it at home. We have no other pot. It is broken into pieces. My mother will thrash me the moment I reach home. I can only weep.' This stark truth moved Swami Akhandananda to pity and he took the girl to a nearby shop and got her an earthen pot for two paise, one half of an anna, and purchased some parched rice for another two paise. The girl was happy and she left with a smile. Akhandananda now had three annas—three sixteenth of one rupee—left with him.

A few boys with hungry bellies and torn clothes had been watching the young monk helping the Muslim girl. They ran up to Akhandananda and pointing to their empty stomachs begged of him to give them something to eat. The Swami purchased fried rice worth the three annas he was left with and distributed the eatables to the children surrounding him.

Then somebody called him to go to the help of an old woman suffering from cholera. Akhandananda rushed immediately and began cleaning the old woman wallowing in dirt. Akhandananda procured some medicine, administered it and procured some food also. He left a couple of days later, only after the old woman had recovered. The old woman, Gaya, said: 'you must have been my son in a previous birth.' 'I am your son in this birth,' was the Swami's reply. All around there were dark shadows of famine. He decided to stay there and wrote a letter to the headquarters for help. This was the first work of famine relief undertaken by the Ramakrishna Mission. That small seed of a quarter rupee—it was a small silver coin—has grown into a mighty banyan tree, and the Ramakrishna Mission spends today millions of rupees every year in famine relief, flood relief, earthquake relief etc. After the devastating earthquake of 2001 in Kutchh and other parts of Gujarat, the Ramakrishna Mission has helped to construct about a hundred school buildings apart from providing houses to hundreds of families.

The idea that was burning in the brain of Swamiji—to start the *machine* for elevating the Indian masses, as Swamiji himself confessed—which in the short span of his life after the finding of the Ramakrishna Mission, came to succeed to a certain extent during that period, has now come to be put into practice in a big way. This is so because, as Swamiji had said, 'God is with me,' in other words, God is with his work. The machine he put to work in 1897 has been in strong working order. He had prophesied the Mission's future working when he had confidently said, "knowing for certain that I have put in a lever for the good of the humanity, in India at least, which no power can drive back. I will sleep without caring what will be next," Romain Rolland (*The Life of Swami Vivekananda*).

Before arriving back in India in 1897, Swamiji had started a centre, each in New York and London. Immediately after he arrived in Kolkata, he had sent his gurubhai Shashi—Swami Ramakrishnananda—to Madras. The five centres of 1897 have now grown to about 150 and are spread from Tokyo in the east to

San Fransisco in the West and from Australia in the south to Moscow in the north. They keep the flag of *Vedanta* flying. The peculiarity of all these centres, particularly in foreign countries, is that unlike Christianity and Islam, there is no proselitising activity at all. The great value of the Vedantic preaching is that it makes a Christian a better Christian, a Muslim a better Muslim. *Vedanta* only injects spiritual strength. It does not boast of being the only way to God.

In spite of this, two enthusiastic persons were initiated into *sannyasa* by Swami Vivekananda before he had returned to India. And the Sevier couple, Miss Waldo, Mrs. Ole Bull and Goodwin had accompanied him to India. Miss Margaret Noble from London though originally hailing from Ireland and Miss Greenstidel from Detroit had followed Swamiji to India to serve India. Miss Noble came to be known as Sister Nivedita and Miss Greenstidel as Sister Christine. They were two devoted and dedicated young ladies. There have been quite a few cases of people in various countries being moved by the message of *Vedanta* and joining the Ramakrishna *Math*. Aldous Huxley and Christopher Isherwood sought solace in Shri Ramakrishna and took refuge in the *Vedanta Centre* in California. A very outstanding example is that of Marie Louise Burke, Sister Gargi, who did tremendous research on the stay of Swami Vivekananda in America and unearthed a lot of material throwing floodlight on Swamiji's stay in America during the period and his magnificant personality.

All this shows the prophetic vision of Swamiji, as foretold by his great Master, Shri Ramakrishna Paramahansa. The Ramakrishna *Math* and the Ramakrishna Mission gave a distinct, new turn to the traditional Hindu religion, tore the veil of many 'dolls' without making any 'Nora' leave her house, inspired political activists and played a major role in uplifting the country from its thousand years' stupor.

True spiritual path is a path of love and service and nothing is stronger than love.

21

Nourishing the Infant

After returning from the Amarnath cave in August, 1898, Swamiji had said that Lord Shiva had given him the boon of death when he wished it. So, his body was fighting against death, yet he wanted to achieve as much as he could, in the short span of life at his disposal. When the consecration ceremony of the new *Math* was taking place, Swamiji was leading a procession of his *gurubhais* and the devotees of Shri Ramakrishna, with a pot of the ashes and relics of their guru on his head. The mood of the procession was laid down by the dancing and *kirtan*-singing Swamiji. The mood was infectious. Most of the people had not dreamt of such an event. Their joy was beyond description. They were not able to foresee the growth of the seedling into a mighty banyan tree, with its branches taking root in various places in the country and in other parts of the world. It was natural on the part of Swamiji to give proper nourishment to the infant sprout by fixing its routine, by laying down rules, regulations and guidelines, by prescribing food and medicine in the form of its curriculum.

A couple of Swamiji's disciples brought one of his *gurubhais*, Swami Adbhutananda, to him. He was seen leaving the *Math* premises. 'Lorenbhai', he said, addressing Swamiji. He changed the initial 'N' of "Naren to 'L. 'I cannot adjust to your fixed timings of getting up, ablutions, bath, meditation etc. I just cannot stop meditating at the stroke of a bell. In fact, I am not used to that kind of life, regulated by outside forces, so I am quitting,' he announced.

'But Latu,' Swamiji replied, calling him by his premonastic name,' Who said that these rules are for you? They are for the novices. You go on living the way you like. Adbhutananda, who was a son of the soil, a cowherd by birth, did not leave the *Math* at that time, at Swamiji's instance. But he could not adjust to a life governed by a clock. Though he continued to visit the *Math* often, he chose a free life, spending most of his time in meditation and preaching, living under a bridge and eating whatever was offered to him. Though totally illiterate and rustic in appearance and mode of living, his spiritual talks uplifted several souls.

Swamiji's teaching was deep and varied. He recalled Sharadananda and with his help and the help of Swami Turiyananda, who was a great scholar and was widely read, the training programme was organized. The *Upanishads* formed the core of studies but the *Vedas* and other *Darshanas*, teachings of the Buddha, teachings of prophets of other religions, history, social sciences, physical sciences and every branch of knowledge had to be imbibed. Group discussions helped to sharpen the intellect of the novices, who had started flocking now. Yogasanas and other physical exercises were also emphasised upon, as a strong mind requires a strong body.

Shri Ramakrishna's birthday was celebrated at the new *Math* in 1899. It was a great event. Many poor people were fed there. Swamiji's heart was moved to see the poor Santhal labourers working hard and exerting themselves as labourers in the construction work. He served them with a proper meal. For him, they were all Narayanas. Another great event was the celebration of Durga Puja in the bright half of the month of Ashvin. Shri Sharada Ma was invited on the occassion. Swamiji told her, "Ma, all these are yours. Move freely, see everything, bless everyone and kindly offer your suggestions." Since, according to the Hindu tradition, *sannyasins* are considered dead persons, the Holy Mother was made the host of the Puja ceremony. Boundless was the joy of Vivekananda and his *gurubhais* on the occasion.

After being widowed, Sharadama had been on a pilgrimage to Gaya and other holy places. She had seen there various *Maths* and the Mathadhipatis—abbots—rolling in wealth, and the sadhus of the different *Maths* were all well-fed and well-dressed. Shri Ramakrishna's disciples at that time were living in the dilapitated Varahanagar *Math* and were eking out a precarious existence. Closing her eyes, she had prayed to Thakur, 'O Thakur, my sons have no proper shelter over their heads, nor they have enough to eat. Thakur, it is my earnest prayer to you to provide them with shelter to protect them from the vagaries of weather, and give a loaf of bread in their plates, so that they do not have to go begging from door to door.' Thanks to the financial assistance of an American disciple of Swamiji, the *Math* had come up. Ma's prayers were thus answered. Naturally she was very elated.

A few years ago, when Swamiji was in America and when Sharadadevi was staying for a few months in the house of Nilambar Mukherjee, she had a vision. Shri Ramakrishna had entered the Ganga and was lost. Naren entered the Ganga soon thereafter and cupping both of his hands together and filling the cup with the Ganga waters, Naren was seen moving in different direction and pouring water every time. Ma understood the significance of the vision and the establishment of the *Math* at Belur: sending Swamis Sharadananda and Abhedananda to the West, Shivananda to Srilanka, and Ramakrishnananda to Madras was nothing but what she had seen in her vision, the spreading of the message of Thakur Shri Ramakrishna.

But there were testing times also. The famine relief work started by Akhandananda called for monetary assistance. The coffers of the Ramakrishna Mission contained hardly anything. People at large were very slow to respond to the appeals issued in newspapers. But Ramakrishnananda sent along with his letter of appeal, some paragraphs from the letters of Akhandananda for publication in Madras newspapers. This moved the people and within no time, the Madras Centre collected a sum of rupees fifteen hundred. The Mahabodhi Society of Kolkata also came forward with regular financial assistance. And the British officer in charge of the relief operations in the district of Murshidabad saw the work being done by Akhandananda and he arranged for the supply of food grains to him at a subsidised rate. Even when the conditions improved after the monsoon, people in the area would not allow Swami Akhandananda to leave. He had started an orphanage for waifs and strays who had lost their parents in the famine and who had none to care for them. The orphanage later on developed into a boarding school, where, besides the three R's, Akhandananda introduced farming, carpentry, spinning and weaving. L'ecole Actif (Activity School) of Adolph Ferrier and Mahatma Gandhi's concept of Basic Education were to be conceived decades later.

In 1898, Kolkata was seized by the epidemic of plague. It was taking big toll of men and women every day. The Ramakrishna Mission undertook relief measures. The Mission also started a big cleansing campaign in the city, particularly in the bustees, the poverty ridden ghettos of the city, where elementary hygienic facilities did not exist. When people saw Nivedita and other Swamis cleansing the streets with brooms and spades and buckets in their hands, they immediately joined the cleansing drive. Houses and shops and streets were disinfected and normalcy was restored.

But this welfare activity caused a financial crisis in the Mission. At one stage things became so critical that Vivekananda had to declare, 'We'll sell our buildings and land and carry on the missionary work. We, sadhus, are accustomed to sleep under a tree.' When the Holy Mother Sharadadevi came to learn this, she said, 'Tell Naren that the property does not belong to him only that he could think of selling it. It belongs as much to those sons of Thakur who would be joining the *Math* in the years to come.' This was the practical sense she exhibited. And fortunately for Vivekananda, help soon poured in and the property remained intact.

Swamiji's diabetes was joined by asthma and both were devouring his innermost recesses. Swamiji was advised to retire to a hill station, so Swamiji went to Almora. A few miles away from Almora, in the quiet of the Himalayas, the Seviers had established their *Advaita Ashrama* at Mayavati. It was a very remote place and in those days the last few miles had to be covered on foot. It was an ideal place for practising the *Advaita* Path. Vivekananda had once said that apparently he was a *Jnani* pursuing the path of knowledge, but inwardly he was a *bhakta*, a person following the path of devotion. Whereas, Swamiji had said, Shri Ramakrishna, his guru, was outwardly a '*bhakta*', but in the heart of his heart, he, Ramakrishna, was a *Jnani*. The advaitins worship no idols, no pictures, no totems. When some one put up a picture of Shri Ramakrishna at the *Advaita Ashrama* at Mayavati, with a view to help meditation, a controversy broke out. Ultimately, the issue, whether to hang a picture of Shri Ramakrishna on a wall of a room of the *Advaita Ashrama*, or not, was referred to Shri Sharadadevi. She immediately replied against the hanging of the picture and said; 'Thakur was an advaitin. His picture could not be kept on any wall of the *Advaita Ashrama*.'

The *Brahmavadin*, a magazine which was started when Swamiji was in America and later on given the name, *Prabuddha Bharata*, 'Awakened India', was shifted to the *Advaita Ashrama*, Mayavati. It has completed a century and is still batting vigorously. The Madras *Math* publishes '*The Vedanta Kesari*,' '*The Lion of Vedanta*,' and spreads the message of *Vedanta* with the same zest and vigour. Many other centres bring out periodicals in regional languages.

While at Mayavati, Swamiji received the sad message of the untimely death of Goodwin, and a cloud of sadness descended on him. 'All that you read as my words, owes its existence to him. But for his devoted service very few things would have seen the light of the day,' Swamiji had said. This news had an effect on his health also.

An important event with far-reaching consequences had taken place, on December 12, ten days before the birthday of Sharadadevi. Sister Nivedita's school was opened on the day and, wonder of wonders, the inauguration was performed by Sharadadevi, who was hardly literate. It was a trend setting event. The small path of girls' education, cut by Sharadama, was to become a highway and more and more girls were to flood the schools. In spite of his failing health Swamiji had participated in the function. The school of Nivedita had another unique feature too. It was being started not by a Christian Mission, but a typical Indian Mission and yet, the head of the school was a European lady. The Nivedita School completed a hundred years of its existence and started at the end of the ninenteenth century it has entered the twenty first century. The school is going stronger and stronger.

All the training of the novices, who were flocking to the *Math*, setting up of guidelines, talking to the incessant flow of visitors, combating the weather with his poor health, strains of the mission activities, tendering advice to the various seekers who flocked to him took its toll on Swamiji's health. He did not seem to come out, at least physically, from the great maelstrom he was caught into. Inwardly he was serene and calm like the waters of the Ganga flowing by in winters. The eddies had, apparently, subsided, but they had gnawed at the physique of the lion. The corrosion had started telling upon him and he was feeling out of sorts and tired. He desired rest very much but it was not possible for him to get it while at Belur or anywhere else in India.

Dr. Durgacharan Nag—Nag Mahashay as he was popularly known—one day walked into the *Math*. He was an exemplary devotee of Shri Ramakrishna and instead of making money out of his medical practice, he spent his time and energy in the service of people. When Swamiji proposed him to join the *Math*, Nag Mahashay replied in the negative and said, 'Thakur had asked me to remain a householder', although he lived like a true *sannyasin*. Girish Ghosh, the great dramatist, used to tell a story about both Nag Mahashay and Vivekananda. If the Universal Mother took any length of rope to catch Swami Vivekananda, the rope would invariably fall short and she wouldn't be able to tie the knot. And if she tried to rope in Nag Mahashay, howsoever tiny the knot, Nag Mahashay was so subtle that he would easily escape the snare of the Mahamaya. The meeting between Swamiji and Nag Mahashaya was a memorable one and everyone who watched it found it very blissful.

For the novices, however, and Swamiji's *gurubhais*, it was not always a bliss. Swamiji wanted the routine to be strictly enforced. The *Math* was not a social club for merry making. He was a hard taskmaster and would, at times, lose his temper. A couple of years ago, when from England he had written to Sharadananda to be with him in England and when Sharadananda was dillydallying, Swamiji had clearly conveyed his displeasure, which had ultimately made Sharadananda take a boat to England. But such outbursts were few and far between. He did not want any sloth, any postponement, any carelessness to enter into the minds of the *Math* inmates. And this was only in the interest of the *Math*. Proper traditions and precedents had to be laid down right from the beginning.

But all this was nibbling at whatever little energy was still left in him. The moisture laden climate was anything but conducive to his health. And he had many calls and callers to attend to. The only way to be free from this ceaseless pressure was for him to go out of the country. And he was medically advised also to do so.

In the short period of two years and four months after his arrival in his home town, he had the solid achievement of building up the *Math* and the Mission to his credit. The buying of land and looking after the minutest detail of planning and construction must have been quite strenuous. The work of training the new entrants was also trend setting. This was the most important part of his work and Swamiji exerted himself to the utmost to solidify the foundation, to lay down precedents and to build up the proper atmosphere. And he had all this to his credit while the bark of his health was slowly sinking. And his journey from Colombo to Almora and Lahore had helped in awakening the people.

22

To the West Again

The humid climate of Kolkata was nibbling at the life of Swamiji. Because of asthma, he found it difficult to breathe. He needed a change very badly. Moreover, that change must be such as would save him from the incessant onslaught of visitors. In a letter to an American disciple, he had written: 'This strenuous work of two years has snatched away twenty years of my life.' The constant moving since he landed at Colombo in mid January, 1897, addressing crowded meetings, nonstop chain of visitors, talking with individuals, speaking to groups, fighting the opposition from some near and dear ones to the establishment of the Ramakrishna Mission, and the task of establishing the twin institutions—the *Math* and the Mission, laying down the routine, training of the brahmacharis... all this had taken its toll on the already poor health of Swamiji. Yet, he had tried to carry on as enthusiastically as possible. But now the tensions had begun to show and he was advised change, change of climate, change in his daily routine. 'Go West,' he was told.

But this departure was fundamentally different from his previous departure. This time he was being accompanied by his learned and pious gurubhai, Swami Turiyananda and Sister Nivedita. Swami Turiyananda was not at first at all willing to go out of the country, but he bowed down to Swami Vivekananda's wishes and became ready for the voyage. Sister Nivedita was accompanying him, mainly, to collect funds for her school. The trio set sail on June 20, 1899.

The monsoon, the life line of India, had already set in, the seas were stormy, winds were lashing and at times, there would be heavy downpours. When the steamer touched Madras, Swamiji's devoted disciple Alasinga Perumal joined the party and accompanied Swamiji upto Colombo, from where he returned to Madras. An orthodox south Indian Brahmin that he was, he was carrying with him fried grams—chickpeas—puffed rice, some fruit etc., and avoided eating any cooked food on the boat. From Colombo, the ship sailed straight to Aden, but all throughout being lashed by the furies of the monsoon, the voyage which should have normally been completed within six days, took ten days.

For Nivedita, it was not a mere journey with Vivekananda, it was a floating academy for her. For, soon after they got settled, Swamiji's encyclopedic intellect took in its grasp various topics of ancient Aryans, the *Upanishads,* the Buddha, Mahavira and Shankara and traced the development of the Indian spiritual thought. The two great epics, the *Mahabharata* and the *Ramayana,* the great Mauryas, particularly, Ashok the great, Alexander's invasion, his meeting of an Indian seer somewhere on the bank of the Sindhu, the influence of the ancient Indian thinking on ancient Greek Philosophies, dramas of Kalidasa and other dramatists, other literary masterpieces, the story of Prithviraj Chauhan and other brave Rajput Princes and Princesses... everything started flowing from the tongue of Swamiji. Both Turiyananda and Nivedita were amazed at the wide range of Swamiji's knowledge as well as by his sharp memory.

When the boat passed by Iran and the Gulf of Iran, ancient Iranian and Babylonian civilizations came into focus. While passing through the Red Sea, the ancient civilizations of Egypt, Judaism, Islam and Christianity must have been the subjects of Swamiji's talks. Christianity is likely to have been with him till their boat reached the shores of Italy. When their ship passed by the island of Corsica, Swamiji remembered Napoleon, one of his heroes. The story of the meteoraric rise and fall of Napoleon would keep any listener spell-bound, particularly when the story teller was a man of Swamiji's stature. Swamiji was struck by the courage and vigour of the Corsican. He condemned the moral cowardice of his countrymen and went to the extreme of prefering the vigour of crime. He condemned the virtuousness of death. As the steamer moved westward towards Gibraltar, the memory of the Moors welled up in Swamiji's mind.

Swamiji was discussing various topics in his cabin or while sitting or moving about on the deck, but the central theme of his conversation was Hinduism in its varied aspects. One very outstanding feature of Hinduism is its diversity of beliefs, diversity of practices, diversity of approaches, and yet its underlying unity, its unique feature of all inclusiveness. One day while talking about the Vaishnava approach of devotion, Swamiji said, 'Vaishnavism preaches realisation of God through senses while *Vedanta* preaches complete control over the senses for realising the Divine. And Hinduism accepts with equal respect both these absolutely opposite points of view! This tolerance is a unique feature of Hinduism!.'

When, on 31st July, 1899, the boat touched London, Nivedita and Turiyananda felt that the voyage had been over too soon. Many friends, admirers and disciples of Swamiji had come to the dock to welcome Swamiji, who was so dear to all of them. The more surprising welcomers were Mrs. Funke with her friend from Detroit in the U.S.A. Their love and respect for Swami Vivekananda was the great moving force, which had emboldened them to cross the Atlantic Ocean in order to see him and be as close to him as possible. They had read some report about Swamiji's health and were very worried about it. This anxiety drilling their hearts had made them cross the Atlantic Ocean to see their revered guru. Mrs. Funke had remarked after meeting Swamiji that he looked like a little baby.

Vivekananda spent two restful weeks in London. There were no public lectures, no hectic movements. However, he did meet small groups and talked to them. After spending two quiet weeks in London, he embarked on a boat from Glasgow for New York on 16th August. He was accompanied by his gurubhai Turiyananda and the two American disciples.

Crossing the Atlantic became a very memorable event for the companions of Swamiji. Mornings were devoted to the readings from the *Gita*, with his commentary on the various verses. It was a new interpretation. This was generally followed by recitations of Sanskrit poetry with translation and commentary. Later on Vedic *mantras* were recited by Swamiji with their special intonations, followed by his translation and explanation of the verses. All these filled the hearts of his companions with indescribable delight and when they arrived at New York, they felt that the voyage had ended too soon.

Mr. and Mrs. Leggett met Swamiji and his party the same evening and their regard and affection carried Swami Vivekananda and his party to Ridgely Manor, about 100 miles upstream on the river Hudson. Vivekananda immediately contacted Abhedananda and asked him to meet him at Ridgely Manor. He was lecturing at different places and had also established a Centre in downtown New York. This was a very pleasing news for Swamiji. Turiyananda was sent to Mont Clair, in New Jersey, close by to New York. Nivedita had joined her guru resting and recuperating at Ridgely Manor. Summer was nearing its end and autumn was setting in. The serene and peaceful atmosphere, the river Hudson flowing by and the Catskil mountain range sending its dry cool air from the West was all what Vivekananda needed very much. On 21st September, Nivedita decided to become a Sannyasini, a nun, and wear ochre clothes. When Nivedita returned from a drive in the evening, her guru put a piece of paper in her hand, containing the poem 'Peace' he had written. It is a very inspiring poem. It must have strengthened her vow of dedication. She was dedicating herself to her guru, his great message of *Vedanta* and to his country.

Swamiji's opinion of the West had undergone a change. He could see that beneath all apparent niceties, there was no depth of feeling. Mammon was the only God, worshipped by the people. The pursuit of lucre was the most predominant factor in the life in the West. 'Social life in the West,' he said to his beloved Western disciple, Nivedita, 'is a peal of laughter; but underneath it is a wail. It ends in a sob. The fun and frivolity are all on the surface; really it is full of tragic intensity '(*The Master as I Saw Him*).

Swamiji's prophetic eye could see the tragedy of the future as if written in bold letters on a wall. Sister Christine, whom Vivekananda addressed as 'violet,' has in her *Remiscences*, quoted Swamiji saying, 'Europe is on the edge of a volcano. If its fire is not extinguished by a flood of spirituality, it will erupt.' And this eruption took place within a decade and a half after this fateful utterance of Swamiji. He could well see the Mephistopheles of the lust for power, greed for cornering wealth and exploitation of poor nations. The natural result was that he was thoroughly disillusioned of the Western civilization. He could very well see the inflammable situation Europe was in.

All this, however, did not prevent him from going to California for preaching his gospel of *Vedanta* and spreading his message of universal love. The climate there was warmer than that in and around New York, Vivekananda went there in spite of 'three parts of' him no longer belonged to this world,' as Romain Rolland has put it in his *Life and Gospel of Vivekananda*.

Unfortunately, there was neither Goodwin nor Nivedita nor anyone else to give us a complete record of what he spoke at various places in California and what else he did there. His letters to Joe McLeod and others, written from various places in California, reveal the trouble he had to take settling some differences, between A in New York (Swami Abhedananda) and others. Mr. Leggett, one of the most trusted friends and benefactors of Swamiji, who was working as President of the New York Centre had resigned. And this must also have added to Swamiji's worries. All this, probably, told on his already poor health and he wrote to 'My Dear Joe' on April 18, from Alamede (*Complete Works*, Vol. VI, p. 431);

'I am so sorry that Mr. Leggett resigned the Presidentship. Well, I keep quiet for fear of making further trouble. You know my methods are extremely harsh and once roused, I may rattle A—too much for his peace of mind.'

These few lines indicate what pain Vivekananda must have been feeling about the disturbing news of the New York Centre. He further wrote in the same letter:

'Work is always difficult; pray for me, Joe, that my work stops for ever and my whole soul be absorbed in Mother. Her works, she knows.' Even though he was a *sannyasin*, above pleasure and pain and a lover of accord, he seemed to have been jolted at the news of discord in the New York Centre. And yet he has written in this very letter:

'I am well, very well mentally.' Is this a hint at his deteriorating physical condition? He continues: 'The battles are lost and won. I have bundled my things and am waiting for the great deliverer.'

'Shiva, O Shiva, carry my boat to the other shore.'

Striking a personal note of pathos, he further wrote:

'After all, Joe, I am only the boy who used to listen with rapt wonderment to the wonderful words of Ramakrishna under the Banyan tree at Dakshineshvar. That is my true nature, works and activities doing good and so forth are all superimpositions. Now I again hear His voice, the same old voice thriling my soul.'

These passionate words of Swamiji indicate how close he was finding himself to death. The very next words in the letter lay bare his soul's desire; 'Bonds are breaking — love dying, work becoming tasteless - the glamour is off life.' How much must Joe have been moved by this pathos dripping words! The finale, she must have felt must not be far away, for, Swamiji had written:

'I come, my beloved Lord, I come.'

Yes, I come. *Nirvana* is before me. I feel it at times-the same infinite ocean of peace, without a ripple, a breath.'

How clear was the vision of his exit from the stage of life! And how calm and serene! 'The infinite ocean of peace' was standing with its arms outstretched, waiting to pick up Swamiji the moment he jumped into its arms and Swamiji was ready for the leap any moment.

Swamiji further goes on to make a startling confession: "Behind my work was ambition, behind my love was personality, behind my pursuit was fear and behind my guidance, the thirst for power. Now they are vanishing and I drift. I come Mother, I come. In thy warm bosom, floating wherever Thou take me—in the voiceless, in the strange, in the wonder—and I come - a spectator, no more an actor."

How stark are the words! They reveal the subtlest petals of Vivekananda's personality. With that poniard, he was dissecting his inner self! This was not the vision Narcissus was looking at. It was also not the vision of Kali, wherein:

The stars are blocked out,
The clouds are covering clouds.

......

The sea has joined the fray,
And swirls up mountain –waves,
To reach the pitchy sky.

Now there were no tornadoes, no typhoons. There was absolute tranquility. There were no struggles. There was total submission. There was no strife. All was in harmony now.

In spite of the sands in the bottle of life slipping down so fast, he was not sitting quiet in California. He gave a series of lectures at Los Angeles and people thronged to hear them. Right from after the time he became a figure of adoration in 1893, the Unitarian Church was very friendly to him. The same church arranged some talks and group discussions and thus helped in the spreading of his message. Swamiji had also visited Oakland, San Fransisco and a couple of other places and spread the message of *Vedanta* before the receptive audiences. Miss Minni C. Brooke was so moved that she donated 160 acres of land to Swamiji in the valley of St. Anton. It was a very uneven land, the soil was rocky and it was veritably a jungle. Before leaving America for Europe, where he was called by his devoted friend Leggett and where he was invited by the organisers of a conference of the History of Religions to be held at Paris, he had stopped at New York for a few days. Turiyananda was doing his work there very efficiently. Vivekananda asked his gurubhai to go to California and develop 'Shanti *Ashrama*' on the land gifted by Miss Brooke. When Swamiji told Turiyananda that it was Jagadamba's desire that he (Turiyananda) should go, Turiyananda said a bit light-heartedly, 'Why don't you say it is your wish? Have you heard Jagadamba speak to you like that? How can we hear Jagadamba's voice?' Swamiji, charged with intense emotion, replied, 'Yes, my brother! We can hear Jagadamba speak as clearly as we hear each other's voice. The only difference is that it requires extremely subtle nerves to do so' Turiyananda made no further argument and proceeded to California, to build the 'Shanti *Ashrama*' there.

While Swamiji was in New York for a few days prior to his departure to Europe, he had addressed a number of meetings. He spoke on the necessity of celibacy and keeping away from lust, if one wanted to attain real piety. 'Being a slave of lust is just animal existence,' he said. He preached conquest of nature, for all progress was achieved by fighting against nature. At times, he spoke in lighter vein and the audience burst into laughter. Some one once asked a silly question: 'Have you ever seen a ghost, Swamiji?' 'Oh sure, he replied with all seriousness, 'it joins us everyday at breakfast in India.' Expressing his great shock, once, when someone had asked him if he was married, he had said that it was the work of Satan and he himself would never submit to the devil. And then he added with all seriousness, 'But I have a very grave objection against this system of *sannyasa*.' Then he paused for a while and with all seriousness proclaimed, 'The system picks up the best persons from the society.' There were peals of laughter.

He left the shores of America in July, 1900, almost seven years after he had first landed on it. The entry, then, was from the West and his exit now was from the east. He reached Paris on the 1st of August and stayed there for four and a half months. Paris, then, was the cultural capital of the West. The Louvre Museum, the Sorbonne University, Notre Dame, the Seine river, Montmartre... everything in Paris had its own attraction. 'Liberty, Equality, Fraternity,' the *mantras* given by the French Revolution a century ago was ringing in Swamiji's ears. In spite of this spell Paris cast on Swamiji, his 'third eye' was able to see the tinderbox all Europe was sitting on and which was to blow off all revelry and pomp of the most powerful continent a decode and four years later.

The Paris Congress was kept confined to merely discussing the History of Religions, simply because the powerful Catholic Church did not have the catholicity to allow free discussions on other religions as at the Chicago Parliament. One Gustav Oppert, a German scholar, who had specialised himself in the study of ancient Eastern studies, and who was suffering from the superiority complex, then so common among the scholars who had stated coming in contact with the religions and cultures of the east, had started that the *lingam*, worshipped as Shiva, was a phallic symbol. Vivekananda argued his case against this prejudiced opinion and quoting from the *Vedas*, showed how it was the symbolic representation of the Brahman. Swamiji gave one more lecture at the Congress. His failing health added to the turning of his face from all affairs on the earth and the narrow outlook of the organisers of the Congress also kept him away. In spite of this, he was impressed by the European scholarship and felt quite grieved at the lack of it in India.

While at Paris, he was invited to visit Lannion in Britany, where Ole Bull was staying. There Nivedita had arrived and it was a very good company for the tattering Swami. When Sister

Nivedita was leaving for England he simply stunned her by uttering, “If I have made you, be destroyed, if the Mother (Jagadamba) has made you, live.”'

He paid several visits to the Catholic churches and on seeing the forms of worship he saw a great similarity between the Hindu and the Catholic forms of worship. He was also struck by many other cultural similarities and he expressed the great need of both to come together to complement each other. ‘A closer contact with Asia,’ he said, ‘would bring about a much needed renaissance in Europe.’ If Asia was to gain material prosperity, the West needed spiritual vigour.

While in Paris, he had the opportunity to meet the great Indian scientist Jagdish Chandra Bose, who had demonstrated experimentally that plants and metals responded like living creatures to various stimuli. Romain Rolland has expressed his regret that only Father Hyacinthe and Jule Bois could meet Swamiji a bit closely while he was at Paris.

Swamiji left Paris on October 24 for Vienna, the then capital of the Austrian Empire. But Swamiji could smell the decay that was soon to overtake Austria and he made a very typical observation when he said, 'If Turkey is the sick man of Europe, Austria is the sick woman of Europe.’ It might be remembred that the murder of an Archduke of Austria had lit the destructive fire of the first World War in 1914.

From Vienna, he went with his party to Constantinople-(now known as Istanbul). His party consisted of Josephine Macleod, Madame Loyson, Jule Bois, Father Hyacinthe and the American opera singer Madame Calve. Father Hyacinthe wanted to bring about a rapproachment between two opposing crusaders, the followers of Islam and those of Christianity. His effort was doomed to failure, because the Khalifa of Constantinople refused permission to Vivekananda to address any public meeting. His fanatic hauteur had been evident right in 1893, when he had turned down the invitation to attend the World Parliament of

Religions at Chicago. It is, of course, not known whether he was seized with the fear of Vivekananda, the hero of the Chicago Parliament and the preacher of equality of all religions, preaching his gospel in the capital of Islam, then. Swamiji tried to meet some Sufi saints there.

From Constantinople, Swamiji and his party left for Athens. November had set in. They spent four days in Athens and saw the ruins of the ancient Greek capital. It was the grave of the once great civilization, enriched by Pericles, Socrates and Plato and many other immortal people. They took a Russian steamer to cross the Mediterranean and reached Egypt. The sight of the very shore of Egypt was cause enough to rake up her hoary past. The great Pharoahs, Semiramis, Cleopatra, the great library of Alexandria raised by the fanatic Arabs and the ancient Indian connection welled up in the mind of Swami Vivekananda. The master story teller that he was, he must have woven the fine muslin of Egyptian history before his companions.

All of a sudden, he felt a shock, the shock of some dear one being snatched away, as if a limb of his own was being amputated. He shocked his companions by declaring that he is cutting his stay in Egypt short and is rushing to India. They could not understand the cause of his hurry. He left them behind and took the first steamer for Bombay. They all felt very sorry. The waters of the Arabian Sea that were carrying the P. & O. liner Swamiji had managed to catch were calm but his heart was being pierced. He landed at Bombay towards the end of the first week of December 1900. There were no receptions, no arches, no welcome addresses. As Romain Rolland has aptly put it, 'he had brought his body back to the funeral pyre.'

23

The 'Last Supper,' And...

It was the late evening of December 9, 1900. The stars were shining in the chilly sky and the Ganga was bearing their reflections on her heaving bosom. The evening *arati* was over in the temple dedicated to Shri Ramakrishna in the Belur *Math*. And some time later, the monks and the inmates of the *Math* were having their evening meal. The gardener suddenly ran up to the door of the dining room and announced: 'Some Sahib has come to the *Math*. Everyone was taken by surprise. Who could the 'Sahib' be, and at this unearthly hour?

But soon the 'Sahib' himself stood in the door frame. And the surprise of the inmates of the *Math* was suddenly turned into great joy. It was Swami Vivekananda! He had come without any intimation, without any information and without any companion. When he saw that they were having 'khichadi'—a mixture of dal and rice cooked together—he immediately joined them. This added to the delight of his *gurubhais* and the other inmates. But they had to control their anxiety on looking at the face of the Swami, which looked a bit swollen and which indicated the poor state of his health.

The sad news of the untimely death of his friend, Mr. Sevier at Mayavati, confirmed the shrill note that the strings of his heart had started producing while he was in Egypt and which had made him take a sudden decision to part company with his friends and catch the first liner sailing to Bombay. So sensitive was his soul. He must run up to Mayavati and console Mrs.

Sevier. But prior to that his own body required rest after his travelling for many days. But the call of his heart took precedence and after sending a telegram, he left the Howrah Station a few days later and arrived at Kathgodam on 29th December. The railway journey to Kathgodam was not a straight one. After changing trains at a junction or two, when he arrived at Kathgodam, there was no one to receive him, only because the telegram he had sent well in advance was not delivered on time at the Mayawati *Ashrama*, a few miles away from Almora and which had got snow bound because of winter. Almora itself is about 1,675 metres above sea level and Mayavati is still higher and, what then connected the two places was called a road in absence or any other name, had got completely snow-bound and the numerous ups and downs, a few of them quite precipitous, and curves, posed great danger. And this was not at all conducive to the fragile health of the asthmatic Swamiji. Fortunately for him, he was being accompanied by Swami Shivananda, a gurubhai and Swami Sadananda, one of Swamiji's first disciples.

Mayavati is 104 kilometers away from Kathgodam and the biting cold winds, the continuous falling of the snow and the low temperature, everything was having an adverse effect on the poor, falling health of Swami Vivekananda. The party, therefore, chose to have a stopover of a night at Kathgodam. Next morning they hired horses and trudged along. The party had to wade through snow a few kilometres, it was quite hazardous for Swamiji. His asthmatic lungs found it very difficult to inhale the cool, thin mountain air. He had to be literally carried by his companions for a few kilometres, when, as a result of the late delivery of the telegram, a party of the inmates of the Mayavati *Ashrama* joined them. He was literally dumped into the *Ashrama*, on the 3rd of January, 1901, on the fifth day after arriving at Kathgodam. At the *Ashrama*, he slowly revived a little bit. He consoled Mrs. Sevier for her loss; it was a personal loss for him also and was also happy to meet her and see the running of the *Ashrama*. Because of the foul weather and also because of the very poor condition of his health, Swamiji could not go out at all to enjoy the mountain air and had to remain confined within the protective walls of the *Ashrama*. But he wrote three articles for the *Prabuddha Bharata* and talked to the inmates, inspiring them and guiding them. The incident of the picture of Shri Ramakrishna on the wall of a room, which had upset him, had taken place at this time, though mentioned earlier. On his return to Belur, he had made a typical remark: 'There must surely be one centre free from dualism.' He had left the Mayavati *Ashrama*, on 18th January, waded for four days through the slippery snow and had returned to the *Math* at Belur on January 26, quite exhausted.

But he wanted to drink life to the lees. As soon as he improved slightly, he responded to the pressing call of people from Dacca and he went there. As usual, there were throngs and throngs of people to hear him. Along with his mother, Bhuvaneshvaridevi, he had a dip in the confluence of the mighty Brahmaputra and the Padma, a tributary of the Ganga. Then they proceeded to Kamakhya in Assam, one of the important centres of Shakti. He visited Shillong, the then seat of the Assam Government, hoping it would be beneficial to him. Unfortunately, his hope was belied, in spite of the services of the British civil surgeon made available to him by Sir Henry Cotton, the then British Commissioner of Assam. Sir Henry was a true friend of India and a great admirer of Swami Vivekananda. But the climate neither proved to be conducive to his health nor was the medical treatment found effective. As a matter of fact, the sands of time were running against him and he was well aware of it. Back to Belur was the only choice.

Since a reference to Swamiji, taking his mother with him on a pilgrimage, has been made, mention might also be made of a letter written by him to the Maharaja of Khetdi earlier, on November 22, 1898. It is a very touching letter revealing one of the tender points in Swamiji's heart. When, as a young *sannyasin* of twenty seven, he had left the *Math* in 1890, he had not cared to visit his own mother to bid her goodbye. The strong feeling of renunciation and the gnawing desire to seek his destiny might have been responsible for it. Yet he made a profession of his love for his mother in his letter to Haridas Desai, he wrote from Chicago on 29th January, 1894: 'Dear Diwanji Saheb, if there is any being I love in the whole world, it is my mother.' It was this love for his mother, whose abject poverty had driven him to pen his letter to the Maharaja, appealing to him for financial assistance for Bhuvaneshvaridevi. Yes, he had cut off all sansaric ties but he was not a hard-hearted brute. If he could help other Daridranarayanas, was his mother not one of them? And she had grown old and his younger brothers were not looking after her. This letter of appeal to the Maharaja for financial help to his own mother is indicative of Swamiji's intense feeling for his mother. It must be made clear that the appeal, though, strikes a pathetic cord, it nowhere exhibits any remorse for having left her in the late eighties of the nineteenth century following the call of Shri Ramakrishna. The spiritual life triggered by his great guru was not there to annihilate love, the binding force of the universe. Swamiji's bonds with the Holy Mother, his *gurubhais*, with the householder disciples of the Paramahansa, with the Maharajas of Khetdi and Ramnad, with Haridas Desai, with Lala Badrishae, with scores of his disciples in the U.S.A and in India, with the Hales of Chicago and the Wrights of Boston, with the Leggetts, the Seviers, with Goodvin and with all he came in close contact with never got severed.

And this love of his turned the Belur *Math* into an *Ashrama* of the old *rishis*, where animals could move freely, Swamiji was taking care of a number of them: Hansi was the she-goat with her kid Matru, who were his favourites. Matru's neck was decorated by a collar of tinkling bells, and with Matru he played as if he himself was a little kid. Then there was a dog, given the ferocious name Bagha – a tiger - who followed Swamiji faithfully. There was a deer, ducks, cows, sheep, geese and a stork.

These animals moved freely and this caused some 'fights.' Swami Brahmananda, who was called 'Raja Maharaj' and who was just next to Vivekananda, was also tending some animals. When these animals crossed into each other's'territories, a war of words broke out between Naren and Rakhal, the two dear 'sons' of Ramakrishna, which provided a great show to the onlookers.

This new band of *sannyasins*, so different from the traditional *sannyasins*, moving in ochre cloth, with a staff in hand, preaching traditional religion and passing from place to place, was not looked upon kindly by many. Swamiji was not a reformist zealot preaching destruction of all old customs and systems. He was a reformer of a different kind. He believed in maintaining links with the past, so he arranged for the Durga Puja Celebrations in October of 1901. Sharadama was specially invited on the occasion and the *puja*, the worship of the Goddess Durga, was performed with eclat and the strict observation of all ceremonies. A huge *pandal* was put up for the occasion and the followers of Shri Ramakrishna thronged there in numbers. The tradition of celebrating all big Hindu festivals now forms a part and parcel of all the Ramakrishna centres in the world and they also celebrate the Christmas and the Buddha Jayanti with equal enthusiasm. After all, God is one and all religions are but paths leading to the same goal.

Reverend Oda, head of the Buddhists in Japan and Rev. Okakura, a Buddhist monk deeply interested in art and culture arrived in India, towards the end of 1901, especially to invite Swami Vivekananda to a religious conference to be held in Japan. But Swamiji's health had been fast deteriorating and he could not accept the invitation. They, however, requested him to accompany them to Bodh Gaya and to Varanasi, the two places so closely connected with the life of the Buddha. Swamiji accompanied them to these two places. It was his last pilgrimage.

Swamiji must have remembered on the way to Gaya that he had run away from the Kashipur house in 1886 to Gaya with a couple of friends without informing his Master, Ramakrishna Paramahansa, slowly inching towards his death. And when, in 1888, he had left the *Math,* his first halt was at Varanasi. At Gaya, the Buddha had achieved Enlightenment and at Varanasi, he had preached his first sermon. Both were places of Swamiji's first pilgrimage also.

Inspired by Vivekananda, a group of young, enthusiastic people had established the 'Ramakrishna Home of Service' for helping, feeding and caring for the pilgrims and sadhus flocking to the holy city and falling ill. Swamiji issued an appeal for funds for this Home. A few years later on when Sharadadevi had been to Varanasi, she was so impressed by the spirit of service there that she gave a donation to the Sevashrama, which had expanded greatly by then. It is, therefore, no surprise that Count Keyserling, after paying a visit to the Sevashrama Hospital wrote in his *Travel Diary*: 'I have never been in a hospital with more cheerful atmosphere. These men are truly real followers of Ramakrishna, the "God-elated," (Romain Rolland: *The Life of Vivekananda,* footnote 1, p.163.)

The sap of his life was fast drying out, yet, the father figure of the *Math* that he was, he kept himself fully occupied in laying down the routine, the guidelines, the path to be followed by the inmates. And he was very strict in its observance. One day, a few minutes after the bell for meditation was rung, he went and found that several people, including a few seniors had not joined. He prescribed a punishment: 'all those who were not present shall not eat the food cooked in the *Math* -kitchen. Everyone of them, without exception, shall go out and beg for food. 'And yet, Nivedita has quoted the Swamiji's own words: 'How often does a man ruin his disciples by remaining always with them? When men are once trained, it is essential that their leader leave them, for without his absence they cannot develop themselves.' (The

Master As I Saw Him, p.327). And he was soon going to follow this, although Nivedita, who was quite closeby and many of his disciples from distant parts of the world gathered around him during the earlier part of 1902 had no idea of this.

The work of the Mission and the *Math* was ever expanding. He had recalled Sharadananda from the West to become the secretary of the Order. Sharadananda was a great organiser. Vivekananda also tried to improve his own health. The diabates had developed into hydropsy. An ayurvedic physician prescribed total stopping of drinking of water. The summer of 1902 was setting in. Yet Swamiji was so firm that not a drop of water would enter his throat while he was gargling his mouth. Even under such hard routine, he continued to take regular classes on various subjects and to meet visitors. At the end of 1901, the Indian National Congress had held its session in Kolkata. Gandhiji, who had been there specially from South Africa and who had been greatly inrpressed by the achievements of Swamiji, paid a visit to Belur to meet Swamiji. Unfortunately, Swamiji's illness had taken him to Kolkata for consultation. But Tilak had been lucky to meet Swamiji a couple of days later.

Towards the end of February of 1902, the *Math* organised the celebration of Shri Ramakrishna's birthday. Crowds had assembled to participate. Many poor people were served food. But Vivekananda's poor health kept him confined to his room and he could only peep at the mass of men from the window of his room on the first floor.

The total avoidance of water seemed to bring about slight improvement in his health. His premonition of his death made him more and more detached from all affairs, yet he resumed his activity of guidance to the novices, of meeting friends and receiving visitors. The service of and sympathy for the poor increased noticeably. The Santhal labourers engaged in the construction work attracted his special attention and he tried his best to serve those daridranarayanas—God in the form of the poor. 'How can we have the heart to put a morsel into our mouths when our countrymen have not enough wherewithal to feed or clothe themselves?' These words of his show, how intense was his feeling for the poor and the deprived. Gandhi, who had missed meeting him, had inherited this sympathy for the poor. Gandhi also shared the same intensity of feeling against untouchability as the Swami.

When a lay disciple of Swamiji a bit shruggingly said that establishing unity and harmony in the country was an extremely difficult task, Swamiji felt annoyed and irritatingly said 'Don't come here anymore if you consider any task too difficult.' He wanted all *Vedanta*, all practising of *tapasya*, all meditation to be put off for the next life. 'Let this body go in the service of others,' he preached. This was the pinnacle of his preaching, indicating very closely how deeply he had inbibed his guru's teaching, *Shivajnane Jivaseva*.'

Nivedita has noted, the Swami had told her: 'As I grow older, I find that I look more and more for greatness in little things.'

He was marching towards his death. It was a 'double march' though no one suspected his sudden departure. He remembered all his disciples from far and near. 'I have done enough for 1500 years,' he had once said. His two pet ideas were the establishment of a Vedic College, giving the knowledge of the *Vedas* and emphasising teaching of Sanskrit, and establishment of a *Math* for ladies in the name of the 'Holy Mother Sharadadevi.' Both came into existence later on.

All through out the spring of 1902, he was going without water and showed how powerful his will was. The same powerful will of his prevented the inmates of the *Math* from seeing how he was sliding to his death. The summer set in, raining intense heat. Vivekananda had so detached himself that he was not worried about the late arrival of the monsoon. He was not worried about anything now. After coming out of the

Amarnath Cave in Kashmir, he had told Nivedita that Lord Shiva had blessed him with the boon of choosing the moment of his death. He asked a disciple to bring a Bengali Calendar and after looking into it, he returned it. He had made his choice. The disciple was totally unaware of it as he suspected nothing.

July of the year 1902 had commenced. The first of the month fell on Tuesday. According to the Hindu calendar, Wednesday the second of July was an *Ekadashi*. He celebrated the day in his own special way. He had invited Nivedita for the special lunch on the day. He told her in a casual manner, 'I am making ready for death. A great *tapasya* and meditation has come upon me and I am making ready for death.' She could not grasp the Swami's preparedness behind the words. To her he looked as normal as usual.

He was fasting strictly on the day. But he had arranged for the special *Ekadashi* meal to be served to Nivedita. He sat opposite to her while she was having her meal and was chatting in a lighter vein on the meal she was having. When she finished eating, Swamiji himself poured water on her hands and when the washing was over, he took her hands and dried them gently with his own towel.

Nivedita felt very awkward and said protestingly, 'it is I who should do these things for you, Swamiji! Not you for me.' The solemn reply of Swamiji shook Nivedita to the backbone: ' 'Jesus washed the *feet* of his disciples!' he said, emphasising the word *feet*.

Jesus had done that, but that was at the time of the last supper, on the day of the Passover. St. Luke has described the event in his Gospel. And what had followed the washing of the feet of his disciples by Jesus was his arrest, ultimately leading to his crucifixion. All this came up in the memory of Nivedita, but she dared not refer to it loudly. Was she witnessing the end which the apostles of Christ had not visualised? Except this symbolic act of washing and drying the hands of Nivedita, the conversation was light and on varied topics.

Two days later, it was Friday, the 4th of July. He had woken up early on the day and he looked more cheerful and full of vigour. He went into the temple and spent full three hours in meditation. He had closed the windows and the door. Was it done so that he could be alone with his Master? When the meditation was over, he sang with his melodious voice a hymn to the Goddess Kali. When he came out of the temple, he looked completely transfigured. He had his meals with the inmates of the *Math* on the day and ate with gusto. Without any rest, he straightway went to teach the novices. He gave a lesson on Sanskrit grammar which lasted for full three hours. The subject was grammar but the teacher was Swamiji, who had the ability to make every lesson a lively one. There were peals of laughter and the learners forgot the intense heat of July so engrossed they had become in the teaching.

Soon thereafter, along with his gurubhai Swami Premananda, he had a pretty long walk on the Belur road stretching outside the *Math*. They walked three kilometres or so and Swamiji discussed with his dear *gurubhai* the plan of the Vedic College he so cherished. He emphasised the importance of the Vedic studies to remove superstitions from the society.

It was evening. He spoke to his dear *gurubhais*, bidding them as it were his last farewell.

The July sun had gone down and the temple bell was pealing for the evening *arati*. Swamiji retired to his room. He sent away the attendant inmate from the room as he wanted his meditation to be undisturbed. After about three quarters of an hour, he called in the attending inmate and asked him to open all the windows. Then he lay down on the floor on his left side. Had he finally come to know who he was? He had willed to depart from the world. Lord Shiva had blissfully fulfilled his desire to do so. It was Maha *Samadhi*.

On the next day, his body was placed on the funeral pyre. The physical matter was transformed into ashes. His *pranavayu* had merged with the eternal, immortal air.

24

A Century After

Vivekananda had not gone to the West to preach Hindu Religion and to convert others to Hinduism. He had not been sent to the Chicago Parliament of Religions as an accredited representative by any of the numerous sects of the Hindu Religion and the Parliament authorities cannot at all be blamed for at first showing him the door. Yet the same authorities of the Parliament took him in in September 1893, on the strength of the recommendation of Professor Wright. And at his very first public speech on November 11, Swamiji proved the prophecy he had made at the Abu Road Railway Station, 'Haribhai, this Parliament is meeting for me.' And he had thumped his chest uttering these words.

His very first speech was an explosion, which had shaken the entire audience in the Columbus Hall. It differed fundamentally from the speeches of those delegates who had preceded him. For, he did not preach Hinduism, he preached tolerance, oneness of God, and he referred to all religions as different paths for the realisation of God. 'No one religion,' he had said, 'can claim superiority over others.'

But this was highly objectionable to most of the Christian sects, whose preachers and priests considered Christianity to be the only real religion and all the 'heathens' to be inferior to them. The Christian priest, like De Nobili, who had followed Vasco Da Gama in India had taken recourse to all means to convert people to Christianity. Vivekananda pricked the balloon of their hollow claims of superiority of Christianity over other 'heathen' religions. A few of the persons like Rev. John Henry Barrows, held in high esteem amongst the organisers of the Chicago Parliament of Religions, sincerely believed that the Parliament would establish conclusively the superiority of Christianity. The manifestation of the phenomenon of Vivekananda thoroughly exposed the hollowness of their irrational claim. Professor Charles Lanman's article in the *Outlook* of July, 1897 was forthright in saying, 'A change of attitude towards non-Christian religions has undoubtedly begun within Christendom. It is a step in advance, clear and great.'

A number of leading intellectuals of the time like William James, Professor Lanman, Professor Wright, Captain Sevier, Paul Deussen and quite a few others could easily understand the idea of equality of all religions and the idea of the superiority of one over another was proved totally untenable. William James, the father of American Philosophy, was no doubt influenced by Swami Vivekananda as testified by Dr. Eugene Taylor. Charles Eliot, who presided over the Harward University for four decades and who also was a learned professor and author of many books, was one of the first individuals to spot the talent of Vivekananda and invite him to be a Professor at Harward. Another Ivy League University, the University of Columbia, had also invited Swamiji to join the university as Professor of Sanskrit. Both were life time posts, not posts on probation or for limited periods.

'The impact of the tremendous spiritual power of Swamiji's personality upon the American mind was such that it brought about a permanent shift in subliminal patterns of thought. Although Vedantic thought had touched, even moved, a few Americans earlier in the century, the American mind as a whole could not digest Swamiji's message without becoming transformed on a deep level of awareness, without its long accustomed view of reality shifting from materialistic outlook to a spiritual one. (I Have Truth To Tell, Marie Louise Burke, in *Swami Vivekananda: A Hundred Years Since Chicago,* p. 193).

Paul Deussen was so impressed by Vivekananda that the latter's two days-stay with him at Kiel did not satisfy him and he joined the Swami going to England, where Deussen spent full two weeks with Swamiji. The Oxford don, Max Mueller, was equally fascinated by Swamiji's all embracing scholarship and his grasp over *Vedanta*. All these were leading luminous stars of the age and all of them are still remembered.

The aim of Vivekananda was not religious conversion but it was spiritual awakening. He rose like a meteor on the American sky in 1893. A meteor doesn't leave any mark on the path it arcs in the sky. The spiritual meteor of Swami Vivekananda did not pass away as a mere flash. It illumined numerous hearts wherever he went. The thirteen articles in the section entitled *Chicago and its Impact on Swami Vivekananda: A Hundred Years Since Chicago,* point out in a modest way, the serene and shining light that Swamiji switched on. If prejudice pours out of every page of the account of the Chicago Parliament presented by the avowedly Christocentric attitude of Barrows, we have the great French savant Romain Rolland's testimony, 'The thought of this warrior prophet of India left a deep mark upon the United States' (*The life of Vivekananda,* 'Prelude', p.5).

When this quite unknown young man of thirty appeared in Chicago at the inaugural meeting of the Parliament of Religions, opened in September 1893, by Cardinal Gibbons, all his fellow-members were forgotten in his commanding presence! 'I am bringing to Europe,—the great French universalist has written, addressing the Western readers of his great biographies of Shri Ramakrishna and Swami Vivekananda, 'I am bringing to Europe, as yet unaware of it, the fruit of a new autumn, a new message of the "Soul"...(*The Life of Ramakrishna,* p.12). And no one expects ungovernable crowds of drunk fans gathering to witness a league football match and indulging in brawls. One Romain Rolland, one Aldous Huxley, one Christopher Isherwood, one Francis Leggett, one Captain Sevier, one Christine Greenstidel, one Margaret Noble, one Mme Calve, one Marie Louis Burke... such individuals, deeply moved and deeply touched by Vivekananda - and Ramakrishna - make up for teeming millions.

And today, in America and Europe, there are about a score of Centres of the Ramakrishna *Math* spreading the great message of *Vedanta*. They do not promise instant *samadhi, samadhi* through sex or ordinary yogic exercises or *pranayama*. But the way for all this was opened by Vivekananda more than a century ago. And the pragmatic business schools and business houses also find it advantageous to put several yogic exercises in their curricula or in daily routine, though their aim is out and out worldly, more efficiency, more production, more money.

The comparative study of religions and philosophies has now become a feature of many universities all over the world. This has led to a better understanding of religions other than the ones the students are born in. These studies help in removal of ingrained prejudices and false belief in the superiority of one's own religion.

The impact of Vivekananda and of Ramakrishna on India was a great one as events of the first half of the twentieth century demonstrated. 'Where the universe becomes a nest', was the motto chosen by Rabindranath Tagore, for his unique educational institution, the Vishva Bharati. Mahatma Gandhi was so moved by the condition of the poor that he cast away all clothes and adopted a loin cloth—'Minus Fours' instead of the 'Plus Fours', as he had so wittily put to the French newspaper reporters, when he was on his way to the Round Table Conference, in 1931. He not only made the word 'daridranarayana,' coined by Swamiji, a current coin, but spent his life in the uplift of the poor of the country. At every prayer meeting of his, hymns of all religions were sung. And his fights in South Africa and later on in India were based on non-violence, truth and love, essentially spiritual in nature. The *Bhoodan*, the land gift, movement of Vinoba Bhave was also based on love and compassion, both of which are spiritual in nature. Vinoba Bhave has written a verse, mentioning the 'gods' of all religions. This verse is used at daily prayer meetings by a large number of schools in India. Martin Luther King, Nelson Mandela and Walessa in Poland are other outstanding examples who had chosen spiritual paths in their own way.

The two World Wars, the incessant fighting in Palestine, violent struggles in some African countries, some countries of South America, the American attack on Iraq, the communal conflicts in India...all these are challenges. Narrow self-interest is the governing factor in life. We come across individuals in all the parts of the world, who rise above them. State polity is generally almost always governed by self-interest. The wolf still devours the innocent lamb, only because the wolf has powerful claws, and its hunger is never satisfied. And as Bernard Shaw has put it in his 'Man of Destiny', every such heinous act of mass murder is sartorically outfitted in a pompous manner. Such acts do succeed in throwing dust in the eyes of some. Inspite of media hype, sensible people are not convinced and some of them dig up the truth. The 'wolves' govern international trade and commerce and take full advantage of exploiting the natural wealth of developing nations.

But there is another side of this bleak picture. Young and old people from the U.S.A. go out as Peace Corps Volunteers in the backward areas of the world and serve the people there. The 'Peacenics,' as the protesters are called, have the spirit and the courage to follow a ship of a powerful country going out to dump hazardous waste in far away seas. They do so at great personal risk. But the spirit in them is undaunted. It is this fearlessness of the spirit in pursuit of truth that was preached by Vivekananda.

The giving up of arms by the Chambal valley robbers at the appeal of Jai Prakash Narayan our courting arrest is another gloring example. Vinoba Bhave had received thousands of acres of land from land lords for distribution amongst the laudcers. The base of all this is love, love for mankind.

When Vivekananda boarded the boat for going to America in 1893, it was more or less a leap in the dark. He was the first *sannyasin,* breaking the bonds of tradition and custom going out to preach. Very few persons in the West then had heard the word 'yoga.' Now, every year, many *sannyasins* of various missions as well as of the Ramakrishna *Math* and several nuns of the Sharada *Math* and other Maths fly to various countries in the world and are heard with rapt attention and due reverence. This royal road was opened to them by Swami Vivekananda.

Index